Cambridge Opera Handbooks

Ludwig van Beethoven
Fidelio

D1647857

Published titles

Ludwig van Beethoven: *Fidelio* by Paul Robinson
Alban Berg: *Lulu* by Douglas Jarman
Alban Berg: *Wozzeck* by Douglas Jarman
Hector Berlioz: *Les Troyens* by Ian Kemp
Georges Bizet: *Carmen* by Susan McClary
Benjamin Britten: *Billy Budd* by Mervyn Cooke and Philip Reed
Benjamin Britten: *Death in Venice* by Donald Mitchell
Benjamin Britten: *Peter Grimes* by Philip Brett
Benjamin Britten: *The Turn of the Screw* by Patricia Howard
Claude Debussy: *Pelléas et Mélisande* by Roger Nichols and Richard
  Langham Smith
C. W. von Gluck: *Orfeo* by Patricia Howard
Leoš Janáček: *Kát'a Kabanová* by John Tyrrell
Claudio Monteverdi: *Orfeo* by John Whenham
W. A. Mozart: *La clemenza di Tito* by John Rice
W. A. Mozart: *Così fan tutte* by Bruce Alan Brown
W. A. Mozart: *Don Giovanni* by Julian Rushton
W. A. Mozart: *Die Entführung aus dem Serail* by Thomas Bauman
W. A. Mozart: *Idomeneo* by Julian Rushton
W. A. Mozart: *Le nozze di Figaro* by Tim Carter
W. A. Mozart: *Die Zauberflöte* by Peter Branscombe
Giacomo Puccini: *La Bohème* by Arthur Groos and Roger Parker
Giacomo Puccini: *Tosca* by Mosco Carner
Richard Strauss: *Arabella* by Kenneth Birkin
Richard Strauss: *Elektra* by Derrick Puffett
Richard Strauss: *Der Rosenkavalier* by Alan Jefferson
Richard Strauss: *Salome* by Derrick Puffett
Igor Stravinsky: *The Rake's Progress* by Paul Griffiths
Giuseppe Verdi: *Falstaff* by James A. Hepokoski
Giuseppe Verdi: *Otello* by James A. Hepokoski
Richard Wagner: *Die Meistersinger von Nürnberg* by John Warrack
Richard Wagner: *Parsifal* by Lucy Beckett
Kurt Weill: *The Threepenny Opera* by Stephen Hinton

Act 2, scene 1 (dungeon scene), Salzburg Festival, 1932.
Leonore: Lotte Lehmann; Florestan: Franz Völker
(Historical Archives, Salzburg Festival).

Ludwig van Beethoven
Fidelio

PAUL ROBINSON

Professor of History
Stanford University

Published by the Press Syndicate of the University of Cambridge
The Pitt Building, Trumpington Street, Cambridge CB2 1RP
40 West 20th Street, New York, NY 10011–4211, USA
10 Stamford Road, Oakleigh, Melbourne 3166, Australia

First published 1996

Printed in Great Britain at the University Press, Cambridge

A catalogue record for this book is available from the British Library

Library of Congress cataloguing in publication data
Robinson, Paul, 1940–
Ludwig van Beethoven, Fidelio / Paul Robinson.
      p.   cm. – (Cambridge opera handbooks)
Includes bibliographical references and index.
ISBN 0 521 45221 X (hardback). ISBN 0 521 45852 8 (paperback)
I. Beethoven, Ludwig van, 1770–1827. Fidelio (1814)
I. Title. II. Series.
ML410.B4R46 1996
782.1–dc20   95–46935   CIP   MN

ISBN 0 521 45221 X hardback
ISBN 0 521 45852 8 paperback

For Stephen Dunatov

Contents

Illustrations

General preface

This is a series of studies of individual operas, written for the serious opera-goer or record-collector as well as the student or scholar. Each volume has three main concerns. The first is historical: to describe the genesis of the work, its sources or its relation to literary proto-types, the collaboration between librettist and composer, and the first performance and subsequent stage history. The history is itself a record of changing attitudes towards the work, and an index of general changes of taste. The second is analytical and is grounded in a very full synopsis which considers the opera as a structure of musical and dramatic effects. In most volumes there is also a musical analysis of a section of the score, showing how the music serves or makes the drama. The analysis, like the history, naturally raises questions of interpretation, and the third concern of each volume is to show how critical writing about an opera, like production and performance, can direct or distort appreciation of its structural elements. Some conflict of interpretation is an inevitable part of this account; editors of the handbooks reflect this – by citing classic statements, by commissioning new essays, by taking up their own critical position. A final section gives a select bibliography and guide to other sources.

Introduction

Fidelio is unique among operas in the standard repertory. It is the only opera by a composer, Beethoven, universally considered among the greatest in Western music. (*Pelléas et Mélisande* is also Debussy's only completed opera, but Debussy doesn't quite enjoy Beethoven's reputation.) Of course many important composers – Bach, Brahms, Mahler come to mind – never wrote an opera. But no composer of Beethoven's stature has failed to produce other operas after the first.[1] Actually, Beethoven himself didn't intend to be a single-opera man, and he never stopped looking for suitable librettos. Yet his inability to find one seems both right and inevitable. *Fidelio*'s true successors are the *Missa Solemnis* and the Ninth Symphony.

Fidelio is also unique in its effect on audiences. It is an opera that many listeners otherwise averse to the genre claim to admire: its intellectual seriousness and humanity, those listeners contend, save it from the frivolity and exhibitionism endemic to opera. By contrast, true buffs are sometimes put off by its vocal awkwardness and tendency to prefer philosophical rumination to dramatic action. For them attending *Fidelio* is less like a night at the opera than a morning in church. John Steane captures this ambivalence nicely: '*Fidelio* . . . can be the greatest of all operas, but only once or twice in a lifetime.'[2] Edward Dent makes a similar point by way of a comparison with Mozart:

Fidelio is perhaps still the most deeply moving opera of the whole modern repertory, and all the more profoundly impressive because it is the quintessence of Beethoven, the culminating work of his second period; but in the general career of Beethoven it stands out as an isolated experiment. Like the concertos, it is great because it is the expression of Beethoven; but for complete mastery and supreme accomplishment in the handling of a definite form we must look to the concertos of Mozart as we do to the operas.[3]

Even its friends admit that *Fidelio* has its longueurs. I have yet to meet anyone who professes to like Rocco's gold aria. More generally, every listener senses the discrepancy between the domestic comedy (and light-weight idiom) with which the opera begins and the emotionally charged, musically resplendent political allegory with which it ends. The usual excuse is that Beethoven lacked practical experience of the theatre and should be forgiven his infelicities in view of the work's philosophical power and musical beauty. One might even argue that *Fidelio* is the best first opera ever written. Certainly it surpasses the first efforts of better known opera composers: Wagner's *Die Feen*, Verdi's *Oberto*, Puccini's *Le Villi* and Strauss's *Guntram* (Mozart's *La finta simplice* seems an unfair comparison, because Mozart was only twelve when he wrote it).

But in an important sense the *Fidelio* we know was not Beethoven's first opera. It might more reasonably be called his third, or at least his second, since the 1814 version was preceded by two earlier versions. The 1805 and 1806 *Fidelios* closely resemble one another, but the changes Beethoven made in 1814 are so radical as to constitute virtually a new work. Willy Hess provides a bar-by-bar analysis of the three versions in *Das Fidelio-Buch* (Winterthur, Switzerland, 1986), and Winton Dean's essay 'Beethoven and Opera', reprinted here as chapter 3, passes judgement on their relative merits. Readers interested in hearing the remarkable differences between Beethoven's first and last thoughts on the subject can consult EMI's recording of the 1805 version (issued under the title of *Leonore*).

Jean-Nicolas Bouilly's libretto, *Léonore, ou L'amour conjugal*, most likely dates from the period after the fall of Robespierre in the summer of 1794.[4] It had already been set three times before Beethoven produced his first version: by Pierre Gaveaux (1798) in the original French and then by Ferdinando Paer (1804) and Simone Mayr (1805) in Italian. Beethoven probably knew the Gaveaux and possibly the Paer (the evidence is discussed by Winton Dean). His librettist for the 1805 version was Joseph von Sonnleithner, secretary of the court theatres in Vienna, who translated Bouilly's text freely into German and added several musical numbers. The relatively modest changes of 1806 (which saw the opera reduced from three acts to two) were made by Beethoven's friend Stephan von Breuning, while the massive overhaul of 1814 was entrusted to Friedrich Treitschke, regisseur and poet at the Kärntnertortheater, where the 1814 version was premiered.

A consideration of the differences between the 1805 and 1814 versions will serve to highlight the features that make the latter such a distinctive and, for some, problematic work. Certainly the most immediately striking difference is that the 1805 version is substantially longer and more leisurely than that of 1814. It contains two numbers cut in 1814, both of which contribute to the Marzelline subplot: a trio ('Ein Mann ist bald genommen') in which Marzelline and Rocco disabuse Jaquino about his marital prospects, and a duet between Marzelline and Leonore ('Um in der Ehe') in which Marzelline anticipates becoming a mother. Just as importantly, all the remaining numbers except the march before Pizarro's entrance are longer in the 1805 version, often considerably so.

Their greater length reflects a second difference between 1805 and 1814: in 1805 Beethoven often lets the music prevail over the drama. He cannot resist the pull of compositional symmetry or formal development, so that the story is frequently stopped in its tracks while a purely musical development is allowed to work itself out to a logical conclusion. In other words, Beethoven in 1805 is an even more 'instrumental' composer than he became in 1814, when, for listeners whose expectations are based on Verdi or Puccini, he still remains too much the symphonist.

The 1805 version is more 'instrumental' than the 1814 versions in purely vocal terms as well: the vocal parts, especially Leonore's, are highly ornamental, given to elaborate coloratura display, particularly at cadences. Thus even more emphatically than in 1814, the music for Leonore and Florestan sounds as if it had been written not for soprano and tenor but for clarinet and French horn. By contrast, the plainer vocal writing and the greater musical succinctness of the 1814 version make it dramatically more cogent – closer to the operatic ideal of *dramma per musica* – than the 1805 original.

Two other changes, however, might be said to have shifted the balance in just the opposite direction. These changes don't necessarily make the opera of 1814 less dramatic than that of 1805, but they transform it from a drama of persons into a drama of ideas. In 1805 the focus is on the individual characters, while in 1814 it shifts to the collectivity. This difference is already implied in the elimination of the two numbers I mentioned a moment ago. But it is seen above all in the more prominent role assigned to the prisoners – musically speaking, the chorus – in the later version. At the same time the prisoners themselves become a yet more transparent representative of all humanity, whose liberation in turn becomes the opera's true subject.

For one thing, the 1814 version has a new chorus for the prisoners as they return to their cells, the exquisite 'Leb' wohl, du warmes Sonnenlicht', which replaces a second revenge aria for Pizarro that had ended the act in 1805. More significantly, a change of scene is introduced after Leonore's and Florestan's 'Namenlose Freude' duet, allowing the final tableau to be set in the bright daylight of the prison parade ground (in 1805 the prisoners and people had invaded Florestan's dungeon). The scene also receives a new choral beginning, 'Heil sei dem Tag', so that the chorus both begins and ends the finale in a celebratory C major, firmly establishing itself as the opera's triumphant protagonist. The world-historical significance of the scene is confirmed by a new speech for the minister, who announces that henceforth tyranny will be banished and brotherhood enjoined.

Just as the role of the prisoners is enhanced – and along with it the opera's philosophical gravitas – the story of Leonore's rescue of her husband is sabotaged by a crucial dramatic (as well as musical) change introduced in 1814. Originally the outcome of the great confrontation between Leonore and Pizarro was left in doubt. At the end of the quartet (no.14) Rocco snatches Leonore's pistol as he departs with Pizarro, and the lovers, still imprisoned, are forced to recognize that their reunion might be their last. As Joseph Kerman remarks, the scene takes on some of the characteristics of a *Liebestod*,[5] a moment of tension and ecstasy that Beethoven realizes in a long and affecting recitative leading into the 'Namenlose Freude' duet.

This intensely dramatic scene was sacrificed in 1814 when Rocco no longer takes Leonore's pistol but instead seeks to reassure the lovers that all is well by gesturing towards heaven. Rocco's dumbshow is supposed to settle every uncertainty about the happy ending, not just for Leonore and Florestan but for the audience as well. The agonized recitative of 1805 is accordingly eliminated, and the 'Namenlose Freude' duet is now launched with only a few lines of dialogue. Most importantly, the duet carries the double (and perhaps contradictory) burden of expressing both the lovers' reunion and their escape. Winton Dean complains bitterly that Leonore and Florestan are thereby stripped of their individuality and become mere 'personifications'. The wonted satisfactions of musical drama give way to philosophical/political generalities that, for Dean, come dangerously close to tub-thumping (see below, p. 44).

Arguably the last act of the 1805 *Fidelio* makes for better conventional theatre than does the end of the 1814 version (although everyone, including Dean, agrees that the earlier portions of the work are greatly improved in their final incarnation). But one might counter that Beethoven had no particular gift for conventional opera – for the musical and dramatic interaction of character we so enjoy in Mozart, Wagner, Verdi, Puccini and Strauss. By contrast, he was an unsurpassed musical philosopher, and the move from individual drama to communal vision effected with Treitschke's aid in 1814 is precisely what puts *Fidelio* in a category by itself. Joseph Kerman is again authoritative: 'What [Beethoven] could do extremely well was project ideas and ideals in his music. . . . In revising his opera in the direction of greater idealization and universality, [he] was leading from strength.'[6] Thus, in spite of its dramatic defects, the 1814 version has rightfully displaced Beethoven's earlier efforts. Not only is it musically superior, but, more importantly, it alone boasts the distinctive moral pathos that separates *Fidelio* from all other works for the lyric theatre.

I have said that the true subject of *Fidelio* as we know it is the liberation of humanity. But the statement unfairly prejudices the question of Beethoven's politics. Doubtless *Fidelio* has long enjoyed a visceral appeal for people on the left as the opera that most fully embodies the ideal of a pacified existence. In his autobiography Stephen Spender reports that as a young man, 'No opera moved me quite so much as *Fidelio*'.[7] But cautionary scholars like Maynard Solomon have argued that Beethoven's political views at the time were at best ambivalent and perhaps expressly anti-revolutionary. David Charlton's discussion, in chapter 4, of the origins of *Fidelio* in French opera of the late eighteenth century shows that Beethoven's source, Bouilly's *Léonore*, was an unambiguously Thermidorean document. Indeed, Bouilly later said that the story was based on a true event in which an aristocratic woman in the Touraine rescued her husband who had been imprisoned by the Terror.[8] There is evidence, in other words, that *Fidelio* is a fundamentally reactionary work, at least in inspiration.

Chapter 5, '*Fidelio* and the French Revolution', seeks to counter this anti-revolutionary reading, not by questioning the incontrovertible findings of Maynard Solomon, David Charlton and others, but by looking to the dramatic and musical logic of the work Beethoven actually wrote in 1814. In *The Principle of Hope* the philosopher Ernst Bloch calls the final scene of *Fidelio* 'the

Marseillaise on the fallen Bastille'. He adds, 'Every future storming of the Bastille is intended in *Fidelio*.'⁹ Bloch's appropriation of *Fidelio* to the cause of revolution is perhaps too explicit and inclusive (does it encompass not merely 1789 and 1848 but also the revolutions of Lenin, Mao and Castro?). Nonetheless, I am inclined to believe that he has correctly identified the ideological and moral appeal that has made Beethoven's only opera uniquely beloved. *Fidelio* holds the stage above all because it so powerfully expresses the hope for a redeemed humanity.

2   *Synopsis*

Characters

Don Fernando, minister of state	Bass*
Don Pizarro, governor of a state prison	Bass*
Florestan, a prisoner	Tenor
Leonore, his wife, disguised as a young man, Fidelio	Soprano
Rocco, jailor	Bass
Marzelline, his daughter	Soprano
Jaquino, doorkeeper	Tenor
First prisoner	Tenor
Second prisoner	Bass

Prisoners, officers, guards, townspeople
Place: a Spanish royal prison, a few miles from Seville
Time: the eighteenth century

* Often sung by a baritone or bass-baritone

Overture

The *Fidelio* overture, famously, is the last of four Beethoven wrote for the opera. It is always described as slighter and more anodyne than its three predecessors (especially *Leonore* No. 2, written for the 1805 version, and *Leonore* No. 3, written for 1806), which are generally thought to render the opera superfluous because they so dramatically realize its fundamental contrast between oppression and liberation. In particular the *Fidelio* overture seems a more appropriate introduction to the comic action of the opening scene. Yet to listen to it alongside the Mozart overtures, with which it might seem to invite comparison, is to recognize its more muscular construction and weightier sonority. It is unmistakably Beethovian, even if drawn on a less monumental scale than the *Leonore* overtures.

A brisk fanfare, which will later serve as the main theme of the Allegro, introduces the piece. It might be associated with the opera's heroic central action. It is answered by a short Adagio of soft modulations in the horns and clarinets, alluding perhaps to the heroine's sustaining hope (which Beethoven often signals with horns). After the fanfare has been repeated in the subdominant, the Adagio sets off on a longer, more anxious harmonic course, rising to *forte* over insistent timpani strokes, until it gives way to the Allegro.

In the sonata-form Allegro the fanfare theme is elaborated in Beethoven's vigorous second-period manner. The movement culminates in a unison *fortissimo* statement of the fanfare, followed by a more elegiac version of the contrasting Adagio. In the final Presto trombones add yet greater weight to the already brassy scoring and help create the sense of affirmation so typical of Beethoven's endings. Thus while the *Fidelio* overture avoids pre-empting the drama as literally as do the second and third *Leonore* overtures (which actually incorporate the liberating trumpet call from the act II quintet), its ending anticipates the exalted mood in which the opera itself closes.

Act I

No. 1, Duet (Allegro, A major), 'Jetzt, Schätzchen, jetzt sind wir allein' (Jaquino, Marzelline)

The courtyard of a state prison. Marzelline is ironing outside her father's house (which, for operatic reasons, is located within the courtyard), while Jaquino is receiving packages through a door in the prison gate. The duet is devoted to Jaquino's attempts to propose to Marzelline and her fending off of his importuning. The contrast between Jaquino's ardour and Marzelline's sarcasm is meant to be amusing, but the effect is curiously disagreeable and, with its many repetitions, tedious. When Jaquino is momentarily distracted with the packages at the door, Marzelline, in a lyrical aside, confesses her love for her father's young assistant, Fidelio.

The duet, in free A–B–A form, is based on a four-note orchestral figure, essentially rhythmical in character, that Beethoven works through the orchestra above or beneath the voices. Both the vocal line and the accompaniment are short-breathed and staccato, save in the middle section where Marzelline expresses her romantic longing in sustained phrases that reach above the stave. The whole has a *faux-naif* atmosphere of chirpy rusticity. In the coda tenor and soprano unite, even though no reconciliation has been achieved (in contrast, say, to the opening duet of *The Marriage of Figaro*), and

Marzelline is set loose on several unmotivated coloratura runs. With its transparent orchestration the number has an archaizing flavour that places us unambiguously in the farcical world of mistaken identity and romantic delusion – in other words, the world of the eighteenth-century domestic comedy.

Dialogue Rocco calls Jaquino into the garden (which the stage directions locate through a door to the right of the courtyard). Alone, Marzelline concedes that she had been quite fond of Jaquino until Fidelio came into the household.

No. 2, Aria (Andante con moto, C minor/C major), 'O wär' ich schon mit dir vereint!' (Marzelline)
    Marzelline's aria was the first number in the 1805 version of the opera. Like the preceding duet, it is very much in the *Singspiel* manner. Marzelline's imaginings begin with the modest wish that Fidelio were already her husband but soon give way to frankly passionate thoughts of their marital bliss. Beethoven marks the shift with a conventional move from minor to major, as well as a faster tempo and fuller orchestration, whose pulsing reflects the hope beating in Marzelline's breast. The second verse conjures up the daily routine of domestic chores but then alludes (rather archly) to the pleasures that will await the couple when night descends. The leitmotif of Marzelline's ruminations is hope, which might tempt us to interpret the aria as a foretaste of Leonore's great outburst, 'Komm, Hoffnung' (no. 9), the opera's only other solo number for female voice. But the common theme of hope serves rather to contrast Marzelline's self-deluding fancies with Leonore's profoundly courageous refusal to despair. The contrast is underlined by Beethoven's music: Marzelline's aria is light, airy and (in its conclusion) cheerful, whereas Leonore's great appeal to hope, in an almost melancholy Adagio, is set to long and weighty *legato* lines, and her concluding Allegro conveys not cheerfulness but ecstatic determination.

Dialogue Coming in from the garden, Rocco asks whether Fidelio has returned with dispatches for the governor of the prison. Leonore, disguised as Fidelio, enters carrying chains (from the blacksmith's) and a box with the dispatches. Rocco congratulates him on the economy of his purchases, promises a reward and hints that the young man's heart is an open book.

No. 3, Quartet (Andante sostenuto, G major), 'Mir ist so wunder-bar' (Marzelline, Leonore, Rocco, Jaquino)

Hushed sustained harmonies in divided violas and cellos, to which clarinets and then flutes are added, introduce this uncanny piece, which rips us from the bumptious world of the *Singspiel*, with its staccato idiom and wordiness, into a transfigured landscape of emotional intensity and relative silence. To be sure, the canon – which is maintained strictly for the first forty bars – hearkens back to a plebeian musical idiom (that of, say, 'Frère Jacques'), but Beethoven's treatment lifts this lowly form to the sublime. Each of the four participants delivers his or her quatrain, beginning at eight-bar intervals, as an aside: Marzelline thinks blissfully of Fidelio's (imagined) love; Leonore sees great danger in the infatuation; Rocco anticipates the couple's domestic happiness; while Jaquino bitterly complains of the betrayal. But the words – often unintelligible because they overlap one another – count for little in this radically musical adumbration of the opera's ultimate resolution. The parallels with the F major Sostenuto assai section of the act II finale are noteworthy.

Dialogue Rocco announces that he intends to make Fidelio his son-in-law but adds that a good marriage needs more than love.

No. 4, Aria (Allegro moderato/Allegro, B flat major), 'Hat man nicht auch Gold beineben' (Rocco)

After the canon's taste of poetry, Rocco's number returns us to the prosaic realm of the *Singspiel*. It is an exercise in petty-bourgeois philosophizing, a sub-Franklinian paean to gold, which alone, Rocco says, can guarantee sustained contentment. The two-strophe aria is in a well established *buffo* tradition in which alternating sections in different tempo and metre (moderate 2/4 and fast 6/8) correspond to the contrasting moods of the singer's encomium, the first anxiously sober (without gold 'life drags on wearily'), the second gleefully philistine (gold brings power and love). In the latter violins mimic the gold's 'ringing and rolling'. Beethoven cut the aria in the 1806 version.

Dialogue Leonore begs Rocco to be allowed to accompany him into the prison's deepest dungeons. Even though the governor has expressly forbidden it, Rocco agrees, but one cell, he says, must remain out of bounds. Searchingly, Leonore asks how long its inmate has been incarcerated, to which Rocco replies, 'More than two years.' On Pizarro's orders the man's daily rations have been steadily reduced. When Marzelline opines that Fidelio could not bear such a gruesome sight, Leonore counters, memorably, 'Why not? I have courage and strength.'

No. 5, Trio (Allegro, ma non troppo/Allegro molto, F major), 'Gut, Söhnchen, gut, hab' immer Mut!' (Rocco, Leonore, Marzelline)
This substantial number, with its stretta-like conclusion, served as the finale to act I in the 1805 version. It marks a sharp departure, dramatically and compositionally, from the domestic concerns and Biedermeier style of numbers 1, 2, and 4. With its forcible motivic development, rhythmic elan, energetic accompaniment (especially in the strings) and soaring vocal lines, it puts us in mind of the works with which *Fidelio* is contemporaneous: the symphonies and concertos of Beethoven's middle period. The music alternates between canon-like imitative passages for the separate voices and concerted moments (especially in the stretta) where the three unite to sing the same, or closely related, words in harmony.

The number's energy derives from our new awareness of Leonore's predicament, which uniquely combines fear and hope: Rocco's remarks have given her reason to believe she has at last found her husband, but he is near death and terrifying obstacles stand between her and his salvation. Nonetheless, she will venture below, she swears, for love (Liebe) can endure great suffering (Leiden). God and justice are on her side, so despite her grief hope restores her. Leonore's tense reflections are the emotional heart of the trio – for several of them Beethoven fashions arching phrases that move to the top of the stave – while the encouraging (but ignorant) remarks of Rocco and Marzelline – he preoccupied with his own mortality, she still caught up in her infatuation – serve to heighten, ironically, our sense of Leonore's isolation. Only Rocco's ominous mentioning of Pizarro ('der Gouverneur') – for which Beethoven momentarily halts the musical flow and shifts evocatively from C major to A major – draws our attention from her.

Dialogue Hearing Pizarro and his retinue approaching, Rocco takes the dispatch box and tells Fidelio and Marzelline to leave. As the March (no. 6) begins, soldiers file in, followed by Pizarro.

No. 6, March (Vivace, B flat major)
The march, accompanies the entrance of Pizarro and his minions. It is a surprisingly genial piece, creating an atmosphere

more of polish than of menace. Particularly striking is its rhythmic deceptiveness, as Beethoven persistently begins the tune on the third beat of the bar, while the two preceding notes – on timpani, *pizzicato* lower strings and contrabassoon – sound like an upbeat and a downbeat (4–1) but actually occur on the first two beats of the measure (1–2). The piece also ends with almost comic abruptness. Like Verdi, Beethoven seems to have had trouble finding the right tone for his operatic marches.

Dialogue Pizarro asks for the dispatches, one of which he proceeds to read aloud to himself. It warns that the minister of state, having learned of 'several victims of arbitrary force' in the prisons under Pizarro's supervision, intends to make a surprise visit. Disconcerted, Pizarro thinks of Florestan, lying beneath in chains, who intended to expose him and whom the minister believes dead. Should Florestan be discovered . . . But Pizarro resolves immediately on 'a bold deed'.

No. 7, Aria with Chorus (Allegro agitato, D minor), 'Ha, welch' ein Augenblick!' (Pizarro)
    The text of Pizarro's aria is apt to put the modern listener in mind of Simon Legree. Pizarro presents himself as a villain unqualified, delirious at the prospect of twisting the knife in his enemy's heart and shouting 'Victory is mine!' in his ear. Indeed, in purely textual terms, evil was never more banal. It is left to the composer to transform this cardboard utterance into a plausible portrait of tyranny. Beethoven's model is the 'vengeance aria' of Baroque and above all French Revolutionary opera, but he raises it to a new level of intensity.
    The minor key and breathless pace provide the basic ingredients. Most of the work is done by the orchestra, with its ominous timpani, whirling strings, syncopated *sforzandi* and near unrelieved brassy *forte*. The vocal phrases are clipped, irregular, and obsessed with the home tone of D natural. Pizarro makes his way through his hateful sentiments twice before he is joined by the chorus of guards, who murmur timorously beneath his fragmentary final outbursts, their voices rising above *piano* only at the end.

Dialogue Pizarro orders a watch to be posted in the tower and a trumpet to sound as soon as an escorted carriage is spotted approaching from the direction of Seville. Then he summons Rocco.

No. 8, Duet (Allegro con brio, A major), 'Jetzt, Alter, jetzt hat es Eile!' (Pizarro, Rocco)

The duet represents Pizarro's seduction of Rocco, whose help he needs to carry out his 'bold deed'. He flatters the old man with a tribute to his years of cool-headed service and the promise of riches before revealing what is now expected of him: 'murder'. Beethoven interrupts the nervous wood-wind accompaniment and sets the word, *mezza voce*, on an eerie downward interval of a seventh. Pizarro tries to shame the terrified jailer by impugning his manhood, but Rocco nonetheless refuses because, he says, taking life is not his duty. Pizarro then resolves to do the deed himself. He orders Rocco to descend 'to that man down there' to dig his grave, after which Pizarro will creep in masked, and, with 'one blow' (ein Stoss), silence the prisoner forever. The two dark voices, heard mainly in dialogue up to this point, now unite in resonant thirds and sixths as if to memorialize the man (Pizarro bitterly, Rocco relievedly) whose death, they aver, will deliver him from starvation in chains. The highly dramatic music of the duet is distinguished by its pictorial effects: 'that man down there' becomes an octave-long descent; the masked Pizarro creeps into the dungeon on a scaly *pianissimo* figure rising and falling nearly an octave; and, most memorable of all, 'one blow' is sung on an uncanny upward third with the orchestra silenced and followed by a fateful pause.

No. 9, Recitative and Aria (Adagio/Allegro con brio, E major), 'Abscheulicher . . . Komm, Hoffnung' (Leonore)

As Pizarro and Rocco leave, Leonore enters from the opposite side and observes the two men with growing agitation, having overheard their plotting in the preceding duet. In her splendid recitative (entirely rewritten for 1814) she calls Pizarro an abomination, whose heart is untouched by human compassion. But just as he seethes with rage and fury, she says, she is calmed by the sweet recollection of old times. The music, with its frequent changes of key, metre and tempo, closely follows her shifting emotions, above all the metamorphosis from anger to tranquility. In the serene Adagio three prominent obbligato horns decorate Leonore's heartfelt prayer to hope, which she begs to illuminate her goal, however distant, so that love can reach it. The Allegro that follows is introduced by a blazing fanfare on the horns, whose energetic commentary accompanies her new-found determination to the end: she will follow her inner drive, the duty of conjugal love, to bring comfort to her fettered husband. The expansive phrases and the long chromatic runs on 'reach' (erreichen) – ultimately up to an exposed high B – in the Adagio, and the killing downward leaps and coloratura passage work of the Allegro make the aria extraordinarily difficult to sing. Just this sort of writing has provoked the complaint that Beethoven's vocal demands are punishingly instrumental. Arguably, however, those demands symbolize the superhuman task Leonore has taken on, and, rendered by the right voice and temperament, the aria can be among the most thrilling in opera.

Dialogue Leonore begs Rocco to let the prisoners out into the garden. He agrees but limits his permission to those in the less secure cells (hence Florestan's failure to appear among them). Rocco leaves to speak with Pizarro, while Leonore and Jaquino open the cell doors and watch the prisoners emerge.

No. 10, Finale

The prisoners' chorus is the opera's ideological core. The men, nearly blinded by the sunlight, straggle onto the stage above quiet unfolding chords in the strings. A hopeful upward-reaching motif, passing from low to high wood-winds, introduces their first tentative words, after which their voices quickly swell to fortissimo as they greet the open air with a rapturous tribute to freedom. The emphatically harmonized choral melody rides above string and wood-wind semiquavers that lend it an optimistic forward momentum, interrupted only by an anxious allusion (on a unison chromatic descent near the bottom of the register) to the tomb-like dungeon they have just left. In the middle section, set in a bright G major, a single prisoner (a tenor) steps forward and, in a lovely, confident melody, sings of his hope that with God's help they will be free, to which the others respond with a series of ecstatic ejaculations. They are brought back to grim reality by a second soloist (a bass) who warns that they are watched. (At this moment a sentry appears on the wall and then departs, presumably to inform Pizarro that the prisoners have been let out.) The opening chorus returns (*piano*), but the prisoners cannot escape their oppressive awareness of being under surveillance, and the number ends, over descending string figures that die away to nothing, with them repeating, 'We are watched with ear and eye.'

The middle sections of the finale, devoted mainly to advancing the plot, are on a less exalted musical level. As the prisoners go into the garden, Rocco returns and reports to Fidelio that Pizarro has acceded to both of the jailor's requests: Fidelio and Marzelline will be allowed to marry and Fidelio can accompany him down to the prison's underground cells that very day. Leonore's joy (at the latter news) is short-lived when she learns that she must help Rocco dig the grave of Pizarro's victim. Their dialogue – up to this point conducted rapidly over a nervous orchestral accompaniment – gives way briefly to a duet, as Leonore reflects on the horror of perhaps digging her husband's grave, while Rocco tries to persuade himself that the man's death will come as a relief. The pace slows, the metre shifts from 4/4 to 6/8, and the key modulates from G to E flat as the dialogue commences again beneath an anxious six-note wood-wind motif that Beethoven subjects to elaborate development. Rocco contemplates the harsh task before them, and when Leonore shows signs of faltering he says he will go alone. But her resolve is soon restored, and the section ends with two voices uniting in a curiously lilting tribute to duty.

The tempo picks up as Jaquino and Marzelline arrive breathlessly warning that Pizarro, furious over the release of the prisoners, is about to descend upon them. To pounding E flats in the full orchestra he storms in and denounces Rocco, who, however, cleverly rescues himself by claiming that his act of magnanimity was inspired by its being the king's name-day (a pompous melody introduced by an orchestral fanfare), and he reminds Pizarro, in an aside, to save his anger for the man condemned to die. Chagrined, Pizarro orders the prisoners returned to their cells.

Their return is the occasion for a second chorus (newly composed for 1814), less well-known than the first but perhaps even more beautiful, which becomes the basis for the closing quintet. It is announced by a luminous B flat chord in the strings. 'Farewell, warm sunshine', the men sing in parallel thirds to a melody that rises achingly over a gently insistent rhythmic motif (a quaver upbeat, a crotchet downbeat) that will accompany the movement to the end and gives it a subtle but inevitable tread with more than a hint of oppression. The five soloists join in an elaborate musical commentary, Leonore, Jaquino and Marzelline sadly shepherding the prisoners back into their cells, Pizarro urging Rocco on to their gruesome task and Rocco agreeing unhappily. In the following section, over a falling and rising melody in the bass, the soloists' lines are set contrapuntally: Rocco trembles at his miserable duty, Pizarro contemplates executing the sentence, Leonore regrets

Pizarro's injustice, Marzelline – her voice twice breaking into coloratura – commiserates with the prisoners and Jaquino wonders what Rocco and Fidelio are plotting. Beethoven has the musical courage and dramatic integrity to end his act recessively, in keeping with the anxious uncertainty of the situation. The singers' lines become more fragmented and softer, until the music expires in a low orchestral murmur.

Act II

No. 11, Introduction, Recitative and Aria (Grave/Adagio/Poco Allegro, F minor/A Flat major/F major), 'Gott, welch' Dunkel hier! . . . In des Lebens Frühlingstagen' (Florestan)

This extended number bears the heavy burden of establishing a major character who has been absent (save in the thoughts of the other principals) from the first half of the opera. Beethoven carefully gives it the same format and dimensions – recitative, Adagio, Allegro – as Leonore's act I solo, thereby suggesting the couple's profound affinity.

In an underground dungeon illuminated by a single lamp, Florestan lies in chains. The long orchestral introduction, with its piercing wind chords, moaning lower strings, ominous timpani, syncopated runs and wandering harmonies, establishes an atmosphere of gloom and foreboding, relieved only by a flicker of light after a D flat major cadence in the middle. Florestan's great recitative begins in desolation, but, as a man of principle and devotion, he recalls God's justice: he will not grumble, he sings, for God determines the measure of human suffering ('Leiden', set on a long modulating melisma that carries the tenor over high A). His disjointed, largely unaccompanied utterances are separated by orchestral commentary, implying his physical exhaustion, and the movement from despair to religious resignation is faithfully captured in the changing harmonic construction and vocal contour of the music.

The Adagio presents Florestan's autobiographical credo. In his life he has spoken the truth, yet chains have been his reward. Still, he takes solace knowing he has done his duty. Broadly conceived in regular four-bar units, the aria's serene melody is rhythmically elusive, with most of its phrases launched on the second or third beat of the bar. The effect is to give the piece a free-flowing unity despite its clearly articulated parts. In the visionary Allegro (new in 1814) the key shifts from A flat to F and the metre from triple to quarter time as Florestan thinks he sees an angel, 'so like Leonore, my wife', leading him to freedom in paradise. His fevered imaginings, carrying the voice ever upward, are set over marching syncopations in violins and horns and accompanied by a sailing oboe obbligato that seems to reach to the heavens. At the height of his ecstasy he collapses in exhaustion, and the orchestra sinks away in a short postlude.

No. 12, Melodrama and Duet (Andante con moto, A minor), 'Nur hurtig fort, nur frisch gegraben' (Rocco, Leonore)

Beethoven borrowed the technique of melodrama, in which declamation is set against orchestral commentary, from contemporary French opera. Most of the lines in the melodrama are spoken between the musical interludes, some of which are as short as one or two bars.

Rocco and Leonore descend into the dungeon with their tools and discover the unconscious prisoner. For a moment they think he is dead, but a slight movement confirms that he is only sleeping (the oboe's recollection of the arpeggiated phrase 'so like Leonore, my wife' from the preceding aria reveals his dreams). As they set to work digging the grave, Leonore tries in vain to make out his features.

The music of the duet depicts their labours. Throbbing string triplets beneath sustained chords in the winds and trombones convey their anxious physical movement, while a sinister rumbling figure in the bass violins and contrabassoon seems to suggest the actual digging. The bass figure also imitates their straining to lift a stone. Beethoven nicely captures the contrast between Rocco's almost business-like attention to duty and Leonore's tense preoccupation with the rescue. Rocco's phrases are dominated by gruff staccato quavers, their effect primarily rhythmic, whereas Leonore's are more contoured and irregular, betraying her inner turmoil. When she looks up from her work to the prisoner, she breaks out of the nervous digging music into a series of passionate melodic arcs, culminating in a long coloratura melisma, to which she declares, in an aside, that she will free the man from his chains no matter who he is. The duet then makes its way busily to its conclusion as a physically and emotionally exhausted Leonore tries to catch her breath while Rocco urges her back to work because Pizarro will be arriving any moment.

Dialogue Florestan awakes. Leonore recognizes him but continues to conceal her identity. He asks who the governor of the prison is and learns that it is Pizarro, the very man whose crimes he had exposed. He begs Rocco to send Leonore a message that he is being held prisoner there. When Rocco demurs, Florestan asks at least for a drop of water. They have none, but Leonore rushes to give him wine instead.

No. 13, Trio (Moderato, A major), 'Euch werde Lohn in bessern Welten' (Florestan, Rocco, Leonore)

The number is a celebration of humanity – primarily Florestan's and Leonore's, but even Rocco's – under circumstances of deprivation and terror. To a broad flowing melody over *legato* string arpeggios Florestan expresses his thanks to the two strangers. As the tune is elaborated, Rocco says he is glad to refresh the poor man, Leonore – her heart pounding – reflects that the decisive moment, which will bring either death or salvation, is at hand, and Florestan marvels that both 'the boy' and the old man are moved to compassion. In the middle section, the accompanying arpeggios – now played *staccato* – turn almost jaunty, as Leonore overcomes Rocco's resistance to offering the man a piece of bread. (Many commentators have noted that Beethoven here expressly invokes the symbolism of the Eucharist with its salvific bread and wine.) Florestan's gratitude brings a return to the opening melody, which Rocco and Leonore promptly join to lend the recapitulation a rich triadic sonority. In the coda the tempo increases slightly, and, to a rising variation of his tune, Florestan regrets that he cannot repay them for their goodness. Leonore fears that the situation is more than she can bear, while Rocco returns to his theme of the prisoner's imminent end.

Dialogue Rocco goes to the back of the stage and signals Pizarro with a whistle. Florestan, wondering if it is his death knell, cries, 'O my Leonore! Then shall I never see you again?' Leonore seeks to reassure him, 'Whatever you may see and hear, do not forget there is a providence.' Pizarro enters, hiding his face with his cloak. After confirming that everything is ready, he draws a dagger.

No. 14, Quartet (Allegro, D major), 'Er sterbe!' (Pizarro, Florestan, Leonore, Rocco)

The quartet encompasses the essential action of the drama. At its centre stands the confrontation – musical as well as dramatic –

between Pizarro and Leonore. To a rising tumult in the orchestra, Pizarro casts off his cloak, reveals his identity and gloats over his triumphant revenge. He lunges toward Florestan with his dagger, but Leonore, seizing the musical initiative, throws herself between them. She then reveals her own identity: 'First kill his wife!' After the briefest moment of recognition (the accompaniment reduced to a rhythmic figure in oboes and bassoons), the already brutal pace is ratcheted up yet further, and Pizarro, overcoming his astonishment, now threatens to kill Leonore as well as Florestan. Just as she produces her pistol, the trumpet call interrupts the musical and dramatic proceedings and stuns everyone into silence. There follows a short choral reflection in which all the principals react to their utterly changed circumstances, and the trumpet sounds again. At the top of the stairs Jaquino, accompanied by two officers and soldiers carrying torches, announces (in a speaking voice) that the minister has arrived. Rocco, surprised but happy, orders the soldiers to 'accompany' the Governor out of the dungeon. With Pizarro's malign power overthrown, the quartet rushes exultantly to its end in a burst of concerted singing. Save at the moment of the trumpet call, the music never abandons its fierce pace or unrelenting *forte*. Violent runs in the strings and blaring chords in the brass provide its essential orchestral texture. During the closing orchestral Presto Pizarro hurries out, preceded by the soldiers and followed by Rocco, who reassuringly grasps Leonore's and Florestan's hands and points towards heaven.

Dialogue Left alone, Leonore assures Florestan that their ordeal is truly over.

No. 15, Duet (Allegro vivace, G major), 'O namenlose Freude!' (Leonore, Florestan)
    Coming after the issue of the drama has been settled (in contrast to the 1805 version, where the situation remains in doubt), this number has the task of giving musical expression to the love that has driven its action. In a sequence of ecstatic outbursts, sung first antiphonally and then together in thirds, Leonore and Florestan rejoice in their triumph over adversity. The arpeggio-like melody of their opening line ('O unutterable joy!') surges into the upper register and sets the breathless tone of the piece, although Beethoven interrupts it with a brief adagio reminder (on a downward, sobbing phrase) of the 'unspeakable sorrows' they have endured. In the

middle section the orchestral texture thins, and to a gentler, less altitudinous motif they delight in being in one another's arms. A quiet, suspenseful passage, in which violins anticipate the opening arpeggios, prepares the recapitulation, where they once again storm the heavens, thanking God for their bliss. As in Leonore's aria (no. 9), the rapid, high-lying vocal lines of the duet have given rise to the stricture that Beethoven makes inhuman demands of his singers.

(In a brief dialogue, almost always cut in performance, Rocco returns to say that Florestan's name is not on the minister's official list of prisoners and that his detention has thus been an act of personal vengeance on Pizarro's part.)

Change of Scene

No. 16, Finale

The parade ground of the prison, as brilliantly illuminated as the previous scene was gloomy. The minister Don Fernando enters with Pizarro and officers. A crowd of townspeople gathers as Marzelline and Jaquino lead in the prisoners.

A long fanfare-like *crescendo*, its orchestration growing thicker as it rocks back and forth between tonic and dominant, introduces a festive C major chorus of prisoners and people. Don Fernando tells them, in a stately recitative, that the King has sent him to dispel the criminal night in which they have all been enshrouded. He breaks into arioso in his final Schillerian phrase, greeting them as brothers.

The next section of the finale, set in A major, disposes of the various unsettled issues of the plot, in music, one senses, that did not receive Beethoven's fullest compositional attention. Rocco presents Leonore and Florestan, still in chains, to Don Fernando, who is astonished to recognize his old friend whom he had assumed dead. Rocco also recounts the heroic exploits that brought Leonore, disguised as a boy, to the prison to free her husband (Marzelline expresses her dismay in a brief outburst) as well as Pizarro's foiled plot to kill Florestan. Here the leisurely recitation – accompanied by a laconic semiquaver figure in the strings – is interrupted by a short, raucous chorus demanding Pizarro's punishment, after which he is led away by guards. Don Fernando then turns to Leonore and, in a beautiful descending phrase, invites her to unlock Florestan's chains.

The unlocking launches an ethereal concerted movement beginning with Leonore's 'O Gott, welch' ein Augenblick!' (O God, what a moment!). It is the musical and emotional heart of the opera. The tempo slows (Sostenuto assai) and the key shifts magically to F major, establishing an atmosphere of hypnotic stillness. Over a long arching phrase, which makes its way repeatedly through the orchestra and is eventually embraced by the voices, each person expresses his or her reaction to the moment of liberation. Although the voices enter separately, they eventually unite in a quintet, supported discreetly by the chorus, in praise of God's justice and mercy.

The celebratory closing chorus with ensemble in C major is based on a line from Schiller's 'Ode to joy', 'Let him who has won a fair wife join in our rejoicing.' We hear the allegro refrain – in increasingly elaborate versions – sung first by the full chorus, next by Florestan over the tenors and basses, and finally by Leonore (the words suitably altered) to the counterpoint of the other soloists. The tempo is then jacked up, and the long stretta begins with a condensed choral utterance of the text set to a thunderous orchestral tutti. The finale makes its ecstatic way to closure as fragments of the tune in the chorus alternate rapidly with more lyrical interventions by the quintet of soloists. Beethoven's opera of freedom ends in a blaze of sound and light.

3 Beethoven and opera

WINTON DEAN

Introduction

The uniqueness of Beethoven's contribution to the operatic repertory must be ascribed to temperament rather than environment. The man who produced his single opera in three versions and equipped it with four overtures, yet complained of the same work that he found it far harder to rethink himself into an old composition than to begin a new one, was clearly not a born opera composer, least of all in the conditions obtaining at the turn of the nineteenth century. Nevertheless he was far from considering himself a one-opera man. He continued for the greater part of his life to invite librettos and plan fresh operas, only to abandon them in the early stages or allow them to lapse through inanition. His potential collaborators included such men of literary distinction and experience as Goethe, Grillparzer, Kotzebue, Collin, Rochlitz, and Rellstab. *Fidelio*, whatever its faults, is a great opera and a work of theatrical genius. Yet not even a mouse followed the birth of the mountain. One might attribute the constant search for librettos to the spur of Beethoven's environment, and its regular frustration to some hidden force in his creative personality. But only a careful study of the opera he did write can suggest an answer to the question what that force was.

The circumstances of Beethoven's life, both in Bonn and Vienna, might have been expected to encourage rather than inhibit an operatic career, or at least an attempt at it. It is true that in neither city during his residence – and especially in his impressionable years – was a composer of the first or even the second rank writing for the stage. But there was plenty of opera; old and new works, home-grown and imported, were constantly on view. In Bonn, where his father was a tenor singer, albeit a drunken one, Beethoven must have learned much of the current repertory in his childhood. In 1783 and 1784, at the age of 12 and 13, he was employed as cembalist in the Elector's theatre orchestra under the Kapellmeister Christian Gottlob Neefe. This service was interrupted by the disbandment of the orchestra on the death of the Elector in April 1784. Even so, the next four years saw a number of visiting companies in Bonn, one of which (in 1785) may have introduced Beethoven to Gluck's *Orfeo* and *Alceste*.[1] Two years later, on his first visit to Vienna, he had a few lessons from Mozart. In the winter of 1788 the Elector Maximilian Franz, brother of the Austrian emperor, established a new opera company at Bonn that gave regular winter seasons lasting several months. Until his departure for Vienna in November 1792 – that is, for four full seasons and part of a fifth – Beethoven played the viola in the orchestra. The repertory consisted almost entirely of light works, whether Italian *opera buffa* (Cimarosa, Paisiello, Sacchini, Salieri, Sarti, Martín y Soler), French *opéra comique* (Grétry, Monsigny, Dezède, Dalayrac), or South German *Singspiel* (Dittersdorf, Benda, Schuster, Schubaur, Umlauf). But it included Gluck's *Die Pilgrime von Mecca* and three operas by Mozart, *Die Entführung aus dem Serail* in 1788–9 and 1791–2, *Don Giovanni* (three performances), and *Le nozze di Figaro* (four performances), both in 1789–90. Practical experience of these scores can scarcely have failed to make a permanent impression on the young Beethoven.

His first ten years in Vienna brought little direct contact with the stage. Although several theatres were in operation, this was not a period of Viennese operatic glory. At the Court Theatre (Kärntnertor), largely confined to Italian opera, the favourite composers were Martín y Soler, Salieri, Cimarosa, Paer, and Zingarelli. It did produce the most successful German opera between *Die Zauberflöte* and *Der Freischütz*, Winter's *Das unterbrochene Opferfest* in 1796; but this singular association of a wildly exotic plot with music of demure domesticity, packed with Mozartian echoes but deficient in structure and characterization, in which a short-winded *volkstümlich* melody may eject without warning a rocket of extravagant coloratura, had little to offer Beethoven.[2] The popular German theatres, Marinelli's Leopoldstadt and Schikaneder's Theater auf der Wieden, specialized in farces and fairy stories, often with an oriental background. These were all *Singspiele* with copious dialogue; indeed, the scenic spectacle and the coarse buffooneries of the spoken text usurped the province of the music, which seldom attempted to impose any unity of

structure or atmosphere. The leading composers were Wenzel
Müller, Weigl, Süssmayr, Hoffmeister, Schenk, and Kauer. Only
Die Zauberflöte, which continued to draw audiences, can have
won Beethoven's respect, and he was not tempted to emulate it,
though he did compose two arias for insertion in a revival of
Umlauf's *Die schöne Schusterin* in 1796. Apart from this and the
ballet *Prometheus* (1801), his only tangible links with the Viennese
theatre at this period are the titles of the operas from which he
chose themes for variations, among them Grétry's *Richard Cœur-
de-Lion*, Müller's *Die Schwestern von Prag*, Wranitzky's *Das
Waldmädchen*, Paisiello's *La molinara*, Winter's *Das unterbrochene
Opferfest*, Weigl's *L'amor marinaro*, Salieri's *Falstaff*, and
Süssmayr's *Soliman II*.

In 1802 occurred an event that changed this picture decisively.
On 23 March Schikaneder produced Cherubini's *Lodoïska* at the
new Theater an der Wien, which had replaced the Theater auf der
Wieden in the previous year. This was the first major opera of the
French Revolution school to reach Vienna; it was also one of
the best, with a solidity of technique, a pulsating energy, and a
flavour of contemporary realism that must have startled Viennese
conservatives. Its success was immediate. Baron Braun, Deputy
Director of the Court Theatre, went to Paris to obtain more French
operas, 'all of which will be performed here most carefully according to the taste of the French'.[3] This journey led to Cherubini's
commission to compose *Faniska* for Vienna. Meanwhile Schikaneder,
encouraged it is said by Mozart's brother-in-law Sebastian Mayer,
an actor and bass singer who was to be Beethoven's first Pizarro,
decided to abandon pantomime and fairy stories for more serious
fare. In the event *Les deux journées* was produced by both
managements under different titles on consecutive nights (13 and
14 August 1802). All Cherubini's other post-Revolution operas
followed, *Médée* at the Kärntnertor on 6 November, *Élisa* at the
Theater an der Wien on 18 December, *L'Hôtellerie portugaise* on
22 September 1803. They were the forerunners of an avalanche of
French operas, many of which became more popular in Vienna
than in Paris. Dalayrac (whose earlier work had long been successful
in Germany), Méhul, Gaveaux, Boïeldieu, Isouard, Berton, and a
little later Spontini conquered the Austrian capital as easily as the
armies of Napoleon. Of the more adventurous operas, Le Sueur's
La Caverne appeared at two theatres within ten days in June 1803,
and Méhul's *Ariodant* followed on 16 February 1804.

Such was the background against which Beethoven's fitful career in the opera house began. Although its early course was inauspicious and in some respects obscure, two things are certain: the agent who established the link was Schikaneder, and the torch that fired Beethoven's imagination was the French opera – or rather *opéra comique* – of the Revolution. His opinion of Cherubini is well known. When the two composers met in July 1805, while the one was working on *Fidelio* and the other on *Faniska* (produced at the Kärntnertor on 25 February 1806), both in collaboration with Joseph Sonnleithner, Beethoven treated Cherubini with marked respect. In March 1823 he wrote to him: 'I value your works more highly than all other compositions for the theatre.' Two months later he sent Cherubini via Louis Schlösser 'all kinds of amiable messages' and an assurance that 'my most ardent longing is that we should soon have another opera composed by him'. His expressions of esteem, often repeated,[4] were not always qualified by restriction to the theatre: he regarded Cherubini as the greatest living composer. Nor was Cherubini the only member of the French school admired by the fastidious Beethoven. On 18 February 1823 he asked Moritz Schlesinger for music by Méhul and in thanking him for an unidentified score pronounced it 'so worthy of him'. Of Spontini he said in 1825: 'There is much good in him; he understands theatrical effects and the musical noises of warfare thoroughly.' He rated the French librettos as high as the music. While he constantly complained that 'the Germans cannot write a good libretto' and told Rellstab in 1825 that he could never compose operas on subjects like *Figaro* and *Don Giovanni*, which he found frivolous and indeed repugnant, he declared in conversation with Julius Benedict in 1823 that the best librettos he knew were those of *Les deux journées* and *La Vestale*.

There is a certain irony in the part played by Schikaneder. No evidence appears to support Emily Anderson's statement[5] that as early as 1801 he offered Beethoven his libretto *Alexander* with which he planned to open the Theater an der Wien (Teyber's setting inaugurated it on 13 June). But he did engage him to compose an opera early in 1803, and on most favourable terms, which included free lodging in the theatre. This commission is first mentioned in a letter of 12 February from Beethoven's brother Johann to Breitkopf & Härtel and thus preceded the concert at which the oratorio *Christus am Oelberge* was first performed on 5 April. The latter may have been a by-product of the same set of circumstances

(Beethoven said he wrote the music in a fortnight); it was taken as evidence of his fitness for theatrical composition. He moved into the theatre in the spring; on 2 August *Die Zeitung für die elegante Welt* published an announcement, under the date 29 June, that 'Beethoven is composing an opera by Schikaneder'. The libretto was *Vestas Feuer*, and Beethoven worked on it for some time, though not very assiduously;[6] production was planned for March 1804. Towards the end of the year he discarded it in disgust, as he explained in an interesting letter to Rochlitz (4 January 1804), adding: 'I have quickly had an old French libretto adapted and am now beginning to work on it.'[7] This was the genesis of *Fidelio*. In the same letter he rejected the first act of a libretto by Rochlitz because its subject was connected with magic. The public were now as prejudiced against such a theme as they had formerly been enthusiastic in its favour: Schikaneder's 'empire has really been entirely eclipsed by the light of the brilliant and attractive French operas'.

That Beethoven was attracted more by the operatic idea than by Schikaneder's libretto emerges from Georg August Griesinger's report to Breitkopf & Härtel (12 November 1803) that though still at work on *Vestas Feuer* 'he told me himself that he is looking for reasonable texts'.[8] *Vestas Feuer* is not a reasonable text. It is a ponderously heroic affair set in ancient Rome (though the names of the characters suggest Parthia or India) and replete with tedious intrigue.[9] Schikaneder had lapsed from pantomime into the stagnant backwash of Metastasio while retaining (in Beethoven's words to Rochlitz) 'language and verses such as could proceed only out of the mouths of our Viennese apple-women'. Beethoven set the opening scene, in which the father of the heroine, inflamed by the dark counsels of a slave and the fact that his would-be son-in-law is the child of an old enemy, at first denounces the lovers, but is won over by their devotion and heroic bearing. The principal movements are a love duet of Mozartian grace and a trio of reconciliation for soprano, tenor, and baritone. Eighty-one pages of autograph survive, but the wind parts are incomplete.[10] The most interesting features of this fragment are the linking arioso passages (it was a grand opera, not a *Singspiel*), which have no exact equivalent elsewhere in Beethoven, the striking parallel with *Fidelio* in the progress from spiritual darkness and conspiracy to the light of joy and reconciliation,[11] and the fact that Beethoven used the material of the trio in the same key for the duet 'O namenlose Freude'.[12] Although the music is characteristic and mature in style, there are no grounds for lamenting the loss of a masterpiece. Beethoven could scarcely have transcended the slough of Schikaneder's later scenes.[13]

His contract was conveniently invalidated by the sale of the Theater an der Wien to Baron Braun on 14 February 1804. By this time he was fully committed to *Fidelio*; in March he was urging Sonnleithner to finish his task by the middle of April, so that 'the opera can be produced in June at latest.'[14] His letter to Rochlitz, already quoted, implies that he himself chose the subject, and this may well be true despite Georg Friedrich Treitschke's statement that the initiative came from Sonnleithner.[15] Baron Braun gave Beethoven a new contract, allowing him to retain his rooms in the theatre, an event that Treitschke places at the end of 1804. This is probably an error, like his assertion that the libretto was chosen after the production of Paer's opera on the same subject (3 October 1804). It is not clear what caused the delay between the spring of 1804 and the summer of 1805, when the bulk of the work was done. The performance, planned for 15 October, was held up by the censorship, which demanded changes in the libretto (the backdating of the action to the sixteenth century dates from this time) and evoked from Sonnleithner a declaration that the empress 'found the original very beautiful and affirmed that no opera subject had ever given her so much pleasure'. The ban was soon lifted, but the delay was disastrous. On 13 November the French army occupied Vienna, which had been vacated by the nobility and most of Beethoven's friends. The opera was produced at the Theater an der Wien on 20 November before an audience full of French officers, and repeated to empty houses on the two following nights. The cast was:

Leonore	Anna Milder
Marzelline	Louise Müller
Florestan	Fritz Demmer
Pizarro	Sebastian Mayer
Jaquino	Caché
Rocco	Rothe
Don Fernando	Weinkopf

The conductor was Ignaz von Seyfried. Beethoven wished to call the opera *Leonore*, but since Paer had used this title and had close connections with the Kärntnertor Theatre the directors insisted on a change. It appeared on the bills as *Fidelio oder Die eheliche Liebe* and in the 1805 libretto simply as *Fidelio*.

The press was far from enthusiastic. The commonest complaint, not wholly without justification, was that the music, though beautiful in places, was 'ineffective and repetitious', especially in the treatment of words.[16] Beethoven's friends recognized this. In December, after he had withdrawn the opera, they organized a complete run-through with piano at Prince Lichnowsky's palace with the intention of persuading him to cut three numbers, the trio for Rocco, Marzelline, and Jaquino ('Ein Mann ist bald genommen'), the duet for Leonore and Marzelline ('Um in der Ehe'), and Pizarro's aria with chorus at the end of the original act II. According to J. A. Röckel it took them six hours to overcome Beethoven's resistance. These pieces, though they disappeared later, were not cut in 1806. Instead, without consulting Sonnleithner, who was busy with *Faniska*, Beethoven brought in Stephan von Breuning to tighten up the libretto. When asking Sonnleithner's permission to print the result under his name (early March 1806) Beethoven added: 'To make the opera move more swiftly I have *shortened everything* as much as possible, the *prisoners'* chorus, and chiefly numbers of that kind.'[17] As will be seen, this was a misleading statement; the 1806 changes were by no means confined to cuts.

Beethoven made another attempt to restore his original title, and the new edition of the libretto appeared as *Leonore oder der Triumph der ehelichen Liebe*;[18] but the directors once more overruled him. The opera was revived on 29 March and repeated on 10 April with the original cast, except that Röckel replaced Demmer as Florestan. Although Beethoven was so late in finishing his score that only one orchestral rehearsal was possible – which no doubt explains his furious complaints in two letters to Mayer[19] that the chorus made dreadful mistakes and many of his dynamic marks were ignored – the reception was much more favourable than in 1805. There are two accounts of what followed. According to Breuning a cabal in the theatre prevented further performances; Röckel, who is more likely to be correct, said that Beethoven, fancying himself cheated of his share of the receipts, demanded his score back just when a lasting success seemed assured. In May there was talk of a private performance at Prince Lobkowitz's palace. It is not known if this took place; but plans to produce the opera in Berlin and later (1808) in Prague came to nothing.

Fidelio slumbered till the beginning of 1814, when Beethoven, to his evident surprise, learned that three singers[20] wished to revive it at the Kärntnertor for their benefit. He agreed on condition that he was permitted to make changes. This time the revision of the libretto was entrusted (with Sonnleithner's permission) to Treitschke, an experienced man of the theatre. Beethoven worked at the score from February until 15 May. He found it an arduous task: 'I could compose something new far more quickly than patch up the old . . . I have to think out the entire work again . . . this opera will win for me a martyr's crown' (to Treitschke, April).[21] The new overture was not ready in time for the first performance (23 May), when that to *Die Ruinen von Athen* was substituted. It made its debut on the second night (26 May). The cast was:

Leonore	Anna Milder
	(Madame Hönig was the first choice)
Marzelline	Mlle Bondra
Florestan	Radichi
Pizarro	Johann Michael Vogl
	(replaced on 18 July by Anton Forti)
Jaquino	Frühwald
Rocco	Carl Friedrich Weinmüller
Don Fernando	Saal

The conductor was Michael Umlauf. The seventh performance on 18 July was for Beethoven's benefit; his advertisement stated that 'two new pieces have been added'.[22] From this revival, followed on 21 November by Weber's production in Prague, the success of the opera was assured.

Gaveaux's *Léonore*

J.-N. Bouilly's libretto *Léonore ou L'amour conjugal*, set by Pierre Gaveaux and produced at the Théâtre Feydeau in Paris on 19 February 1798, was, like his *Les deux journées* of two years later, based on a historical incident during the Reign of Terror.[23] Bouilly, serving in an official position at Tours, found himself in the role of Don Fernando; it is strange to reflect that the real-life Léonore and Florestan may have survived and even witnessed their translation to operatic fame. To prevent precise identification Bouilly moved the action to Spain, but acknowledged its authenticity by adding the words 'fait historique' to the title.[24]

The work is an *opéra comique* in two acts with thirteen musical numbers (apart from the overture) and much spoken dialogue. Roc, Marceline, and Jacquino talk in dialect. The general outline of the plot remains unchanged in Bouilly's libretto and Beethoven's three versions and is too familiar to need summarizing here; but there are significant shifts of emphasis. While Bouilly's act-division corresponds to that of the 1814 *Fidelio*, the course of events, the placing of the musical numbers, and the dialogue are closer to 1805. Five of the seven numbers in Bouilly's first act – Marceline's *couplets*, her duet with Jacquino, Roc's *chanson*, the duet for Marceline and Léonore in which the former looks forward to the birth of their first child while the latter dissembles, and the prisoners' chorus – were retained by Sonnleithner with little change. The other two he combined in a single movement. Léonore has two consecutive solos, a *romance* in which she is sustained by conjugal love and addresses her lost husband, and an air apostrophizing hope; they are separated by dialogue in which she learns from Roc of Pizare's orders that the prisoner is to be killed for reasons of state and to preserve the honour of one of the noblest families in Spain. Pizare has not revealed this to the audience; he whispers to Roc and briefs him offstage. Léonore has an awkward moment after the duet with Marceline, who has heard her talking in her sleep; she has to pretend she is looking for her lost father. Although Marceline speaks of letting the prisoners out for their daily exercise, it is Léonore who does this on Roc's orders, as a cover for their descent to dig the grave. The prisoners' chorus contains a solo, but none of the named characters takes part or is on the stage.

Sonnleithner also kept the first four numbers in Bouilly's second act: a recitative and *romance* for Florestan, the grave-digging duet for Léonore and Roc (during which she resolves to rescue the prisoner whoever he may be), their trio with Florestan, and the duet for husband and wife. There is no quartet in Gaveaux's opera; the important action here, including the trumpet call, takes place in dialogue. Pizare is heavily disguised and has to change into uniform to receive the Minister. Roc, whose orders were to admit a masked man, is at first ignorant of his identity as well as his motives. Léonore reveals herself before Pizare, who after unmasking tosses Roc a second purse of gold. When Pizare's assault on Léonore has been frustrated by her pistol and the trumpet call, Roc snatches the pistol and goes out with Pizare, closing the door on the lovers. Léonore, her weapon gone, collapses in despair. During the duet Florestan, still bemused, calls her, but cannot reach her on account of his chains. She revives slowly, taking some time to grasp that he is indeed her husband. The movement ends in mutual rapture. As Léonore explains how she entered the prison an offstage chorus is heard demanding vengeance. This is combined with a second duet in which the lovers, convinced that their last hour has come, resolve to die together. The denouement reverts to dialogue. Roc after exculpating himself restores the pistol to Léonore and throws both purses at Pizare's feet: he is cured of his lust for gold. Dom Fernand recommends the women in the audience to take Léonore as an example.

Bouilly tells an intensely dramatic story in clear straightforward terms. The compound of realism, low life, and earthy humour on the one hand (Roc is a close-fisted French peasant with an eye to the main chance) and heroic endeavour, a last-minute rescue, and an elevating moral on the other is typical of French opera in the revolutionary decade. So is the confined space and darkness of the setting. *Léonore* contains many premonitions of Romantic opera. It is as far as possible removed from the stagey conventions almost universal in contemporary German and Italian opera, whether serious or comic. Therein lay part of its appeal to Beethoven.

Gaveaux's *Léonore*, like many of the *opéras comiques* of Grétry and his school, is as much a play with songs as an opera. The fact that Pizare is a spoken part[25] is enough to prevent the drama permeating the score. Nevertheless the music, influenced as much by Cherubini as by Grétry, is not negligible.

Of particular interest are the strong indications that Beethoven knew Gaveaux's score, which had been published in Paris.[26] Half a dozen movements seem to contain the germs of ideas that Beethoven brought to full flower; this, not chance thematic resemblance, is the significant debt that genius owes to the second-rate. Among such passages are the headlong string scales in the coda of the overture, strikingly prophetic of *Leonore* Nos. 2 and 3, though more symmetrical; the alternating minor and major strains of Marceline's *couplets* (an interesting early experiment in local colour marked 'Tempo di Minuetto Seguidilla'); the cut of the melody of Roc's *chanson* (ex. 3.1); the use of a solo horn to introduce Léonore's *romance*; the combination of ostinato and repeated chords in the accompaniment of the grave-digging duet; and most of all the

Example 3.1

Maestoso marqué

Sans un peu d'or, un peu d'ai - san - ce, Re - te - nez bien cet - te le - çon

treatment of the prisoners' chorus. As in Beethoven, the slow-moving harmony, long pedals and gradual climb in pitch and volume from an initial *pianissimo* express the wonder of the prisoners as they creep out of their cells and peer into the light (ex. 3.2).

Example 3.2

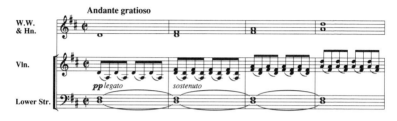

The Operas of Paer and Mayr

Between the inception and the performance of *Fidelio* two other operas based on Bouilly's libretto, both in Italian, came to birth. The libretto of Paer's *Leonora ossia L'amore conjugale* (Dresden, 3 October 1804), by G. Schmidt, preserves much of the detail of the story at the expense of its spirit. The part of Marcellina is expanded, evidently for a favoured singer boasting a top D and E flat. She has two substantial arias in the first act as well as several ensembles; like Gaveaux, Paer seeks to establish the locality, setting her initial aria in bolero rhythm. Her ambitions are thrust inappropriately into the foreground not only in the first finale but in the dungeon scene, where she appears catastrophically (having stolen the key from Rocco) between Pizarro's exit and the reunion of the lovers. She brings news of the Minister's arrival and refuses to budge without specific and repeated assurances of Fedele's love. Leonora is forced to comply in an extended duet in the presence of her husband. He is the only prisoner; there is no chorus, and Pizarro (a tenor) has no solo, though he sings in ensembles. On the other hand, the librettist does attempt to construct viable musical numbers from Bouilly's dialogue. There is a *buffo*[27] trio for Marcellina, Giacchino, and Rocco (both basses) at the point corresponding to Beethoven's 'Ein Mann ist bald genommen', and another trio when Pizarro, watched by Leonora, orders Rocco to follow him to receive secret instructions. Paer has a quartet in the second act, beginning when Leonora reveals her identity, but not in the first.

His score is more ambitious than Gaveaux's, but has less character. The style might be described as sub-Mozart; the duet for Marcellina and Giacchino is heavily indebted to *Figaro*. The dramatic scenes for Leonora in act I and Florestan in act II are on an enormous scale, bigger indeed than those in Beethoven's opera. Each has several linked movements comprising recitative, cavatina, and cabaletta; Leonora's contains a motive used in the overture.

Richard Engländer in an emphatic article[28] has argued that Beethoven and Sonnleithner knew Paer's opera and that all three versions of *Fidelio* are considerably indebted to it. Beethoven certainly possessed a copy of the score, though there is nothing to indicate when he acquired it. Engländer conjectures that it was Paer, on a visit to Vienna early in 1803, who brought the subject to his attention, and claims his Dresden *Leonora* as a vital link between Gaveaux and *Fidelio*. It is true that Paer's and Beethoven's librettos share certain features not found in Bouilly, for example the trio for Marzelline, Jaquino, and Rocco near the beginning, Pizarro's angry return in the first finale, and the dungeon quartet; but these are predictable moves for any librettist anxious to strengthen the links between music and drama. The one unquestionable point of contact concerns the 1814 version of *Fidelio* and is mentioned below. Engländer's musical parallels are for the most part period clichés and quite unconvincing. An exception is the resemblance between the chorus 'Wer ein holdes Weib' (ex. 3.3b) and a theme in Paer's finale (ex. 3.3a).

Example 3.3a

Suon di gio - ia in si bel gior - no [etc.]

Example 3.3b

Wer ein hol - des Weib er - run - gen, stimm' in un - ser'n Ju - bel ein

This is certainly striking, and it is conceivable that some visitor from Dresden whistled – or bellowed – a little Paer outside Beethoven's window.[29] On the other hand, the sketchbook shows him hammering out his melody by the usual laborious process,[30] and the date '2 June' among the sketches for this finale probably refers to 1804 (before the production of Paer's opera) rather than 1805.[31] Paer's *Leonora* did not reach Vienna until March 1806, when it was given privately at the Lobkowitz palace. Beethoven attended its first public performance (in German) on 8 February 1809.

Simone Mayr's *L'amor conjugale*, a one-act *farsa sentimentale* (a cross between Italian *farsa* and French *opéra comique* with the *buffo* element played down), saw the light at Padua in July 1805.[32] The librettist, Gaetano Rossi, transferred the action to Poland, doubtless under the influence of *Lodoïska*, which Mayr had already set twice in Italian. His text reduces the realism and potency of Bouilly's plot to a caper with the conventions. The political content vanishes: Pizarro's motive is love for Leonora, who is rescued by the fortuitous arrival of her brother-in-law.[33] Jaquino does not appear, nor do the prisoners; Rocco patronizes the bottle (Mayr, unlike Paer, keeps the gold aria). In place of the grave-digging duet Leonora sings a strophic romance in popular French style, hoping that Florestan will recognize her voice. Unlike Gaveaux and Paer, Mayr binds together the closing scenes in continuous music, beginning with a quartet when Rocco signals to Pizarro that the grave is ready. The climax of this is delayed by a slow cantabile in E flat, typical of Mayr and his Italian successors, including Rossini, after which the pistol and the trumpet signal restore the tempo. The finale contains an angry aria for Pizarro, very like Dourlinski's in act III of Cherubini's *Lodoïska*, which gives it a collateral relationship with Beethoven. Mayr's style is not unlike Paer's; he, too, concentrates on big dramatic monologues for Leonora and Florestan. When Florestan begins to think of his wife, two cors anglais (a favourite instrument) introduce a melody that oddly anticipates the main theme of Beethoven's 1814 overture. As usual Mayr is most individual in his treatment of the orchestra, especially the solo wind instruments. His function in the history of music was to provide a bridge between Mozart on the one hand and Rossini and Donizetti on the other. No one has suggested that Beethoven knew his opera.[34]

The 1805 version of Beethoven's opera

Beethoven's opera is by far the closest to the letter and the spirit of Bouilly. Sonnleithner's libretto is largely a translation with additional musical numbers. He divided Bouilly's first act into two, with no change of scene until the second finale, which he moved from the prison courtyard to another part of the fortress. Act I has three inserted numbers, a trio ('Ein Mann ist bald genommen') in which Rocco and Marzelline dash Jaquino's hopes of marriage, the canon quartet, and the trio for Rocco, Leonore, and Marzelline (no. 5 of the 1814 score), after which the curtain falls. The first three numbers in act II, the March, Pizarro's aria with chorus, and his duet with Rocco, are new. Pizarro posts the trumpeter before his aria and briefs Rocco on stage in the duet, but is not overheard by Leonore. Sonnleithner retains the long scene for Leonore and Marzelline, including the duet (without the passage, redolent of Papageno and Papagena, in which they speculate whether their child's first words will be 'Maman' or 'Papa') and the dialogue about Leonore talking in her sleep. The recitative before Leonore's aria ('O brich noch nicht, du mattes Herz!') is translated from Bouilly and very different from 1814; the apostrophe to hope is not in the 1805 libretto, but was probably inserted before performance. The scene changes at the end of the aria, and the finale follows at once. Marzelline lets the prisoners out in the ordinary course of her duties. Sonnleithner extended their chorus into a substantial finale. Rocco orders them back to the cells before telling Leonore the outcome of his interview with Pizarro. The Governor's wrath, warning of which is brought by Marzelline alone, is provoked not by the release of the prisoners but by Rocco's delay in digging the grave. He hustles the jailer and his assistants out and ends the act with a second aria, supported by male chorus, that involves much sabre-rattling, but does not advance the plot.

Act III follows the model closely, apart from the insertion of the quartet and the connection of Bouilly's last two numbers with the intervening dialogue in a continuous movement. The final section of Florestan's aria, as in Bouilly, is addressed to Leonore's portrait. Pizarro enters masked and disguised, but he reveals himself before Leonore and does not offer Rocco a second purse. The dialogue linking the quartet to the lovers' duet becomes a recitative. In the finale the chorus denounce Pizarro's sentence as too lenient, and Don Fernando decides to leave the decision to the king (was this one of the changes demanded by the censorship?). Pizarro is silent throughout. Leonore does not mention Marzelline's dowry, and there is no homily to the audience from Fernando or anyone else. These two details are essentially French, the former of all time, the latter characteristic of the Revolution period (compare Bouilly's ethical conclusion to *Les deux journées*: 'Le premier charme de la vie, C'est de servir l'humanité'). Perhaps in compensation Sonnleithner (or Beethoven) introduced a slightly modified quotation from Schiller's *Ode to Joy* in the couplet beginning 'Wer ein holdes Weib errungen', thereby linking the opera with the finale of the Ninth Symphony. Both works carry the same message; it is even possible that the one put the other into Beethoven's head.

Sonnleithner's chief aim was to increase the opportunities for expressing drama by musical means. In this he is often successful, especially in the two quartets and the development of Pizarro's part. The finales of the second and third acts, though not wholly satisfactory, are moves in the right direction. What is effective in Bouilly he preserves. The obvious flaw is the enormous expansion of the first and less dramatic half of the story. The exposition of the Marzelline subplot, leisurely in Bouilly, is further retarded by the new musical numbers. The first act merely outlines a situation; the action has yet to begin. Of the three central characters, Leonore does not appear until half-way through act I, Pizarro until act II, Florestan until act III. Up to Pizarro's first exit Sonnleithner has deployed nine musical numbers (excluding the overture), several of them developed at considerable length by Beethoven, against Bouilly's three. After this the drama sags again in the superfluous scene for Leonore and Marzelline; nor does the second finale draw all the threads together. The lightweight opening in the jailer's household, whose function is to set the scene, has usurped the prominence of the main plot. When the last act begins it is too late to redress the balance.

This defect is accentuated by Beethoven's music.[35] Though never dull, its regular periods are geared to abstract musical design rather than dramatic pace; consequently it lags behind the action and seems on occasion diffuse and repetitive. This must be ascribed to lack of practical experience in the theatre. The movements are all longer – some of them much longer – than in the 1814 score,[36] and there are more of them. The trio 'Ein Mann ist bald genommen' in act I and the duet 'Um in der Ehe' in act II are dramatically otiose, especially the latter, which enlarges on a false situation of which we have already had more than enough and disperses the tension when it has at last begun to accumulate. The old-fashioned concertante layout with solo violin and cello, for all its charm, belongs to a more leisurely type of pre-Revolution rescue opera, that of Mozart's *Die Entführung*. In recommending the omission of these two numbers and Pizarro's second aria, the weakest music in the score, Beethoven's friends showed sound judgement, as he tacitly acknowledged when he followed their advice in 1814. The musical idiom, especially in the early scenes, is much more Mozartian in 1805 than in 1814. The 1805 overture, *Leonore* No. 2, might be criticized for its lopsided construction, especially when compared with its successor; but Beethoven's intention seems to have been to supply a graphic summary of the action rather than a formal overture. The result is a piece of programme music that ranks as a mighty forerunner of the symphonic poems of Liszt and Strauss.[37]

The original third act is a different matter. Although this, too, contains passages, especially in the finale, where the music clogs the wheels of the drama, it is less a primitive attempt at what Beethoven achieved in 1814 than a volley at a different target. This change of aim is discussed below. Meanwhile the music that did not survive 1805–6 demands comment. The andante un poco agitato F minor conclusion to Florestan's aria, though it lacks the radiance of his F major vision in 1814, has a defiant stoicism that is not only most movingly expressed but enlarges our view of Florestan's character. Anyone can see his beloved in a trance; it takes a hero to look back on his past happiness and accept his fate. There is some doubt whether the *Melodram* before the grave-digging duet formed part of the 1805 score. Prieger and Hess include it; Jahn ascribes it to 1814. Certainly its surviving form cannot belong to 1805, for it quotes the F major (1814) section of Florestan's aria when he stirs in his sleep. Yet there are sketches dating from 1804 as well as 1814. The most likely solution is that it was performed in 1805 in a version since lost, and rewritten in 1814. The sketches prove that the allusions to the 6/8 section of the Leonore–Rocco duet in the previous finale ('Wir müssen gleich zum Werke schreiten') were part of Beethoven's original plan.

Example 3.4

Allegro ma non troppo

From the end of the quartet onwards the 1805 score (following Bouilly) has a dramatic tension and a vividness of characterization, both fully realized in musical terms, that are almost entirely absent from 1814. When Pizarro goes out, in response to the more florid trumpet call of the No. 2 overture, Leonore throws herself at Rocco's feet with a spoken appeal against the closing bars of the orchestral ritornello. Rocco snatches the pistol from her and disappears; the quartet ends with a *fortissimo* diminished seventh as she utters a piercing cry and falls senseless. The long recitative in which Florestan tries to reach her, she slowly recovers, and each at last grasps the truth, is a superb stroke of musical drama. Based on a beautiful melody for solo oboe (ex. 3.4), it builds up gradually over seventy-six bars to the passionate discharge of the duet 'O namenlose Freude'. The music has a quality of dawning suspense paralleled only by that which introduces the finale of the Fifth Symphony. It launches the duet with a tremendous impact, reinforced by the fact that both voices enter together and the melody is carried up to the top B. This may be instrumental vocal writing (the words are a much poorer fit than in *Vestas Feuer*), but it releases the full emotional content of the situation. Of Beethoven's three versions of this melody the second is by far the most exciting in its context because it has been so thoroughly prepared (see ex. 3.5).

Moreover the whole ambience of the duet is transformed by the fact that the lovers have no reason to believe themselves out of danger. They have lost their only weapon and naturally take the distant cries of vengeance, supported by trombones behind the scenes, as directed against them. These and the incursion of the whole tumultuous crowd into the dungeon produce another splendid theatrical climax, which may well have reminded early audiences of the storming of the Bastille. The finale contains some rather commonplace rejoicing, though Fernando's solos have a Sarastro-like nobility, and is undeniably static. The F major Andante assai, twice as long as in 1814, is a tribute to the continuity of Beethoven's development: its principal theme comes from the *Cantata on the*

Example 3.5

(a) Vestas Feuer

(b) 1805

(c) 1814

Death of the Emperor Joseph II, composed in Bonn as early as 1790.[38] The original words are significant, and may have suggested the borrowing; but the simple dance-like accompaniment shows no sign of the later polyphonic resource (ex. 3.6).

Example 3.6

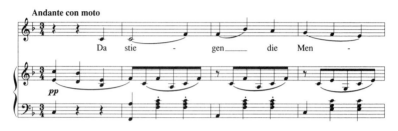

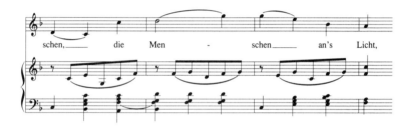

The 1806 version[39]

The changes made in 1806 are generally dismissed as hasty cuts to serve a temporary emergency. This does less than justice to Beethoven and Breuning. Although some of the excisions are crude and were later restored, it is clear that the authors had a shrewd idea what was the matter with the opera. They reduced it to two acts by combining the original acts I and II, but made a change of scene at the old act-break. They altered the order of movements and events in the new first act. Rocco's aria was omitted, but not before Breuning had supplied it with new words;[40] when it was eventually restored, the text was a fusion of these and Sonnleithner's. Pizarro now posts the trumpeter *after* his aria (a good touch). Leonore enters in great agitation immediately after the Rocco–Pizarro duet; she has observed their conference, but is uncertain whether Rocco has obtained permission for her to enter the dungeon. Her recitative and aria (no. 11 in 1805) follow; then the scene with Marzelline, including the duet 'Um in der Ehe' (no. 10), *preceded* by the conversation about Leonore talking in her sleep. Jaquino overhears the end of the duet. Leonore, seeking a pretext to escape, asks if it is not time to let the prisoners out for their exercise and hurries off. Jaquino flies into a jealous rage, leading to the trio with Rocco 'Ein Mann ist bald genommen' (no. 3), which like the other trio (no. 6) is followed by a change of scene. Leonore enters with keys, delighted to release the prisoners and wishing she could do the same for Florestan. But Rocco does not send the prisoners back to the cells after their chorus; they go into the garden, as in 1814, and we do not witness their return. It will be seen that several improvements usually attributed to Treitschke date from 1806.[41] Breuning also clarified a number of points in the dialogue and stage directions.

In act II he added the direction about shifting the stone during the duet and made the words of the trio 'Euch werde Lohn' more graphic. Leonore's reference to her beating heart and Florestan's observation that the boy as well as the man seems moved are new. In the quartet Pizarro opens his cloak instead of taking off his mask. Leonore's first half-conscious words in the recitative before 'O namenlose Freude' were changed from 'Gebt ihm mir!' to 'Todt! Dahin!' There were several amendments to the finale. Just after Don Fernando raises Leonore to her feet Jaquino has a brief exchange with Marzelline. His hopes revive on the instant, and she encourages him too readily with a reference to the trio in which she refused him in act I. This cannot be called good psychology, and it disappeared in 1814 in favour of Marzelline's single cry of distress. The long section in which Don Fernando pronounces sentence on Pizarro, Leonore and Florestan appeal for mercy, the chorus demand greater severity, and Don Fernando decides to refer the matter to the king was replaced by a short recitative: Fernando disposes of Pizarro with a terse 'Hinweg mit diesem Bösewicht!'[42] Breuning had to supply Leonore with a new quatrain in the closing ensemble. In 1805 she was mute for the last 132 bars of the opera. Beethoven carved a top line for her out of the choral soprano part and rewrote Florestan's music here in more florid form.

Rocco's aria and the *Melodram* were the only movements to disappear entirely. But most of the others were shortened, some of them drastically.[43] Both trios in act I suffered something approaching mutilation, and so did the opening of Florestan's scena: the recitative was rewritten, by no means for the better, and the Adagio deprived of its ritornello.[44] Leonore's aria lost fourteen bars in the coda, including an elaborate and taxing cadenza. An interesting change here was the insertion of the words 'O Hoffnung, O komm', marked *sprechend oder singend*, against the ritornello of the Adagio. The orchestral introduction to the grave-digging duet was shortened by seventeen bars, but the double bassoon was added to the score.[45] Beethoven rewrote the trio 'Euch werde Lohn' in much terser form, modifying the anacrusis of the main theme, removing a long roulade for Florestan on the word 'Dank!' (bar 94 of the 1814 score), and transplanting the next section, where all three voices sing together just before the change of tempo, back into the middle of Florestan's first solo, where it replaced the earlier statement of the same material. This destroyed the balance of the movement at both points; Beethoven rectified it in 1814. He severely compressed 'O namenlose Freude' and its recitative, reducing a total of 291 bars to 185, but lengthened and improved the orchestral coda, which reached its 1814 form in 1806. Leonore's part in the duet was eased by the removal of two slow chromatic-scale passages climbing to top C, possibly at the request of Milder. Both finales were considerably shortened, the first by 122 bars, the second by 154. This affected all their principal movements. The prisoners' chorus was pruned of much repetition. In the second finale the offstage chorus lost its trombones[46] and the F major section its long opening quintet for soloists. A more positive change was the substitution of the No. 3 overture for No. 2 and the consequent simplification of the trumpet calls in the quartet. Tempo alterations suggest that several movements were taken too slowly in 1805. The prisoners' chorus was marked up from Allegretto to Allegretto con moto, Pizarro's second aria from Allegro ma non troppo to Allegro con brio, the trio 'Euch werde Lohn' from Andante con moto (leading to Più mosso) to Allegro (leading to Un poco più allegro), the dungeon quartet from Allegro to Allegro con brio, the opening of 'Wer ein holdes Weib' from Maestoso to Maestoso vivace.

While the effect of these alterations must have been beneficial in speeding up the action, they did not go to the root of the problem, the undue prominence of Marzelline, and some of them were ill-judged. It is not surprising that Beethoven returned to the attack eight years later.

The 1814 version

Treitschke's statement that he rewrote the dialogue 'almost wholly anew, succinct and clear as possible' is disingenuous; he preserved a great deal of both Sonnleithner and Breuning, though he made cuts and a few small insertions. His changes were, however, radical in several important respects. He tackled Marzelline firmly, omitting the trio and duet shifted in 1806 and the conversation about Leonore talking in her sleep. He transposed the order of the first two numbers, obtaining a more effective launch into the drama. He abolished both changes of scene in this act. Leonore now overhears Pizarro's duet with Rocco and reacts to it in the new recitative 'Abscheulicher!' This is the one episode in *Fidelio* that undoubtedly echoes Paer's libretto, where the corresponding scene begins (in the German translation): 'Abscheulicher Pizarro! Wo gehest du hin? Was denkst du? Was hast du vor?' and the aria contains the line 'Des Meers empörte Wogen'.[47] It is at Leonore's special request that Rocco lets out the prisoners. Treitschke worked much more action into the finale. At the bass prisoner's solo 'Sprecht leise' a sentry appears on the wall and goes off to inform Pizarro. Jaquino as well as Marzelline brings warning of the Governor's wrath, which is more formidable because more strongly motivated than in 1805. Rocco takes a less abject stand. His excuses include the subtle one that since Pizarro's particular prisoner is to die the others can surely be allowed to enjoy the sunshine and celebrate the king's name-day. He has, however, to recall them from the garden and lock them up. This makes room for their second chorus and the ensemble based on it.

There are few changes in the first half of act II, except that Florestan, instead of addressing Leonore's portrait, has a delirious vision of her as an angel summoning him to freedom in heaven. (Treitschke left a vivid account of Beethoven improvising the music of the new F major section as soon as he received the words; nevertheless it appears in its proper place among the sketches.) The quartet is interrupted after the second trumpet call by the arrival of Jaquino and soldiers, to the unconcealed delight of Rocco. This effectively circumscribes Pizarro's movements, but destroys the effect of Beethoven's modulation. At Pizarro's exit Rocco, instead of disarming Leonore, seizes her hand and Florestan's, presses them to his breast, and points to heaven before hurrying out. In the dialogue that replaces the recitative Leonore assures Florestan that all their troubles are over. Rocco returns after the duet and informs them, in dialogue, that Florestan's name is not on the official list of prisoners; his detention was therefore illegal. The scene changes to the parade-ground, where the chorus, including the prisoners, acclaim the long-awaited day of justice. Don Fernando brings from the king a pardon for all the prisoners and makes a political speech: tyranny is at an end, let brother seek the hand of brother. He is astonished when Rocco produces Florestan and Leonore (Rocco does not throw down the purse, and he tells Don Fernando a good deal that we already know). Pizarro asks permission to speak, but is refused and led off *before* the removal of Florestan's fetters.

Treitschke's treatment of act I merits unstinted applause. The drama begins to move earlier, gathers momentum from Pizarro's first appearance, and retains a tightening grip until the end. The changes in act II produce exactly the opposite effect. Rocco's character is sentimentalized. The lovers' secure confidence saps the excitement of the duet, which in the absence of the recitative makes a standing instead of a flying start. The spoken conclusion (generally omitted today) is feeble in the extreme. The change of scene, which Treitschke regarded as the healing of 'a great fault' in Sonnleithner's libretto, fails to achieve one of the most resounding anticlimaxes in the history of opera only because Beethoven capped it with a hymn to freedom of surpassing nobility.

We must, however, recognize that this was the result of deliberate choice. Sonnleithner, like Bouilly, concentrates on the personal drama of Leonore and Florestan; the other prisoners are little more than a background. The moral is not emphasized, but allowed to emerge through the action. Treitschke and Beethoven raise it from the particular to the universal and ram it home so hard that the hollow reverberations of a thumped tub are all but discernible. (In a letter of April 1814, already cited, Beethoven told Treitschke that he was setting the text 'exactly in the way you have altered and improved everything, an achievement which every moment I am recognizing more and more',[48] but it must be assumed that they had already agreed on the main trend.) The prisoners, no longer restricted to a single chorus, play a much larger part and obviously symbolize for Beethoven the whole of suffering mankind. The finale with its general amnesty becomes a pattern of the day of judgement. Moreover the change of scene gives the opera a neatly symmetrical plan: act I moves from light into darkness, act II from darkness into light. But although this idealized content finds ample utterance in the music, it does not spring convincingly from the plot; the symbolism is stretched beyond its implications. We have little reason to suppose that all the prisoners had been unjustly incarcerated, or that their crime was political (though Pizarro's anonymous letter does hint that Florestan may not be the only innocent victim); they could be a set of thieves, murderers, and delinquents. In delivering this mighty paean Beethoven comes closer still to the spirit of the Ninth Symphony,[49] but he drains his characters of individuality and smudges the portrait of the hero and heroine so movingly drawn in 1805. They become personifications, and since Pizarro alone stands for evil the mottled personality of Rocco must be white-washed into benevolent conformity.

The musical changes in 1814 nearly all bear witness to richer maturity. The splendid new E major overture supplies a more fitting introduction to the light tone of the first scene than *Leonore* No. 3, whose massive stature throws much that follows into shadow. The key may have been chosen to pick out the E major of Leonore's aria. The 1805–6 versions have a clear C major home tonic; the first and last vocal movements each move from C minor to C major, and the words of Marzelline's aria, 'O wär' ich schon mit dir vereint', announce at the outset one of the central ideas of the story. The rearranged order and the new overture indicate a different tonal plan. Beethoven made further changes in all the numbers he retained. Many of them are small cuts, involving the elision of idle bars and florid ornamental passages, especially at cadences. Their cumulative effect is considerable, and reflects a powerful urge, typical of late Beethoven, to break down exact symmetry of phrase; at the same time they accommodate the expression and declamation of the music strictly to the ebb and flow of the drama. Hess, though full of complaints that Beethoven destroyed the perfection of his 1805 design, rightly points out that in such movements as the duet in which Pizarro and Rocco plan the murder he took a substantial stride towards the flexible methods of Wagner. There are numerous improvements in detail. These, like the sketches,[50] throw much fascinating light on Beethoven's creative processes; only a few can be mentioned here. It is clear that he did indeed rethink the whole score from the beginning. While he accepted most of the 1806 cuts, in three movements, the two surviving trios and the recitative and ritornello of Florestan's aria, he made a partial return to the longer text of 1805, though not in identical form.

The canon quartet, slightly modified, lost a single bar. Pizarro's aria was improved by the insertion of sixteen bars with a bold new modulation and a new rhythm at the first entry of the chorus. Leonore's aria, apart from its more striking recitative, emerged in much terser and more concentrated form. The ritornello was shortened, the voice part simplified and pruned of adornments, the first twenty-two bars of the Allegro con brio with an arresting passage for horns cut altogether, thereby altering the whole balance of the aria, and the *più lento* mark added at the words 'in Fesseln schlug'. Milder told Schindler that she had severe struggles with Beethoven over 'the unbeautiful, unsingable passages, unsuited to her voice' in the Adagio and finally refused to sing it in the old form. This did the trick. A comparison of the final bars indicates what she achieved (ex. 3.7).

Beethoven made an interesting change – or rather two successive changes – to the tenor prisoner's solo in the chorus 'O welche Lust'. In 1805 he set the third and fourth lines as shown in ex. 3.8. The pause of nearly two bars, punctuated by shy *staccato* arpeggios on the wood-wind, gives a touching emphasis to the words 'wir werden frei', as if the singer scarcely dare utter them. In shortening the whole passage for 1806 Beethoven reduced this to a momentary hesitation, emphasizing 'frei' with a *sforzando* (ex. 3.9). In 1814, though the accompaniment is virtually unchanged, he modified the declamation and dynamics (ex. 3.10). 'Frei' carries more weight,

Example 3.7

(a) 1805

(b) 1814

Example 3.8

but the pause has gone, and it is impossible not to feel that something has been lost. The later part of the finale from shortly after Pizarro's return, including the exquisite chorus 'Leb' wohl, du warmes Sonnenlicht', is all new. The formal and the tonal balance is strengthened: the 1814 finale, though it makes an impression of greater spaciousness and mass, is the shortest of the three.

Florestan's aria has many differences in addition to the restoration of the ritornello and the new F major conclusion. The introduction and recitative were refashioned for the second time, and the Adagio extended. The only musical alteration to the grave-digging duet (the words were touched up towards the end) was the

Example 3.9

Example 3.10

new semiquaver bass figure for the shifting of the stone. Beethoven again rewrote the trio 'Euch werde Lohn', bringing it much closer to 1805 than to 1806. There were many changes to the vocal lines of the quartet, especially in Pizarro's part, and to the scoring of the last section. Leonore's top note at 'Tödt erst sein *Weib*!', which had been B natural (despite the accompanying harmony) in 1805, became B flat,[51] and her top B flat at 'und du bist *todt*!' an octave above the trumpet entry fell to a low F below it. The second trumpet call was now unaccompanied, and the two introductory bars were added after the spoken interruption, perhaps to help the voices. In 'O namelose Freude', the one movement unmistakably weakened, the voices sing the modified melody in succession instead of together. Whereas in 1805 the duet expresses the joy of reunion and the A major episode of the finale the sense of release as the spiritual light of freedom bursts into the dungeon, in 1814 the duet has to carry a double response to reunion and rescue, and the A major music (with new words) is played in full daylight after all is over. Nevertheless the new finale is musically a great improvement. The opening chorus and Don Fernando's solo are new; from·the A major section onwards everything is rewritten on the old material. The F major Andante assai, now Sostenuto assai, begins not with a quintet (as in 1805) or a chorus (as in 1806), but far more movingly with solos for Leonore and Florestan expressing wonder. Beethoven had second thoughts about several of the tempos altered in 1806: the first prisoners' chorus is now Allegro ma non troppo, the trio 'Euch werde Lohn' Moderato, 'Wer ein holdes Weib' Allegro ma non troppo (Presto molto instead of Allegro con brio in the coda).

A certain mystery surrounds Beethoven's advertisement of two new pieces for his benefit on 18 July. One of them was Rocco's aria, not heard since 1805. Treitschke conflated two versions of the words; Beethoven slightly shortened the 6/8 sections, removed the trumpet and drum parts, and changed the tempos from Allegretto moderato (2/4) – Allegro non molto (6/8) to Allegro moderato – Allegro. The other insertion was a new aria for Leonore; Beethoven reported to Treitschke early in July that 'Milder got her aria a fortnight ago'.[52] Treitschke says it held up the action and 'was again omitted' (after one performance?); the *Allgemeine musikalische Zeitung* also considered the act had 'become unnecessarily long'.[53] Despite certain inconsistencies in the press notices this was almost certainly the aria we know today. But if so, what had Milder sung at the first six performances? A dated manuscript libretto in the theatre archives, unquestionably prepared for the 1814 revival, contains a different version of the 'Abscheulicher' recitative (eight lines, the last four quite unconnected with the seven that took their place),[54] followed by the words of the Allegro con brio in the 1805–6 setting (beginning 'O du, für den ich alles trug'); no sign of 'Komm, Hoffnung'. (A later hand has inserted the familiar words, and those of Rocco's aria.) This agrees precisely with Treitschke's statement that the aria 'received a new introduction, and only the last movement, "O du, für den ich alles trug", was retained'.[55] It seems likely that an earlier 'Abscheulicher', from which the entire 'Komm, Hoffnung' section was struck out, was sung six times and subsequently lost. Some support for this conjecture may be found in another manuscript libretto[56] of very recent discovery, which also omits Rocco's aria and has the earlier form of 'Abscheulicher'. Its margins are covered with Beethoven's annotations (words, music, indications of scoring and tempo), which clearly reflect his first thoughts on receiving the text early in 1814, before sketching began. Against the last two lines of 'Abscheulicher' he wrote 'Corni (6/8)', an indication that corresponds with no surviving version.[57] It is true that there is no sign of a lost aria in the sketches; but those for the first finale before the chorus 'Leb' wohl, du warmes Sonnenlicht', which would have immediately followed any such aria composed in the spring of 1814, are likewise missing. The sketches for the familiar 'Abscheulicher' come very late, after those for the overture, which was not ready for the first night.

In 1925 Hans Joachim Moser suggested the construction of a fourth version of the opera, combining all that is best in the first and third. This is neither practicable nor desirable.[58] But there is no need to regard the later version as a replacement of the earlier; both are viable, and the labours of Jahn, Prieger, and Hess have made 1805 as accessible as 1814. Our preference can remain a matter of taste. It is perhaps worth commenting on the custom, introduced in the nineteenth century, popularized by Mahler, and followed by Toscanini, Klemperer, and other conductors, of interposing the No. 3 overture between the dungeon and parade-ground scenes. This cannot be defended on the score of authenticity; but neither can it be condemned as dramatically injurious, for the drama is dead. The overture repeats in summary what we have just witnessed; it scarcely affects Beethoven's paean to liberty. And it may bridge an awkward lacuna while the scenery is changed.

4 *The French theatrical origins of* Fidelio

DAVID CHARLTON

Like any traditional myth, the fable of Leonora is at once simple to summarize but very complex in its human implications. We cannot know the stages by which the ancient myths reached their now-familiar forms. But with *Fidelio* this process is open to view. Beethoven's opera derived, with few changes, from a recent operatic text by a young lawyer and administrator with an inborn love of storytelling: Jean-Nicolas Bouilly (1763–1842).

The constituent elements of *Léonore, ou L'amour conjugal* were not the invention of Bouilly: subject, genre, dramaturgy, dramatic motifs (the prison; female singer in male role; liberation) all drew on recent French traditions. Furthermore, *Léonore* was performed at a theatre with a particular social and political reputation; and its score was written by the composer of the most notorious political song of the mid-1790s: 'Le réveil du peuple'. This musician, Pierre Gaveaux, took the role of Florestan in his own opera. In short, the Paris *Léonore* of 19 February 1798 contained a host of political associations and theatrical memories. It engaged with French history by dramatizing a political crime at a sensitive juncture in the Directory (1795–9) and by claiming to be historically self-referential: to show (under the lightest mask of disguise) events that had occurred in recent life. This claim was part of its political terms of reference.

Viennese theatre was no stranger to Parisian opera with spoken dialogue. For forty years the French had nurtured a new style of *opéra comique*, using solos, ensembles and choruses developed musically out of the experience of Italian *opera buffa*. This fertile regeneration of a national art form drew particular strength from Enlightenment Paris. The capital had always acted as a magnet for writers; it provided salons where they could develop ideas; its publishers disseminated endless new material (stories; novels;

travel writing; poems; plays, etc.) and of course music. Opera and theatre before 1790 operated from day to day at a modest distance from royal control, though there was universal censorship. A spirit of enthusiasm and invention prevailed, which projected itself in *opéra comique* through a powerful repertory of works, the best of which maintained themselves on the stage. So, as Bruce Brown has well shown, French *opéra comique* was familiar as a series of fictions (perhaps more than as a musical repertory) through different modes of assimilation throughout the theatrical cultures of the civilized world from 1760 on.[1]

In fact, the decline of the *ancien régime* formed a piquant counterpoint to the undisguised vigour of its theatre. Some writers quickly learnt social criticism from the tradition of the English stage, so that *opéra comique* in particular developed a small but important repertory of works which obliquely addressed topical questions, for example, the power of landlords; the loyalty of their tenants; the power conferred by inheritance, or by the privilege of a career in Church or army.[2]

The path taken by Bouilly was thus unsurprising: trained in law at Tours and Orléans, presented in 1787 at the bar of the Paris Parlement, he was obviously thrown into constitutional debates and actively continued the theatre career he had begun with the comedy *La Matinée à la mode* in 1782. Politics could not be escaped. In 1790 Bouilly virtually lectured the audience in his libretto on Peter the Great (*Pierre le Grand*, set by Grétry) by pointing out that he saw the figure of Peter as analogous to Louis XVI, and that of Peter's Swiss mentor, Admiral Lefort, as analogous to Louis's Swiss financial adviser, Jacques Necker. Peter – supposedly like the French monarch – 'disdained the splendour and pleasures of his throne, to dedicate himself completely to the happiness of his peoples'. Rarely had a librettist, in a published preface, nailed his royalist colours so firmly to the mast.

In demonstrating considerable early skill as a musical dramatist, Bouilly also announced his aesthetic apprenticeship to the doyen of *opéra comique* authors, Michel-Jean Sedaine (1719–97). In his unreliable memoirs, Bouilly claimed that Sedaine personally unlocked for him the secrets of his dramatic art.[3] Sedaine was the presiding genius of *opéra comique* between 1759 and 1789, being elected to the Académie Française in 1786. Of unprivileged birth and education, he retained – in spite of the prolonged opposition that certain of his works encountered – a staunch independence of mind. He was clearly of the reforming camp: his best-known play is entitled *Le Philosophe sans le savoir* (1765).[4] The theme of unjust detention runs through key Sedaine texts from 1762 onwards, and so these can be regarded as forming the foundation of a drama-turgical mentality that was congenial to Beethoven (whose years in the Bonn orchestra were spent in part playing French *opéra comique*) and crucial to *Fidelio*.

In Sedaine's *Le Roi et le fermier* (1762; music by Monsigny) Jenny is ensnared within Lurewell's chateau, defends her virtue, and escapes by using her wits. In his *Le Déserteur* (1769; also by Monsigny) the unfortunate soldier Alexis finds himself in prison and under sentence of death for desertion. He is eventually saved by the extraordinary courage of his fiancée, Louise, who petitions the king. The whole of act 2 and much of act 3 are set in the interior of the place of detention. Sedaine's adaptation of La Fontaine and Boccaccio (*Le Magnifique*, music by Grétry, 1777) features the release of the heroine's father from years of slavery, to which he has been subjected by a malefactor. The adaptation of the *chantefable Aucassin et Nicolette* portrays an escape from a fortified tower, and the same motif shortly afterwards formed the resolution of *Richard Cœur-de-lion* in the setting by Grétry of 1784. (Beethoven wrote piano variations on the Romance which occurs throughout this opera, 'Une fièvre brûlante'.)

It is interesting that Sedaine, almost with each work, valued the historical authenticity of his source material. *Le Roi et le fermier* merely originated in Robert Dodsley's English play, but *Le Déserteur* stemmed from a reported incident in actual life.[5] The thirteenth-century *Aucassin* was hallowed by age anyway, while *Richard* was of course based on the imprisonment of Richard I of England on his return from the Third Crusade. Most of these works held the stage to 1790, all were published, and many were performed on a wide scale.

Sedaine was certainly concerned to educate audiences by creating art from life, though he never makes his moral verbally explicit. Clearly, acts of humanity – sometimes retribution – were of the essence. But at the same time Sedaine seems to have wanted to impart a 'mythic' level to his work. In *Aucassin* he handles material of elemental intensity; in *Richard* he was so conscious of the parallel between Blondel (who finds King Richard by singing the Romance) and Orpheus that he makes Blondel himself refer to Orpheus' musical journey into Hades.[6] And in the text for his Bluebeard opera (*Raoul Barbe-Bleue*, 1789) he worked in a relevant allusion to the myth of Cupid and Psyche. Thanks to this kind of approach, actions and stage settings could carry unusual symbolic weight.

Sedaine's closest anticipation of *Léonore/Fidelio* contains both a 'mythic' and a historical underpinning: *Le Comte d'Albert* (1787). This opera, set by Grétry, betrays the closest structural connection with *Fidelio* since it is in two acts, focussing on the climactic release of a prisoner (d'Albert) by his wife. Critics noted that the basic story derived from events in 1721, when one Count d'Albert (possibly a Flemish citizen) was imprisoned for duelling but escaped thanks to a daring stratagem.[7]

Countess d'Albert is pictured as devoted and courageous: she risks danger by appearing to cause her husband's escape, using a knife to make it seem as though she has obliged Antoine (a street porter) to exchange clothes with her husband, and so allow the latter to flee. Earlier on, d'Albert and his wife are shown, in a substantial musical duet, to be exemplars of conjugal love, and indeed it may well have been this unusual dramatic feature (for *opéra comique*) that inspired Grétry to his best musical efforts. However, conjugal love exists in the work in parallel to the 'mythic' matrix, which was taken from La Fontaine's fable 'The Lion and the Rat'. As a concealed allegory, Sedaine explained, the repayment of a virtuous deed by the low-born Antoine to the higher-born d'Albert (the 'lion') was the secular gospel within the story.

The curtain to act 2 – as in *Fidelio* and *Le Déserteur* – rises to reveal a prison cell containing the male leading character alone. In *Le Déserteur* Alexis is at first defiant (D minor) then evokes his Louise (wind instruments predominating) by reading a letter from her. D'Albert in the later opera is accorded a sombre C minor orchestral prelude (see ex. 4.1), before his subdued opening words, 'Quelle fatale journée'. Such orchestral music now metaphorically reflects the consciousness of an imprisoning space and in fact 'overwhelms' the vocal utterance. Later, as the music shifts to E flat, d'Albert's mind turns to the memory of his wife and children.

It is not certain that Beethoven knew *Le Comte d'Albert* at first hand. However, it is recorded by Thayer that two years before the composer left Bonn, late in 1792, one of the works staged at the Court theatre there was entitled 'Kein Dienst bleibt unbelohnt', which could easily refer to Sedaine's opera. And the work went on being acted in 1790s Paris.

Beethoven cannot, however, have been ignorant of *Le Déserteur*; Bonn performances apart, it had been – in 1776 – the most frequently performed stage work in Germany *in any genre*; the relevant survey included works by Lessing, Goethe, Shakespeare and Mozart.[8] We forget the European familiarity with *opéra-comique* at our peril.

Example 4.1
Act 2.   Le Théâtre représente l'intérieur d'une Chambre de Prison.
             (The stage depicts the interior of a prison chamber.)

Herbert Lindenberger reminds us: 'Most of the great historical dramas are centrally concerned either with the transfer of power from one force to another, or with the means by which a force already in power manages to stabilize itself against the onslaught of contending forces.'[9] History plays and historical operas had already been advocated by writers in France as suitable means for educating her citizenry, following the example of Shakespeare. (Conversely, the use of classical subjects had been denigrated by radical progressives.) Around the time of Bouilly's arrival in Paris the monarchy's predicament was already provoking politicised reactions in historical opera; one example was Dalayrac's opera *Sargines* (1788). Taken from an incident in mediaeval French history, it indirectly solicited support for Louis XVI. A yet closer harbinger of Revolution opera was Nicolas Dezède's *Péronne sauveé*, given at the Paris Opéra (no less!) in 1783. It was radical enough to portray a woman of the people who saves the nation through her quick-witted courage. This woman, Marie Fouré, had been a historical figure during the actual siege of Péronne in 1536. Therefore it was natural that when the revolutionary wars brought their own sieges, catastrophes and military victories, operas should have taken over realistic formats in order to bring such events into the theatre and help generate patriotic support. History was brought up to date, as it were, and a number of generic labels were adopted to signal that the works in question derived from the annals of life: *trait historique*; *fait historique*; *drame historique*; *pièce patriotique*; and so on.

At the same time, the new legislators in the National Convention were breaking the mould of privilege which had always kept the number of official theatres in France to a minimum. From 1791 anyone was permitted to open a theatre and stage any genre of work. There followed an explosion of activity, and librettists and playwrights sought inspiration in the world around them to fill new stages with new material. By April 1795, when the following words appeared in the *Journal des théâtres*, this practice was already stale:

If [the young author] wants to start a dramatic career, he should no longer follow the path of most modern writers, who faithfully consult all the newspapers to find a subject usable in the theatre. He will understand that the virtues displayed by a few characters cannot be instructive: one applauds them, but on leaving the theatre, no one makes it their duty to imitate them.[10]

The important thing (Sedaine might have argued) was not to preach too much.

Inevitably, the different phases of the Revolution gave rise to different fashions in opera and drama. The early years, 1789 to 1792, gave rise to works espousing hope in the equality of citizens, hope for constitutional monarchy, and for the self-determining unity of the French nation. The Terror years, 1793 to 1794, gave rise to intense didactic works about sacrifice and patriotism, and of course works celebrating military victories. Then the fall of Robespierre (9 Thermidor II/27 July 1794) saw a resurgence of counter-revolutionary movements of all kinds; some contained old-fashioned royalists, others, constitutionalists; all were united against the memory of Robespierre and his 'drinkers of blood'. Politically, the government amounted to a balancing act called the Directory, for 'It is easier to describe the Directory's enemies than to define its adherents,' as one historian puts it.[11] The *Léonore* libretto falls into this last period, the 'years of Thermidorean reaction'. That is what makes it difficult and fascinating to construe. *Léonore* was born of a time characterized not by any single revolutionary didacticism but by shock and fear after the traumas of 1792/93 (the end of the monarchy) and 1793/94 (the revolutionary dictatorship).

Ten years of theatrical invention cannot be adequately summarized in a short space; but it is perhaps fair to assert that images of the prison, and release from imprisonment, occurred throughout the whole 1789 decade in a variety of genres – even musical comedy (as in the popular *Le Prisonnier*, music by Della-Maria). Is not the same *topos* present in popular fiction today, on the large and the small screen? Before 14 July 1789, the Bastille was not just a mediaeval fortress supposedly holding state prisoners; it had become a symbol of arbitrary detention imposed by the monarch who could (ultimately) overrule all judicial and ecclesiastical process. Michel Foucault has stressed that the later *ancien régime* especially identified this mode of punishment with princely power (as against judicial power). It became 'a ceremonial of sovereignty . . .; it uses the ritual marks of the vengeance that it applies to the body of the condemned man; and it deploys before the eyes of the spectators an effect of terror [evocative of] the physical presence of the sovereign and of his power'.[12]

Any serious fiction deploying a prison scene in France therefore carried the whole conceptual and emotional burden of '1789': the collision of absolute monarchy with democracy. And yet, over the next five years, prisons would be filled to overflowing by the revolutionary authorities too: after the fall of Robespierre some 10,000 detainees were released in a matter of days.

Alexis's and d'Albert's prisons were not themselves portrayed by Sedaine as instruments of physical pain. But the requirements of 1789 soon changed this convention. No one wrote an opera directly about detention in the Bastille, but the image of the political prison was readily co-opted in making modern myths out of contemporary history. A first example: in July 1793 anti-Jacobins in the port town of Toulon took control of it, imprisoned its leaders (including one Beauvais), and invited in the English enemy. The French revolutionary government sent a military force which, after bombardments, relieved the town on 19 December. Beauvais was released but, exhausted, died a few days later. At least fifteen stage works were written celebrating these events, thirteen of which were seen in the theatre. Most of the eight surviving texts dramatized the release of Beauvais. Five of the fifteen were musical works of different kinds.[13]

In the play *Le Cachot de Beauvais* (Beauvais's dungeon), a one-act *fait historique* by Ribié staged in Rouen, the action is set in two contiguous cells. Beauvais is finally hailed as a Christ-like saviour, 'after four months of suffering', when a victorious French officer releases him from captivity with the following pronounce-ment: 'Your glory has [already] survived you . . . You are born again a second time.'[14] That is, on a mythic level; the historical Beauvais, through the agency of drama, was indeed able to 'rise again from the dead'.

A second example: modern 'prison' myths were equally co-opted by the anti-Jacobin reaction after Thermidor. One such was the story of Cange, a prison governor under the Terror who performed acts of personal generosity. In one of several drama-tizations seen in autumn 1794 we find the type of coded events and language also present in Bouilly's *Léonore*, early in 1798. (Only the text of the following piece survives; the music was by the highly talented Hyacinthe Jadin.)

Scene 17:   Cange leads in Durand (whose suffering and whose family he has personally relieved). Fellow-prisoners of both sexes emerge: they 'offer mutual congratulation, they embrace one another, they betray the liveliest satisfaction'.

Durand: 'Thanks to the fortunate revolution that has occurred, justice, humanity, all the virtues are at last the order of the day, now that our country is delivered from those tigers . . .'[15]

The fortunes of stage works at this date were volatile. Jadin's collaborator, A. P. Bellement, produced a reasonably stageworthy text. A rival *Cange*, music by Dalayrac (18 November 1794), was poor enough in places to cause laughter, a fact which prompted at least one critic to address the general problem of staging 'modern moralities', as we might call them.[16] Solid musico-dramatic values still counted more than bad propaganda. A mere nine days before Dalayrac's unsatisfactory *Cange* was premiered, the Opéra-Comique had revived *Raoul, sire de Créqui*, Dalayrac's very successful and effective 'prison' opera from the days of 1789. To stage this was to evoke the epoch of support for the late king; notwithstanding the opera made no pretence of being adapted from history: it was set in a fictional mediaeval past. Because it was a durable operatic fiction, in which a feudal ruler (at least in the 1789 version) is supported and rescued, it too implied support for the old monarchist *status quo*. Such was its coded significance that the new government, evidently fearful of demonstrations, ordered its performance on 29 November to be suspended.

It is not hard to see why *Raoul, sire de Créqui* was such a potent precursor of *Léonore/Fidelio*, politically as well as dramatically. The mainspring of this three-act dialogue opera is the feud between the cruel lord Beaudouin (who is never actually seen) and Raoul of Créqui. The latter, thought to have died in Palestine, has in fact been a prisoner in his own castle for six months. In the course of the work Raoul's destitute family acknowledges its dependance on the common people, who subsequently help to restore Créqui by force. A pivotal scene which was one model for *Fidelio* – directly or indirectly – occurs in act 2. The curtain rises to reveal Raoul's roofless prison cell. The prisoner is shown wet through, long-bearded, in great misery. He is forced to exist on small amounts of black bread. His jailer is the drunkard Ludger, whose two children take pity on Raoul and, with utmost courage, in scenes of considerable dramatic tension, steal Ludger's key from his pocket and so free the prisoner.

When Raoul first sings (scene 3) it is in the form of a solo scena:

Ritornello	C minor	(Disjointed and turbulent)
Recitative	C min/Eb major	He wakes
Cantabile	Eb/Bb	He recounts dreaming of his wife and son
Recitative		(Transition)
Allegro moderato	C minor	He relapses into desperation

The swings in mood are much more extreme in Dalayrac's *scena* here than they had been in Grétry's music for Count d'Albert. But the 'prison' key is once again C minor (close, but not identical, to the tonality Beethoven would select for Florestan's solo scene), and the power of the orchestra's introduction seems based upon a mimetic concept of convulsive violence (ex. 4.2).

Raoul's *Cantabile* is openly affecting and Italianate in melodic style; but his first sung words, against hushed chords, represent a thoroughly weakened spirit. In 1789 this Raoul 'meant' Louis. In 1795 he may have 'meant' different things to different viewers. At any rate, on 29 November 1794, when *Raoul* was taken off by order, Dalayrac's *Cange* was the work substituted.

Beethoven's *Fidelio* was not the only non-French adaptation of a 'prison' opera of the Revolution decade. Dalayrac's *Raoul, sire de Créqui*, with new music (some adapted from Mozart), and new libretto, reached the Theatre Royal, Drury Lane, London, on 18 October 1792. Entitled *The Prisoner*, 'A musical romance', this show took the exciting second-act incidents from Marsollier (Dalayrac's librettist) but planted them in a picaresque, war-dominated setting, in which two women disguised as soldiers take the leading roles.[17] Clara is seeking her brother, Marcos (the Créqui role), who has been incarcerated for two years. She has also lost touch with her lover, Bernado. He turns out to be Marcos's captor. Clara's friend Nina takes the secondary *travesti* role. In the end the soldier-women reach Bernado, and, after a recognition scene, all is resolved.

The case of *The Prisoner* is more interesting for its combination of cross-dressed female roles with the motif of male imprisonment than for any intrinsic dramatic value. Even so, the depiction of Marcos in his act 2 prison and the sense of unrest and displacement are striking.

'Warrior women' in English history, balladry and theatre have been described by Dianne Dugaw,[18] who reminds us that Sheridan's play *The Camp* (1778) had responded to actual events in which fashionable women, dressed as soldiers, had attended troop exercises. In French theatre there was a parallel tradition of female actors playing adolescent males and young men. Both spoken and sung roles were potentially involved. This was a somewhat secondary tradition in *opéra comique* (where younger male lovers were sung by men), but women still regularly sang male adolescent roles at the Comédie-Italienne, the home of French *opéra comique*. A noted

Example 4.2
Act 2, scene 3. Seul dans sa Tour, il étend les bras, regarde autour de lui,
secoue ses pauvres vêtemens que la pluie a percés, touche ses chaînes, les
agite et se met sur son séant. Il porte une longue barbe, son habit est celui
d'un Esclave, il doit avoir tout le caractère de la Misère la plus profonde.
(Alone in his tower, [Raoul] stretches his arms, looks about him, rubs his
inadequate, rain-soaked clothes, touches his chains, shakes them, and sits
on the ground. He wears a long beard; he is dressed as a slave; he shows
every appearance of being in most profound torment.)

specialist was Mlle Carline, who sang the young chevalier in Grétry's *Le Rival confident* in 1788, and also Tell's son in the same composer's *Guillaume Tell* in 1791. In 1798 at least one critic looked back appreciatively at Carline's career when she took the page's role in Dalayrac's opera *Primerose*, exchanging clothes with a female lover in order to secure the latter's release from detention.[19]

The Paris *Léonore, ou L'amour conjugal* was not, however, performed at the Comédie-Italienne (often simply called Opéra-Comique). It was designed for the rather different company – and clientele – of its great rival, the Théâtre Feydeau. Any material distinctions are not very apparent when one looks, say, at printed scores or librettos produced for one or the other company. Beethoven's collaborators may or may not have been fully aware of the Parisian resonances. But the fact is that the Feydeau had started life in 1789 as an ultra-royalist institution, insofar as it had court backing, was named 'Théâtre de Monsieur' (the title of the King's brother), and catered to elitist taste in the shape of the latest *Italian* opera. By and large, right-wing associations were to remain a characteristic of the Feydeau in the public mind.

Italian opera was an art-form that had been sedulously excluded from general French experience before 1789 by combinations of vested interests. The Théâtre de Monsieur provided an energetic spate of productions, which came to a halt only when its Italian singers left France in August 1792. The character of the company altered under revolutionary pressures; a change of name was immediately thought prudent. At the same time, its young resident Florentine genius, Luigi Cherubini, made a huge impression with his first *opéra comique*, based on a recent novel: *Lodoïska* (1791). Cherubini was to remain faithful to the Feydeau company in his later French works: *Eliza* (1794), *Médée* (1797) and *Les Deux journées* (1800).

The Feydeau was distinguished in other ways from its rival theatres. It had always laid great emphasis on having the best possible set designs and scene-painters, and the best effects (such as the explosions and fires which destroyed Lodoïska's imprisoning castle in Cherubini's opera). Furthermore, it boasted the finest Parisian orchestra; and, not least, it had at the centre of its troupe the two performers for whom the musical roles of Bouilly's Florestan and Léonore were conceived: Pierre Gaveaux and Julie-Angélique Scio.[20] In 1797 they had created the parts of Jason and Medea, in

Cherubini's opera, and their stage partnership continued up to the dissolution of the Feydeau in 1800, for example, as the husband and wife Armand and Constance in the same composer's *Les deux journées*. (The text of this last opera was immediately recognized as Bouilly's masterpiece.)

Madame Scio (1768–1807) was, simply, the outstanding actor-singer of the decade, capable of comic roles, cross-dressed roles, and anything between these and Medea, which to this day remains the most heroic female role ever conceived for a French dialogue opera. In it, she also declaimed classical alexandrines with perfect success. The following is typical of the poems written for her by her devotees, not least to welcome her back after bouts of ill-health:

> Douce *Palma*, jalouse *Calypso*,
> Fière *Médée*, espiègle *Matelot*,
>   *Léonore*, épouse touchante,
> Et toujours aimable Scio,
>   Après une si longue attente,
> Sur la scène à nos yeux enfin tu reparois . . .[21]

Pierre Gaveaux (1760–1825) was known to contemporary Paris for more than his acting, singing or operatic compositions. (Apart from *Léonore*, his best-known scores were *Le petit matelot*, 1796, and a series of one-act comedies between 1800 and 1805.) Gaveaux was notorious as the composer and performer of the inflammatory anti-Jacobin song 'Le réveil du peuple' (The people's awakening). This he first sang publicly on 19 January 1795, some two months after the *Cange* operas mentioned earlier. The words of the song were by J. M. Souriguère de Saint-Marc, who would be deported for royalism in September 1797,[22] and its composition came in the wake of the shutting down of the Jacobins' club (11 November 1794) and a consequent reaction by right-wing groups to purge Paris of the memory of its immediate past. Unlike the Marseillaise or the 'Ça ira', Gaveaux's song 'was the first symbolically significant [political] song to be closely and meaningfully associated with its author, and [to be] the song of a party',[23] that is, a specific minority group, the reactionary *jeunesse d'orée*.

Over the coming months and years, 'Le Réveil du peuple' was sung in opposition to Republican songs (like the Marseillaise) in contexts varying with the ebb and flow of political currents. Theatre audiences skirmished, and the government agonized over the precise official attitude it should take to each song. Gaveaux was some-times at the centre of disturbances: on 14 January 1796, loud factions at the Feydeau clashed over his position both as political figurehead and as executor of political songs.[24]

The text of Gaveaux's song is replete with the coded language ordinarily employed by the Right to refer to Jacobins and their allies: 'brigands', 'monstres', 'buveurs de sang humains', 'agents du crime', 'égorgeurs'. As an example of a Thermidorean opera employing the same language, we need cite only *Le Brigand*, music by Rodolphe Kreutzer (Opéra-Comique, July 1795). Set in the time of Charles I of England, it was immediately recognized as taking a position, for example, in the humorous poem published the same month in the *Journal de Paris*.[25]

It can hardly be denied that Bouilly's *Léonore* is also a Thermidorean work, even discounting the symbolic presence of Gaveaux as its composer and impersonator of the role of the tortured Florestan. We need not take into account the Spanish setting either, since the designated genre of *Léonore – fait historique* – tells us that its story has more immediate relevance. Let us discount the knowledge that Bouilly and Gaveaux were both inscribed as members of the Société Philotechnique, 'formed by politicians and men of letters "to oppose the ravages of vandalism . . . and bad taste"'.[26] The language alone of *Léonore*, in the context of 1797–8, makes it clear that an audience probably saw Gaveaux/Florestan as an unambiguous symbol of political reaction. In the dungeon, he refers to his guiltless conscience; Pizarre, whose 'crimes' and 'abuses of authority' Florestan has virtuously reported, is referred to as 'un tyran', 'un monstre exécrable', while Dom Fernand will conclude the drama not by celebrating the victory of *la patrie*, or 'fraternity', let alone 'sacrifice', but instead by urging the audience to celebrate the end of an era: 'Let us hasten to remove the memory [of crime unmasked] by the immutable return of justice and truth.'

Bouilly, as we saw at the outset, was a liberal intellectual. By 1798 he was too wise to repeat any explicit political allegorizing, as in *Pierre le Grand* he had done in 1790. In a series of revealing articles, David Galliver has amply shown how much Bouilly himself had to hide after acting as public prosecutor near his home town of Tours under the Terror.[27] He saw both sides because he had been on both sides. Small must be the sum of librettists who have signed a death-warrant on a fellow human being. Bouilly was one such person.[28] Bitter experience doubtless helped give *Léonore* its peculiar economy and power. Its economy stems from the masterly condensation of motive and incident, as compared with, say, the otherwise similar *Le Comte d'Albert*. Its power, too, derives from its economy and focus; but these are in fact inseparable from the uncommon ferocity and evil of Pizarre. Sedaine's operas had concentrated on the victims of unjust detention, not the perpe-trators. Revolution operas either functioned similarly (e.g., *Raoul, sire de Créqui*, or *Cange*), or else showed their tyrants to have believable motives related to their desire to seduce women (as Dourlinski in Cherubini's *Lodoïska*) or otherwise coerce them. But Bouilly's villain is a purely malign and repugnant force. His – as we would say – sadistic cruelty in starving Florestan by degrees was picked out for comment by reviewers.[29] Once decided upon by Bouilly, this motif of cruelty could be dramatized using the devices of the prisoners' chorus and of the monologue in the dungeon.

Just as Grétry and Dalayrac did in their prison scenes (discussed above), so too Gaveaux used C minor tonality, horn tone and extremes of orchestral dynamics and texture to provide the fullest musical metaphor for the condition of suffering.[30] Beethoven would in his turn increase that metaphorical power, but the desire to employ exceptional means at this point is not less present in Gaveaux's music. He requests the two orchestral horns to play with their bells placed next to one another (see ex. 4.3). This musical gesture, possibly derived from Gluck's *Alceste*, symbolized the proximity of death. It was the first notated instance of such a way of playing and was soon imitated in operas by Le Sueur and Catel in analogous contexts.[31]

There is no surviving musical model for Gaveaux's prisoners' chorus, although, as we saw earlier, Dalayrac's *Cange* (which is lost) may have contained one, and H. Jadin's *Cange* had shown emerging prisoners (explicitly as victims of the Terror), even though Bellement's text here did not provide for musical setting. Gaveaux's prisoners are seen to 'fill the stage' and then leave as the act ends quietly.[32]

This scene was not discussed by the Parisian critics, though they were impressed by the opera in general. The most consid-ered review of the work was probably that by Poisson de La Chabeaussière of the *Décade Philosophique*,[33] and we will benefit by translating some of his final sentences, which confirm the aesthetic and indeed political impact of Bouilly's fable in a startlingly honest manner.

Example 4.3
Act 2. Florestan seul (Florestan alone.)

This work, as we see, certainly has all the 'English' [='Gothic'] colour of the blackest *drames*, and one cannot rightly conceive by what strange verbal misuse one is still forced to describe these types of composition as *opéras comiques*. [He goes on to condemn *drames* in general.]

But if the writer merely had the aim of scaring us and wringing from us a few painful tears, he has succeeded. They even say that the basis of the anecdote that he has put on stage is a veritable fact: so much the worse for humanity, if we absolutely require great crimes in order to demonstrate great virtues. However, we can only be grateful to Citizen Bouilly for wanting to reveal – to our eyes at least – a fine example of conjugal piety, which is a sublime sentiment: one which the tyranny of fifteen months, of which we were victims, nevertheless revealed to be much less rare than is ordinarily supposed.[34]

In other words, this review proves that the model for *Fidelio* was seen as an image of the excesses of 1793–4, and in no way as a verdict on the *ancien régime*.

5 Fidelio *and the French Revolution*

1

Fidelio has always posed difficulties for operatic interpreters. On the literal level it is straight-forward enough, much more so, certainly, than its great Mozartian predecessor, *The Magic Flute*. It tells the unproblematic story of a wife, Leonore, who disguises herself as a boy in order to rescue her unjustly imprisoned husband. In the prison she obtains a job with the jailor, Rocco, whose daughter proceeds to fall in love with her (in spite of being promised to the prison gatekeeper). The central action is triggered when the governor of the prison, Don Pizarro, learns that the minister (representing the central monarch) has set out to visit the prison, suspecting that it harbours several 'victims of arbitrary force'. Pizarro is terrified that the minister will discover one particular inmate, Florestan, who had threatened to expose his crimes and whom the minister believes to be dead (we, of course, have no difficulty recognizing him as Leonore's husband). Pizarro thus resolves to murder Florestan. In the second act Rocco and Leonore precede Pizarro into the dungeon to dig the victim's grave, and there Leonore ascertains that the condemned prisoner is indeed her husband. When Pizarro descends for the kill he is confronted by Leonore, who tells him he will have to kill Florestan's wife first and pulls a gun on him. At exactly this moment a trumpet call announces the minister, whose arrival dissolves the dramatic situation with breathtaking suddenness: Florestan is rescued, husband and wife are reunited, and Pizarro's tyranny is broken. In the final scene all the prisoners are liberated, Pizarro is banished (presumably to face imprisonment himself), and the minister, learning that his friend Florestan has been saved by his wife's courage, invites her to unlock his chains. The opera ends with a choral tribute to wifely devotion.

Unfortunately, only the bare plot of *Fidelio* boasts the virtues

68

of simplicity, logic and consistency. Around its clear, if unremarkable, lines have emerged numerous confusions and uncertainties. Most of these focus on inconsistencies of dramatic tone and musical style. Put baldly, the opening scenes belong to the world of eighteenth-century domestic comedy, in which attention is directed to character and human relationships, but by the end of the opera these characters and their predicaments have been utterly forgotten – indeed, the actual figures with whom the opera begins have become almost invisible. Instead, dramatic interest has been lodged in the liberated prisoners, who come to stand for all humanity and express their joy over their new estate. The conventional operatic world of romance, mistaken identity and intrigue has been displaced by one of ideological celebration. In musical terms, the disciplined classical style of Beethoven's first period, which is the dominant idiom of the opening scenes, gives way to the extravagant musical gestures of his heroic period (the last movement of the Fifth Symphony in particular comes to mind), and there are even anticipations of the choral outbursts of the Ninth Symphony and the *Missa Solemnis*. The whole, for many critics, is dangerously contradictory – an opera whose conclusion explodes its musical and dramatic premises.

Even if not excessively bothered by these anomalies, analysts seem generally uncomfortable with the discrepancy between the simple melodramatic story and the overwhelming emotional burden that Beethoven has imposed on it through his music. Not surprisingly, therefore, virtually every critic of the opera feels the need to interpret it, to ask what *Fidelio* is 'really' about, because the music tells us that it cannot simply be about a wife rescuing her husband. In their efforts to account for the discrepancy between subject and form, plot and manner, critics have come to a variety of conclusions. They agree only that the real subject of *Fidelio* must be weighty enough to account for its musical riches and emotional power.

Some of this interpretive energy does not take us very far from the specific of the plot. Most obvious in this respect have been attempts to link the story to Beethoven's biography, particularly to his long, frustrating and ultimately unsuccessful pursuit of a wife. The subtitle of Bouilly's original libretto was *L'amour conjugal*, and one needs little hermeneutic daring (or psychological acumen) to explain at least part of Beethoven's emotional investment in the opera in terms of his preoccupation with Leonore, a fantasy figure from the deepest regions of desire, the Immortal Beloved, the idealized mate. A Freudian variation on this theme (suggested gently by Maynard Solomon and heavy-handedly by Editha and Richard Sterba), argues that Beethoven in fact identified with Leonore – that she was for him a means of giving expression to powerful feminine feelings, which were later to find a biographical outlet in his unhappy relationship with his nephew.[1] Alan Tyson offers a more venturesome psychological interpretation when he suggests that Beethoven identified not with Leonore but with Florestan, and in particular that he equated the latter's imprisonment with his own deafness. Just as Florestan is isolated in darkness, Beethoven was imprisoned in silence.[2] Among the attractions of this hypothesis is that it allows us to interpret the opening utterance of Florestan's aria, 'Gott! welch' Dunkel hier' (God! What darkness here), as a thinly disguised *cri de coeur* and thus explain, in part, why Beethoven invested it with such incisive musical articulation.

The main weakness of these biographical analyses is that, while they deepen the characters of Leonore and Florestan, they say nothing about the transformation of a simple rescue story into something approaching a myth of universal liberation – the sea change that the work undergoes between its modest domestic beginnings and the communal shout with which it concludes. In other words, the attempt to lend weight to the story through psychological interpretation ignores the opera's sociology, which, if we can judge from the musical attention Beethoven gives it, was anything but peripheral to his concerns. The ideal of marital devotion and the agonies of deafness could have been addressed in a decidedly more intimate format; neither of them requires the liberation of an entire prison, to say nothing of the whole of humanity. And yet it is on precisely this collective material that Beethoven lavishes much of his best music in the opera, from the prisoners' chorus in the first act to the choral apotheosis at the end.

Perhaps we should turn then to interpretations that explore the social or communal dimension of the opera, interpretations that take us beyond the psychological dramas of romantic frustration and deafness. Maynard Solomon proposes a Freudian analysis that touches on this domain. His interpretation is rich and more than a trifle confusing, so let me begin by quoting him in full:

Fidelio opens in a Mozartian Eden, a sunlit Arcadia in which a good father (Rocco) seeks to bring about the marriage of his daughter (Marzelline) to the young man she loves (Fidelio). But things are not what they seem. The Eden surface gives way to a darker substratum; the good father is a jailer; Fidelio is Leonore in disguise seeking her husband, Florestan, who lies imprisoned for an unspecified 'crime' in a dungeon beneath the ground they walk upon. Thus light masks darkness. Marzelline's innocent love unconsciously conceals a forbidden attraction. The good Rocco, protesting, agrees to cooperate in the murder of Florestan by Pizarro as the price of the latter's approval of his daughter's marriage. And Leonore's conjugal fidelity leads her to two conjugal betrayals: of Marzelline, to whom she pledges her love, and of Florestan, whose wife now embraces another. Rocco and Leonore descend into the tomb to prepare Florestan's grave; in a sense, Leonore is cooperating in the murder of her husband. The rescue fantasy is only apparently an inversion of the Oedipus myth: the impulses behind myths of killing and saving are ultimately identical; but in the rescue fantasy the murder (and guilt) is averted by a *deus ex machina*, here the minister of state, Don Fernando. Florestan's place in the dungeon is now taken by the evil 'father' – Pizarro – and the prisoners (sons) who planned the patricidal crime ascend into the light of freedom while Leonore resumes her sexual identity and receives the plaudits of the multitude for her heroism and fidelity.[3]

Part of the interest of this reading is that it draws attention to what might be called the vertical dimension of the opera: its pre-occupation with a world divided between above and below, 'surface' and 'substratum', light and darkness. But in terms of explaining the collective dimension of *Fidelio* the most important move in Solomon's analysis is the attempt to link the opera to Freud's patricidal myth in *Totem and Taboo* – that epochal tale of brothers who band together to slay their father and take his place with the liberated women, their mother and sisters. Freud believed that the memory of this primal crime was lodged in the collective unconscious, passed from generation to generation by a kind of psychic Lamarkism. Solomon's interpretation, too, seems to presume such a shared unconscious implication in the idea, at least if it is to account for the power of the opera's collective theme, not only for Beethoven but for his audience as well. The proposition should not be dismissed merely because it can never be proved. Nonetheless one might complain that the emphasis on aggression and guilt fits rather badly with the unambiguously affirmative tone of the opera's conclusion. Solomon could plausibly respond that the affirmations are in fact overemphatic and actually serve to repress the brothers' consciousness of guilt. But his interpretation ultimately comes unstuck over the figure of Pizarro, who makes an improbable father. Beethoven originally wanted to spare Pizarro, and the brief choral episode in which the crowd urges his punishment in the 1814 version is decidedly inferior to the rest of the finale. Beethoven's heart, one senses, simply was not in this retributive gesture.

Solomon himself does not seem to feel particularly confident about his Freudian reading, because he proceeds to displace it with an entirely different interpretation, although one that again transcends the arena of individual psychology. The terms here are drawn from myth, and one suspects an intellectual debt to Northrop Frye, or Sir James Frazer:

> *Fidelio* can be seen as an opera about resurrection as well as rescue. Florestan is not only imprisoned but entombed; Leonore and Rocco descend with their spades not to dig his grave but to exhume him from his sepulchre. A mythic pattern intrudes here: the dying vegetation god (the meaning of Florestan's name becomes clearer) lies awaiting the arrival of the bisexual goddess (Leonore/Fidelio) and the princely hero (Fernando) to restore him to life and to youth, to mark his passage from the dark ground into the sunlight. The winter god (Pizarro) is slain, replacing Florestan in the tomb, and mankind celebrates the arrival of the New Year with hymns to marriage.[4]

Here the collective element ('mankind') is invoked by linking the narrative, at the deepest level, with the seasonal mythology of an agrarian society, where the rhythms of individual and communal life are at once reflected in and deeply dependent on the cycle of death and rebirth. *Fidelio* thus becomes an opera of germination. Like Solomon's psychoanalytic reading, this mythic interpretation draws its interest from the vertical dimension of the opera – the descent into death, the rise to new life – and, also like the psychoanalytic reading, it is not susceptible of proof. It is, however, more suited to the affirmations of the finale than is the menacing image of Freud's band of parricides. Solomon finds support in Irving Singer, who also sees the opera as essentially mythic or sacramental, and who likewise stresses its preoccupation with death and rebirth. *Fidelio*, writes Singer, 'is the passion according to Beethoven'; at its heart stands 'the mythic rebirth of Florestan, his return to life through his courage and the efforts of an angelic woman'.[5]

The appeal of this interpretation is the light it sheds on the collective dimension of *Fidelio*. It makes sense of the opera's inexorable movement from the individual to the community, and it also helps explain the work's deep emotional resonance. But against these virtues one must regret that Solomon and Singer say nothing about the music (they treat the opera as if were no different from a stage play) and that they force us so very far from its manifest content – or, for that matter, from anything that one might reasonably argue Beethoven had in mind. There is about their readings an obvious sense of desperation, of reaching well beyond the textual evidence in order to identify an interpretive register appropriate to the opera's effect.

In the body of this essay I want to argue that a political interpretation of *Fidelio* – and, more precisely, one that links it explicitly to the French Revolution – allows one to avoid the extremes to which Solomon and Singer seem forced. Such a tack deals comfortably with the opera's shift from the individual to the communal, and it also supplies the intellectual freight for which the work seems to beg. But perhaps its chief attraction is that it is supported by evidence from the opera itself. It permits one to argue from the score as well as the libretto – from the musical as well as the verbal record – which, in my common-sensical view, is the hallmark of any good operatic interpretation.

I should not suggest that *Fidelio* has been without its political interpreters. The literature contains countless allusions to its ideological subtext, and one even finds it expressly linked to the French Revolution.[6] But I have come across no sustained attempt to interpret it in terms of the Revolution. Furthermore, an important tendency in recent commentary on the opera's politics – and on Beethoven's political ideas in general – has tended to shift attention away from the Revolution to the Enlightenment. Once again, the redoubtable Maynard Solomon has been an authoritative figure in this development.

Solomon argues that Beethoven's political views were formed in Bonn during the 1780s, when under Elector Maximilian Franz 'the ideas of the Enlightenment virtually became the official principles of the Electorate'.[7] In political terms this meant that Beethoven subscribed to an ideal of reform from above – enlightened absolutism – in which a good prince would lead his people towards freedom, brotherhood and peace: 'Reliance upon the notion of an aristocratic redeemer remained central to Beethoven's beliefs until his last years.'[8] Solomon sees this conviction entering Beethoven's music in a number of places, notably the early *Funeral Cantata on the Death of Joseph II*, the Incidental Music to Goethe's *Egmont* and the 'Eroica' Symphony (Napoleon, the original dedicatee, being for Beethoven, until his disillusionment, another of these princely saviours). Moreover, Solomon doubts that Beethoven was in fact sympathetic to the French Revolution, noting that, 'apart from his subscription to a volume of Eulogius Schneider's poems, there is no sure sign of such sympathy on Beethoven's part'.[9] In terms of *Fidelio*, Solomon explicitly denies that the opera exhibits Revolutionary enthusiasms:

> The opera's themes of brotherhood, conjugal devotion, and triumph over injustice are basic to his ideology, but they do not signal his devotion to a Jacobin outlook. On the contrary, the 1798 French libretto by Bouilly that was adapted for Beethoven's use, based on an episode that occurred under the Terror, can be seen as a critique of the Jacobin persecutions of the French aristocracy.[10]

The libretto was indeed based on an incident from the Terror, in which an aristocrat incarcerated in Touraine was saved by his wife. Beethoven, however, knew nothing of this historical derivation, as it was revealed by Bouilly only in his memoirs, published in 1836. Solomon is technically correct when he identifies Florestan as 'an imprisoned noble'[11] – we know this from a single reference of Rocco's to 'Don' Florestan – but Beethoven virtually ignores such social distinctions in the opera. There are, admittedly, musical residues of the two-couple convention, with its connotations of social elevation and inferiority: Florestan and Leonore, with their *opera seria* style arias, are descended from Tamino and Pamina and from the Count and Countess in *Figaro*, just as Jaquino and Marzelline are descended from Papageno and Papagena, and from Figaro and Susanna. But Beethoven takes remarkably little interest in social discriminations, just as he seems uninterested in specific political convictions, whether conservative or radical. In social and ideological terms the story has been hollowed out, leaving us with such abstract categories as 'tyrant', 'victim', 'victim's devoted wife', 'minister' and 'prince'. Appropriately, *Fidelio* has come to serve as an all-purpose opera of liberation, performed at the Congress of Vienna to celebrate the defeat of Napoleon and at the reopening of the Vienna State Opera after the victory over the Nazis.

By identifying Florestan as an aristocrat, and by linking the opera to its historical source in the Terror, Solomon intends to suggest that it is an anti-revolutionary rather than a revolutionary document. *Fidelio* comes to stand to the French Revolution in much the same relation as Burke's *Reflections*. But Solomon is more eager to remove the opera entirely from the revolutionary debate (whether pro or con) and instead to associate its political values with the tradition of enlightened absolutism. He therefore stresses the central role of the minister, the emissary from the 'bon prince', whose arrival is signalled by the trumpet call and who holds forth benevolently in the final scene. There is no reason to dispute the presence of this theme in the opera, but the musical and dramatic evidence hardly suggests that it was central to Beethoven's conception. In terms of the amount of time he spends on stage and the music Beethoven composes for him, the minister can only be described as a secondary figure, whom most opera-goers quickly forget. He has no aria, only a few bars of recitative, which are yet further diminished by being set within the heightened choral exclamations of the finale. To make him the ideological centrepiece of *Fidelio* would be to conclude that Beethoven had little notion of how to give his most important ideas compelling musical expression. As we shall see, Don Fernando's princely gesture must be set against the labour, both dramatic and musical, of Leonore in determining where effective agency in the opera resides. In the meantime, arguing that *Fidelio* is an opera about enlightened absolutism involves transforming a dramatically and musically marginal character – really a comprimario – into something approaching the work's protagonist.

2

At the ideological centre of *Fidelio* stands the abstract idea of freedom. It is not expressly connected with any particular political movement or social group, nor is it elaborated into particular freedoms such as freedom of speech, religion or the press. Rather it is freedom *tout court*. One can identify it with the French Revolution only in the general sense that during Beethoven's lifetime the Revolution became, for virtually all Europeans, the single most important locus of this idea and its realization. Indeed, in 1805 one would need to be politically illiterate not to know that an opera trumpeting the idea of freedom would automatically be associated with the Revolution, albeit at the highest level of generalization. Moreover, that Beethoven should have appropriated the *idea* of the Revolution rather than its historical reality – that he should have composed *Fidelio* rather than, say, *Andrea Chénier* – is utterly in keeping with the response of his generation of German intellectuals to the phenomenon of the Revolution. The historian R. R. Palmer, in his magisterial *Age of the Democratic Revolution*, documents the way German thinkers and artists transformed the Revolution into categories of mind, discarding its political particulars and elevating it into a grand abstraction.[12] Hegel is the central figure in this development, and there is an unmistakable affinity between Hegel's tribute to the French Revolution as 'a glorious mental dawn'[13] in the *Lectures on the Philosophy of History* and Beethoven's paean to liberty in *Fidelio*.

Let us now consider several instances from the opera where the idea finds expression. They were identified more than half a century ago by Ludwig Schiedermair in a monograph entitled *Die Gestaltung weltanschaulicher Ideen in der Vokalmusik Beethovens* (Leipzig, 1934). All of these moments are characterized by a heightened musical interest that indicates Beethoven's deep intellectual commitment to the idea.

The first comes in the famous prisoners' chorus. Virtually every commentator on the opera – indeed, virtually everyone who has seen or heard it – recognizes the importance that Beethoven attached to this scene. While present in the original Bouilly libretto, it is, strictly speaking, dramatically gratuitous, thereby calling attention to its ideological character. Leonore begs Rocco to allow the prisoners into the fortress garden while the weather is so lovely, and the jailor gives in to her request. It is, in other words, a transparently symbolical or allegorical moment.

The word 'free' (or 'freedom') makes three significant appearances in this scene, and its mantra-like repetition over the course of the movement gives it almost leitmotivic weight. It is introduced in the very first verse of the chorus:

> O welche Lust! In freier Luft
> den Atem leicht zu heben!
>
> [Oh what joy! In the free air
> to breathe with ease!]

The crucial phrase 'in freier Luft' is placed at the musical apex of the chorus's opening period. It comes at the culmination of a four-bar *crescendo*, and Beethoven marks it *fortissimo*. It is accompanied by a strongly-felt ascending figure in the cellos and basses, giving it a firm musical lift – an almost physical elevation appropriate to the elevating idea. The phrase also marks the climax of the melodic and harmonic trajectory of the opening musical gesture: on the word 'Luft' the upper voices (tenors) move to their highest note, a sustained G (scale degree 6 of the B flat tonality), and the harmony shifts onto an exalted subdominant – a move that becomes practically a harmonic code for the idea of freedom in the opera. The phrase thus impresses itself on every listener's mind, so carefully has Beethoven underlined it through manipulations of volume, pitch, melody, harmony and orchestration. Musically italicized in this fashion, it emerges almost as a concept. When the opening couplet is repeated some sixteen bars later, the musical treatment of 'in freier Luft' remains unchanged: the phrase is once again firmly located at the centre of the melodic and harmonic proceedings.

Next, a single, anonymous prisoner steps forward and sings:

> Wir wollen mit Vertrauen
> auf Gottes Hülfe bauen.
> Die Hoffnung flüstert sanft mir zu:
> Wir werden frei, wir finden Ruh!

> [With trust we will
> build on God's help.
> Hope whispers gently to me:
> We shall be free, we shall find rest!]

Here the phrase 'Wir werden frei' is made the musical crux, and Beethoven deploys virtually the same methods that he had moments earlier to highlight 'in freier Luft'. As before, the phrase comes at the apex of a gradually ascending melodic line, and the word 'frei' itself is given even greater prominence by being set to the highest and longest note the prisoner sings. At the same time, the vocal effort the tenor must exert to produce this relatively high and protracted note lends it a sense of reaching, of aspiration. Most important, this plangent, high-lying phrase is set on repeated upper E's – scale degree 6 of the passage's G major tonality – and the harmony, as with 'in freier Luft', shifts to the telltale sub-dominant with its distinctively Beethovian pathos.

The remaining prisoners respond to their fellow inmate's words in a choral passage of mounting excitement. So great is their emotion that they are reduced at first to broken ideological ejaculations:

> O Himmel! Rettung! welch' ein Glück!
> O Freiheit! O Freiheit, kehrst du zurück?

> [O Heaven! Salvation! What Joy!
> O Freedom! O Freedom, will you return?]

Beethoven sets these hushed outbursts over evocatively pulsing semiquavers in the strings, and, as we now fully expect, the musical proceedings culminate in the repeated *forte* cries of 'O Freiheit!' The second sounding of the words comes on the longest note in the passage, to an upward interval (from D to E flat), and at a moment of striking harmonic progression, from G major to

C minor – the minor subdominant, which creates an even more decisive italicizing effect than the move to the major subdominant chord in the two preceding episodes. It is a moment of great intensity, in which Beethoven completes what might fairly be described as his musical lecture on the idea of freedom.

When, finally, the original chorus is repeated, its opening musical line again climaxes on the phrase 'in freier Luft'. Now, however, Beethoven asks that the entire passage be sung quietly, for the prisoners have grown conscious of being watched: 'Sprecht leise, haltet euch zurück! / Wir sind belauscht mit Ohr und Blick' (Speak softly, restrain yourselves! / We are observed by ears and eyes). These terrifying thoughts, which have an almost Foucauldian ring to them, cast a shadow over the scene, as exhilaration gives way to fear. Freedom has only been imagined. We must await the finale for its realization.

The idea of freedom is again set before us in the concluding F major Poco allegro of Florestan's aria in the second act. The imprisoned husband, in his delirium, imagines he sees his wife as an angel coming to rescue him:

> Ein Engel, Leonoren, der Gattin, so gleich,
> der führt mich zur Freiheit ins himmlische Reich!
>
> [An angel so like Leonore, my wife,
> who leads me to freedom in the Heavenly Kingdom!]

Here 'Freiheit' receives an even more pointed musical treatment than it had in the prisoners' chorus. At the climax the word is repeated no less than eight times within a dozen bars – bars that take less than half a minute to perform. As the final line is sung over and over, Beethoven insists on doubling the phrase 'zur Freiheit', almost as if he were lecturing to a particularly obdurate or inattentive audience. The italicizing is musical as well as textual. While the very highest note Florestan sings, a B flat, is reserved for the word 'Reich', most of the repetitions of 'zur Freiheit' hover in the area of high G, and they are twice sustained for two beats on that altitudinous note. More exactly, the most prominent utterances of the phrase are set midway in a relentlessly ascending vocal line, beginning on F at the top of the stave and moving stepwise through F sharp, G, A, to B flat. The climactic final note lands us in the by-now familiar subdominant, as Beethoven again resorts to his wonted harmonic code. Moreover, for most tenors who sing Florestan, this B flat represents the uppermost limit of their range. As a result the passage conveys that sense of reaching, of aspiring, that we heard in the lone prisoner's singing of 'Wir werden frei' in the first act. Finally, each of these vocal ascents is marked *crescendo*, and every conductor I have heard takes the opportunity to increase not merely the orchestral volume but the already brutal pace as well. Beethoven thus manipulates volume, melody, harmony, tessitura and textual repetition to give the idea of freedom incomparably exalted expression.

The third instance of his preoccupation with the idea comes in the immediately succeeding duet between Rocco and Leonore. The two have descended into the dungeon and are in the process of digging the prisoner's grave. Leonore has not yet been able to determine whether the man is in fact her husband, and, as she seeks to get a better look at him, she sings (aside):

> Wer du auch seist, ich will dich retten,
> bei Gott! Du sollst kein Opfer sein!
> Gewiß, ich löse deine Ketten,
> ich will, du Armer, dich befrei'n!

> [Whoever you may be, I will save you,
> by God! You shall not be a victim!
> For certain I'll loose your chains,
> poor man, I will free you!]

It is a significant assertion for our understanding of Leonore, because in it she announces her adherence to the humane principles for which her husband has been imprisoned. She is motivated, in other words, not simply by wifely devotion but also by a more impersonal and categorical imperative. The passage has a distinctly Kantian ring to it, and we know that Beethoven admired Kant as a moral prophet. One should also note the reference to chains, which are a recurring material symbol in the opera. When we first see Leonore in the opening act she is returning to the prison with chains she has just bought, and in the final scene her unlocking of Florestan's chains provides the occasion for the most ecstatic passage in the opera, the fugal quintet beginning 'O Gott! welch' ein Augenblick!' It is perhaps not inappropriate to hear in these allusions an echo of the famous first sentence of Jean-Jacques Rousseau's *Social Contract*: 'Man is born free, and everywhere he is in chains'.

Leonore's ideologically loaded pronouncement terminates in the verb 'befreien' (to free), which, because Beethoven chooses to repeat the second couplet in order to underline its importance, is sounded twice. The first occasion comes at the end of a melodic line, marked crescendo, that ascends from C in the middle of the soprano's register to a sustained F at the top of the stave. It is a strong, if not especially pointed, musical setting. The repetition of the word, however, is transformed by Beethoven into a grand coloratura display, its significant second syllable stretched out over two and a half bars and carrying the voice over a twenty-four note melisma. The sequence of triplets swoops down nearly an octave from high F and then ascends to a sustained G above the stave. It is the only coloratura writing for Leonore outside the concluding Allegro of her act I aria, calling attention to itself by its singularity as well as its length, range and vocal athleticism. One might complain that it comes dangerously close to preachiness. But Beethoven is never shy about his convictions, and he is fully prepared to risk this sort of musical underscoring. His commitment to the idea of freedom was apparently unqualified.

3

On the evidence, then, liberation is a central concern of the opera, its reigning conceit, deeply embedded in the text and richly articulated in the music. But, as noted, Beethoven's conception of liberation is abstract and categorical. It is linked to no particular historical moment or political agenda. As such, it can be associated with the French Revolution only by way of the now unfashionable invocation of the *Zeitgeist* – by chronological proximity, as it were. Indeed, one might even argue that linking the opera's liberationist theme to the events of the Revolution violates its universalist spirit and thereby diminishes it.

I wish to propose, however, that *Fidelio* and the French Revolution share a number of important structural affinities, and these affinities lend plausibility to our otherwise only vague suspicion that the two are somehow connected. Almost by definition, affinities never constitute proof, of either authorial intent or historical influence. Rather, their appeal must rest on their ability to illuminate, to explain matters that otherwise seem confused or unaccountable. The identification of affinities between *Fidelio* and the French Revolution provides, I believe, just such a heuristic service.

The most profound similarity between *Fidelio* and the Revolution resides in the conception of historical time they both embrace. Earlier I mentioned that several commentators have drawn attention to the opera's vertical dimension, its preoccupation with above and below, surface and substructure, light and dark. But equally striking is the distinctive horizontal pattern of the opera: its no less obsessive concern with before and after, the beginning and the end, the old order and the new. Indeed, more emphatically than any other opera I can think of, *Fidelio* conveys a sense of historical transformation, of movement from one realm of existence to another, from a defective to a pacified world.

This conception of historical time is precisely the conception that inspired the French Revolutionaries. Recent historians of the Revolution such as François Furet and Keith Michael Baker have laid great emphasis on the distinctive historical consciousness of the Revolutionaries, finding in it perhaps the deepest source of their extraordinary and unprecedented actions. In Furet's phrase, the notion of a 'radical break', a conscious dividing of the historical continuum between the Old Regime (a label invented by the revolutionaries themselves) and the new order created by the Revolution, served as the most powerful agent of revolutionary praxis.[14] The quintessential embodiment of this dichotomous historical consciousness was the new Republican Calendar: the institution of the Republic on 22 September 1792, the Revolutionaries announced, marked the beginning of a wholly new temporal dispensation, the first day of the Year I. It thereby displaced the birth of Christ as the 'break' dividing the old order from the new, the City of Man, as it were, from the City of God.

The literary critic M. H. Abrams sees this same historical conception at work in the poetry and philosophy of the entire generation of European thinkers and artists who came of age in the Revolutionary period. In *Natural Supernaturalism* he explicitly identifies the French Revolution itself as the main contemporary source of the idea, which was then internalized in the poetry of Wordsworth and the philosophy of Hegel, among others. The essential feature of this sensibility for Abrams is the notion of history as 'right-angled', as sharply divided between two orders, an old and a new, the latter being ushered into existence by a dramatic event or sequence of events.[15]

One distinctive feature of *Fidelio* immediately suggests the pertinence of this conception to an understanding of the opera. I refer to the manner in which its dramatic continuity is sharply interrupted at a single moment in the unfolding of the action, namely, at the arrival of the minister in the middle of act II.

Beethoven acknowledges this moment by bringing the frenetic musical and dramatic proceedings to a sudden halt in order to introduce a solo trumpet call. As countless viewers and critics have observed, it is an intervention of uncanny effectiveness. The unadorned tones of a descending and then ascending B flat major arpeggio, sounded on a single, archaic horn, are like a voice from above. The trumpet call marks an instantaneous and utter reversal of the dramatic situation, an upheaval that the principals (Leonore, Florestan, Pizarro and Rocco) memorialize in a short but moving chorale. It marks, in other words, the operatic counterpart of the Revolutionary Year I, the time-line that categorically separates past misery from future happiness. Significantly, *The Magic Flute*, which shares *Fidelio*'s moral earnestness, boasts no such transformative moment. Tamino's passage from ignorance to wisdom is portrayed as a gradual ascent, a progressive education, in which no single episode can be construed as a turning-point. Only *Fidelio*'s moral trajectory is right-angled.

We see this bifurcated sense of history in *Fidelio* most obviously if we focus on Florestan and the prisoners. The opera begins with them in a state of oppression, and through its dramatic action it brings about their deliverance. Beethoven contrives to draw this antithesis to our attention above all through the prisoners' chorus: the men's melancholy and timorous aspirations create an unforgettable sense of the repressive present, just as their transformation into the jubilant assembly of the opera's final scene marks the institution of a new regime of freedom and brotherhood. But to focus on the prisoners, significant though they are, overlooks a deeper and structurally more compelling link between the opera and the historical consciousness introduced by the Revolution. For it is not just the specific depredations suffered by the inmates that *Fidelio* aims to transcend. Rather, it is the whole order of being that we meet in the opera's opening scenes. The world of Rocco, Marzelline and Jaquino – the world of bourgeois routine – has been veritably abolished in its concluding chiliastic celebrations. The opera thus depicts the redemption not merely of the prisoners but of the entire social universe to which it introduces us. In its overarching contours, *Fidelio* conforms to the pattern of radical break and right-angledness that Furet and Abrams have identified as the hallmarks of the French Revolution.

Not least among the attractions of this interpretation is that it turns what has generally been regarded as a weakness of the opera into a strength, namely, the putative inconsistency between its beginning and its end. The opera does indeed start in one realm and conclude in another. But we should perhaps contemplate the possibility that this discrepancy is very much to the point. Beethoven has not dawdled in the jailor's household simply because he can think of nothing better to do, or because he must 'set the scene' for the significant actions that follow, or even because he is adhering to the conventions of the rescue opera genre. Rather, he is here creating the first term of his grand historical argument, the lapsed world of imperfect beings and relationships that will be utterly transformed in the work's conclusion. We can feel the power of that transformation only if the old order is firmly established in our minds as the *terminus a quo* of the opera's trajectory.

The sense of moving from an unreconstructed to a redeemed order is in fact the single most powerful impression that *Fidelio* conveys to its audience. This dichotomous experience, furthermore, is as much musical as dramatic. It is perhaps most readily appreciated by considering, in close juxtaposition, the opera's beginning and its end.

Three of the first four numbers in *Fidelio* serve to establish the old regime: the duet 'Jetzt, Schätzchen, jetzt sind wir allein' between Jaquino and Marzelline (no. 1), Marzelline's aria 'O wär' ich schon mit dir vereint' (no. 2) and Rocco's gold aria (no. 4). The world they depict is neither hellish nor depraved, but it is decidedly egoistic and provincial. It is also tension-ridden, even alienated. The long opening duet is devoted to unpleasant bickering between former lovers. It pits Jaquino's peevish resentment against the cruel annoyance of Marzelline. In the middle of it Jaquino is further angered by repeated knocking at the prison door, thereby drawing our attention to his menial job and his less than gracious fulfilment of it. Marzelline's aria expounds on her infatuation with Fidelio, which we are made to feel is naive and self-indulgent. Rocco, for his part, holds forth with bourgeois satisfaction and pedagogic self-importance on the virtues of money: gold alone, he says, can guarantee a good marriage. In effect, we are introduced to a world of narrow horizons and dim perspectives, a cramped, grey, mindless world of personal antagonism, illusory desire and selfish materialism – a world sorely in need of redemption.

Beethoven's music for these opening numbers is well suited to convey their shallow sentiment and petty conflicts. It is trivializing music, whose restraint and formality nicely suggest the emotional claustrophobia of the prison household. Some have called it Mozartian, and certainly it has an archaizing flavour about it. But it is Mozart without much spirit. The effect is not bubbly or excited (one thinks of the opening of *Figaro*) but nervous and insubstantial. Perhaps the most distinctive feature of the music is Beethoven's insistence on *staccato* effects: neither orchestra nor singers are permitted the sort of broad *legato* expansion that might suggest deep passion or strong conviction. Instead everything is short-breathed and choppy. Sometimes Beethoven even inserts rests between the individual notes of the vocal line, as in the opening phrase of Marzelline's aria. There is a similar feeling of restraint in the harmonic choices, which incline towards automatic alternations of tonic and dominant. Throughout these numbers the singers stick to the middle of their range and rarely venture beyond *mezzo forte*. The few exceptions, such as the thirteen-bar period in the middle of the duet where Marzelline reflects on her love of Fidelio, serve mainly to highlight the prevailing sense of constraint. It all sounds undernourished, especially if we have occasion to make mental comparisons with the powerful and expansive music Beethoven had written less than two years earlier for the 'Eroica'. Jaquino, Marzelline and Rocco are untouched by the heroic style, and Beethoven's deliberate withholding of his compositional powers results in their sounding spiritually impoverished.

The contrast with the dramatic and musical language of the opera's conclusion could hardly be greater. Admittedly, the ends of operas are often different from their beginnings, with a larger number of people on stage and the music louder, faster and more elaborately composed. But Beethoven categorically exceeds the limits of this expectation, especially if we compare his practice with that of the Mozart finales. Where the opera begins with particular characters singing discrete, self-contained musical numbers, it ends with a chorus of undifferentiated individuals, singing what for all practical purposes could be the conclusion of a cantata, a mass or (significantly) a choral symphony. Instead of half a dozen identifiable figures, we see (in a major opera house) up to a hundred choristers. To be sure, the most important personages from the body of the opera are still on stage, but they have been transformed into a vocal ensemble very much like the vocal quartet that Beethoven uses in both the Ninth Symphony and the *Missa Solemnis* to offset the massed voices of the chorus. That is, the bulk of their singing is devoted not to individual actions or sentiments but to the collective musical articulation of generalized ideas and emotions. Their words are largely interchangeable, and a line originally assigned to one voice will as often as not find itself taken over by the others. The scene is nearly devoid of action, the only important exception – Leonore's unlocking of Florestan's chains – being itself a symbolic rather than a real event. Indeed, there is hardly any reason for the proceedings to be on stage at all, and directors rightly opt for an essentially static deployment of their huge choral forces, who behave exactly as would their robed counterparts standing on risers in a concert performance. They are the secular counterpart of Bach's redeemed chorus of believers.

The scene begins with what amounts to a prolonged orchestral fanfare, thirty bars of hammering dotted figures whose essential purpose is to announce the finale's resolute C major tonality. Beethoven associated the key with triumph and celebration, as in the last movement of the Fifth Symphony. The introduction is composed out of almost comically mechanical alternations of tonic and dominant, reaching a deafening intensity between bars 16 and 19, where the entire orchestra screams this rudimentary antithesis in unison. If it were not so robust and aggressive, one might almost suspect it of having been composed by Rossini, especially in view of the long *crescendo* that dominates its first half. The orchestral music here does not so much set a dramatic scene – in the manner of, say, Verdi or Wagner – as announce a state of mind, namely, unqualified affirmation. Any hint of ambiguity or tension has been banished from the philosophical, not to say religious, proceedings about to get under way.

The orchestral build-up allows Beethoven to march his singers on stage and array them in a tableau. The stage directions call for the choristers to be divided into two groups, the prisoners and the people, the latter of whom have been neither seen nor mentioned before in the opera (stage directors sometimes pretend they are the friends and relatives of the liberated prisoners). In the opening chorus Beethoven maintains the dramatic fiction that these two groups are somehow differentiated: the two-voiced 'Chor der Gefangenen' is set on different lines of the score from the four-voiced 'Chor des Volkes'. But the tenors and basses of the prisoners' chorus sing exactly the same words and notes as the tenors and basses of the people's chorus. Moreover, throughout the rest of the finale Beethoven gives up all pretence to verisimilitude

and refers simply to 'the Chorus' without qualification. The real
purpose of the original distinction was to excuse the introduction
of sopranos and altos onto the stage, thus providing the composer
with the full vocal complement needed to produce the massed
choral effects he has in mind. Once again, dramatic considerations
give way to musical ones, which in turn stand in the service of
ideology. The full four-voiced chorus is a more adequate
representative of humanity, which is the finale's real protagonist.

The music it now intones might be described as a kind of all-
purpose shout. The text reads as follows:

> Heil sei dem Tag, heil sei der Stunde,
> die lang ersehnt, doch unvermeint.
> Gerechtigkeit mit Huld im Bunde
> vor unseres Grabes Tor erscheint!
>
> [Hail the day, hail the hour,
> long yearned for but unforeseen.
> Justice in league with mercy
> appears at the threshold of our grave!]

The mention of the grave is passed over briskly, and the listener
is impressed mainly by the repeated outbursts of 'Heil sei dem
Tag' with its significant allusion to the sunlit open air of the
parade ground where the scene is set. The German brings to mind
'heiliger Tag', and it is a holy day indeed. We are at the outset of
a sacramental act.

The officiating priest is the minister Don Fernando, who now
steps forward to deliver his brief monologue:

> Des besten Königs Wink und Wille
> führt mich zu euch, ihr Armen, her,
> daß ich der Frevel Nacht enthülle,
> die all' umfangen, schwarz und schwer.
>
> Nein, nicht länger knieet sklavisch nieder,
> Tyrannenstrenge sei mir fern!
> Es sucht der Bruder seine Brüder,
> und kann er helfen, hilft er gern.
>
> [The command of the best of kings
> leads me here to you, poor people,
> that I may uncover the night of crime,
> which, black and heavy, enveloped all.
>
> No longer kneel down like slaves,
> stern tyranny be far from me!
> A brother seeks his brothers,
> and gladly helps, if help he can.]

Characteristically, Don Fernando turns from a consideration of the dramatic specifics in the first stanza to moral generalization in the second. His peroration is composed as a dignified recitative, commented on by a wood-wind choir. Coming after the noisy assertions of the opening chorus, it marks an unmistakable moment of relaxation. Beethoven takes noted musical interest only in the humane sentiments of the last couplet (which anticipates the apostrophe to brotherhood in the Ninth Symphony). It is set to Don Fernando's most eloquent musical line, which is warmed by doubling in the wood-winds and the reintroduction of the strings. After a final choral exclamation of 'Heil sei dem Tag', the couplet is repeated, to identical musical material, thus confirming its ideological importance.

The second large section of the finale, set in A major, is devoted to unravelling the plot. It is the only part of the finale that is truly operatic, in the sense of addressing itself to the resolution of the specific dramatic issues raised by the libretto. The most important thing to be said about Beethoven's response to those issues is that it is thoroughly uninspired, both dramatically and musically. Here, one senses, is precisely the material that Mozart would have developed into a virtuoso display, such as he produced in the finale to the second act of *Figaro*. It is, in fact, ideally suited to such treatment, consisting of a sequence of revelations, clarifications, reunions and expulsions, for each of which Mozart might have fashioned a brilliant musical realization. Beethoven, however, treats these events in the most perfunctory fashion imaginable. Certain obvious dramatic possibilities, such as the presumed reconciliation of Jaquino and Marzelline, are ignored altogether. For the rest, they are disposed of largely in a narrative for Rocco, who recounts the opera's story for the illumination of Don Fernando. A less dramatic device can hardly be imagined. Beethoven composes this section in an utterly recessive manner, organizing it around an oft-repeated five-note noodling figure in the orchestra, interrupted only by the brief choral outburst that ushers Pizarro off the stage. Transparently he wants to rid himself of these tedious narrative reponsibilities with as little fuss as possible, so that he can get on to the important ideological work ahead.

Only Don Fernando's last two lines capture the composer's interest, and that because they belong emotionally and intellectually to the extraordinary musical passage that follows. Beethoven brings the obsessive noodling to a halt, a hush falls over the orchestra, and the minister turns to Leonore in two serene descending phrases:

> Euch, edle Frau, allein
> euch ziemt es, ganz ihn zu befrei'n.
>
> [You, noble lady, you alone
> should be the one to set him wholly free.]

This is the signal to begin the third section of the finale, the splendid Sostenuto assai in F major. The textual basis for this extended musical episode is not very promising. It consists of a sequence of unspecific emotional ejaculations and theological platitudes:

> O Gott! O welch' ein Augenblick!
> O unaussprechlich süßes Glück!
> Gerecht, O Gott, ist dein Gericht!
> Du prüfest, du verläßt uns nicht.
>
> [O God! O what a moment!
> O inexpressibly sweet happiness!
> Righteous, O God, is Thy judgement!
> Thou dost try, but not forsake us.]

The first line is intoned by Leonore, the second by Florestan, the third by Don Fernando, and the last by Marzelline and Rocco. But there is no compelling reason for any of these figures to be uttering the particular words assigned to them, and Beethoven quickly abandons any pretence to dramatic appositeness in order to mould his characters into a vocal quintet that sings the whole of the text in a series of overlapping musical repetitions. After their original statement the words become unintelligible, as so often happens in vocal ensembles. But this is of no consequence, because the quintet is a musical, not a textual, event. It is in fact an extended musical tribute to Leonore as an agent of liberation, an angel of freedom.

Nothing in the quintet itself indicates that it serves this function. Indeed, nothing in the text tells us what the quintet is about at all or why Beethoven has lavished such extravagant musical attention on it. Audiences instinctively recognize its importance, but I doubt that they are able to link its solemn and intense music to any precise idea or purpose. Doubtless they feel, in a vague way, that it is somehow appropriate to the opera's lofty sentiments. Its fifty-six bars are dominated by a beautiful arched phrase that Beethoven repeats, either in the voices or on various instruments, no fewer than eight times. It consists of an upward leap of a fourth or a fifth followed by a seven-note descending scale of crotchets. The soaring upward interval recalls the reaching effect that Beethoven uses to evoke the idea of freedom in the prisoners' chorus and in Florestan's aria. The cumulative effect of its repetitions is at once mesmerizing and exalted, and the mood it creates can legitimately be described as religious or liturgical. We have reached the heart, one senses, of Beethoven's inspiration.

Scholars have discovered an important hint as to the quintet's meaning for Beethoven. The melody, they have shown, is taken directly from a passage in the *Funeral Cantata on the Death of Joseph II*. In 1924 Alfred Heuss dubbed it Beethoven's *Humanitätsmelodie*.[16] Beethoven used it in the cantata to give musical expression to his vision of human transcendence:

Exsurgunt, ad lucem, revolvitur feliciter orbis circa solum, atque sol eradiat fulgore divino.

[Then did men climb into the light, then the earth spun more joyfully around the sun, and the sun warmed it with heaven's light.]

This music clearly had profound philosophical associations for Beethoven. In the context of *Fidelio*, we are able to ascertain its specific import only from Don Fernando's couplet at the end of the preceding section. His lines explicitly name Leonore, the 'edle Frau', as the subject of this sonic tribute, and they also specify, with a precision known only to music, that liberation is its theme. The minister's final word – indeed, the significant second syllable to that word – marks the exact moment at which this episode is launched: 'befrei'n', the ideological code-word whose repeated musical elaboration in the earlier parts of the opera we have already examined. Here it is italicized even more emphatically than before. At its sounding Beethoven introduces a sudden and breathtaking transformation in the musical fabric. The tempo is slowed, the metre shifts from common time to 3/4 and, most spectacular of all, the music modulates unexpectedly to F major. Every listener feels the magic of this change. Time seems suspended, and there is a sense of being transported to some remote and ethereal realm, as Beethoven begins his campaign of musical repetitions.

Viewed symphonically, the F major segment of the finale might be compared to the lyrical third movement of the Ninth Symphony. It serves to set off, by contrast, the unbuttoned celebrations of the choral Allegro that follows and brings the opera to a conclusion. There is, furthermore, a specific textual link between this fourth section of the finale and the last movement of the Ninth: it is based on a quatrain whose first two lines are taken, with only slight modification, from Schiller's 'An die Freude';

> Wer ein holdes Weib errungen,
> stimm' in unsern Jubel ein.
> Nie wird es zu hoch besungen
> Retterin des Gatten sein.
>
> [He who has won a noble wife
> may join in our rejoicing.
> Never can we praise too highly
> the saviour of her husband.]

(The corresponding lines in the 'Ode to Joy' are: 'Wer ein holdes Weib errungen, / mische seinen Jubel ein' [He who has won a noble wife, let him mingle his rejoicing with ours].) The quatrain supplies the basic textual material for a large and complex musical composition, in which the individual phrases are repeated so many times that it makes no sense to count them – or, for that matter, even to listen for them. Save for the occasion when they are sung alone by Florestan, they remain largely unintelligible, set as they are for the massed voices of the chorus or the equally opaque concertato grouping of the vocal sextet (Leonore, Marzelline, Florestan, Jaquino, Don Fernando and Rocco, who here become simply two sopranos, two tenors and two basses). Just as in the preceding F major passage, Beethoven's argument in this final section is musical rather than textual. It is, in effect, an extended essay in musical affirmation, an uninflected expression of joy. In this respect it might be compared to the last movement of several of the symphonies, notably the Third, the Fifth and the Seventh. The text, one feels, merely supplies an excuse to add the heft and sonority of a hundred-voice choir to the orchestral goings-on, much as happens in the closing movement of the Ninth. We have travelled light years from the insipid, textually responsible music of the opera's beginning – travelled, in effect, from the quotidian to the sublime, from the old regime to the new.

The attentive reader will have noticed that, in this contrast between *Fidelio*'s cramped beginning and its expansive end, I have passed over the so-called canon, 'Mir ist so wunderbar', the third number in the opera and in the minds of many (including myself) the most beautiful piece in the entire work. The canon represents a challenge to my interpretation of *Fidelio* as the opera of the French

Revolution, because its music conveys the sort of exalted transcendence that we don't hear again until the finale of the second act and that I want to associate with Beethoven's musical portrait of a new order of freedom and brotherhood.

Actually, the canon poses a problem even for interpreters who don't view the opera from the particular historical perspective I do. Its musical beauties seem unrelated to the thoughts being expressed by the four characters who sing it: Marzelline, Leonore, Rocco and Jaquino. To be precise, the four characters give voice to their individual thoughts – all of them are singing 'asides' – and in the case of each those thoughts are very different. Marzelline, who sings first, indulges herself in a happy fantasy of union with Fidelio; Leonore, who comes in next, expresses anxious foreboding about Marzelline's infatuation; then Rocco gives voice to his satisfaction at the prospective marriage between Fidelio and Marzelline; while Jaquino, who enters last, frets angrily at Rocco's betrayal. Yet in spite of their diverse emotions, Beethoven makes no effort (such as Verdi does in the famous *Rigoletto* quartet) to differentiate among the four musically. On the contrary, because this is a canon, all four are given the identical vocal line, as each repeats the same basic melody.

My hypothesis – perhaps too conveniently – is that the canon is a kind of visionary moment in which we are given a foretaste of the music, and the world, of the future, the music of the opera's conclusion. It is a kind of musical promise, a down-payment, as it were, and has the effect of alerting us near the start of the opera that something much more significant is in store for us than we would be inclined to expect from the trivialities of the opening duet and Marzelline's aria – the only two pieces we have heard up to this point.

Among the most striking features of the canon is the way its music resembles that of the great slow section, marked Sostenuto assai, of the second act finale, the passage beginning 'O Gott! welch' ein Augenblick!' Both are set in slow triple metre, both are punctuated by bass *pizzicati* on the third and first beats of the bar, and both have the same sort of long-breathed, arching phrases, although in the canon this essential *legato* is created more by the orchestra (especially the wood-winds) than by the voices. Most important, the canon and the slow section of the finale create the same sense of stillness and transfiguration, the same sense of having entered an altered universe. The main difference is that in the canon this stillness gives way gradually to exaltation, as the overlapping vocal lines grow more agitated and are allowed to soar upwards and as the underlying accompaniment becomes more excited, whereas in the Sostenuto assai Beethoven maintains the stillness to the end, because he wants to create the greatest possible contrast with the frenetic movement of the closing Allegro that follows.

The canon, in sum, must be bracketed off from the numbers that surround it. It anticipates the world in which *Fidelio* ends, but it does not fundamentally disturb the opera's bipolar structure – our sense of moving from a discredited past to a redeemed future.

4

The principal affinity between *Fidelio* and the French Revolution is their common right-angled conception of history. But they exhibit an equally remarkable similarity in the way they view the transition from the old order to the new. Admittedly, for both of them the movement from oppression to liberation is categorical and swift. But it is in no sense easy. On the contrary, the passage is marked by anxiety, even despair. It is managed only in the face of opposition and through struggle. Indeed, the revolutionary break is accompanied by violence and profound conflict.

Much of the middle portion of Beethoven's opera is devoted to a dramatic and musical representation of this antagonistic process of transition. We are repeatedly made aware of its heavy psychological costs, particularly in Leonore's frequent expressions of anxiety and in the general intimation of terror that hovers over the action. Beethoven constructs his most concentrated musical portrait of the fear and despair attending the revolutionary struggle in the long orchestral prelude to Florestan's prison aria – a musical essay of symphonic dimensions and intensity. The dark, minor tonality, the piercing brass and the low moans in the strings, giving way to anxious staccatos, all conspire to create an impression of blackest depression.

The central figure in Beethoven's representation of conflict and struggle in the opera is Pizarro. He is usually thought to be a personification of evil, and in the minds of many he comes dangerously close to comedy in this regard. Even for a conventional rescue-opera villain, he is a decidedly cardboard figure, speaking a melodramatic language that borders on caricature, nowhere more so than in the opening lines of his aria:

> Ha! welch' ein Augenblick!
> Die Rache werd' ich kühlen.
> Dich rufet dein Geschick!
> In seinem Herzen wühlen,
> O Wonne, großes Glück!
>
> [Ah! What a moment!
> I can wreak my vengeance.
> Your fate calls you!
> To run him through the heart,
> what bliss, what great joy!]

One is tempted to say that Beethoven was not aesthetically equipped to represent evil, certainly not in the persuasive manner of a later artist like Wagner (Hagen is the genuine item, and he seems both psychologically and musically altogether outside Beethoven's orbit). It is a shortcoming he shares with Mozart and, perhaps more generally, with the entire European Enlightenment.

Pizarro is a more impressive achievement if we think of him as the incarnation not of evil but of power. Power, unlike evil, is very much within Beethoven's aesthetic vocabulary. The idiom of the heroic period in particular is ideally suited to its representation. Thus, while Beethoven fails to persuade us of Pizarro's vileness, he is superbly successful at conveying his enormous oppositional force. The libretto is of very little help in the enterprise. Rather, as the embodiment of intense negative energy, Pizarro is strictly a creation of Beethoven's music. It alone convinces us of the formidable obstacles that Leonore must overcome in her mission of liberation.

Beethoven realizes Pizarro in this oppositional sense most effectively in his aria and in the opening music of the dungeon quartet that leads to the opera's climax. In both instances he uses the identical device. He forces Pizarro to plant his voice over and over again on the tonic. Not insignificantly, that tonic is the same note in both the aria and the quartet: a D, which is the home tone of the aria's D minor key, just as it is of the quartet's D major. The note conveys a sense of power, first, because of the almost compulsive manner in which Beethoven forces his singer to return to it and repeat it and, secondly, because it lies fairly high in the baritone's range. When the singer is obliged to sustain the note and to emit it over and over again, the effect is decidedly strenuous. We are conscious of his effort, even of a sense of strain. In other words, the vocal power needed to produce Pizarro's reiterated upper Ds is experienced by the listener as a sonic metaphor for personal power.

'Ha! welch' ein Augenblick!' comes about as close as imaginable to being a one-note aria. The way Beethoven sits on upper D in the piece is altogether astonishing. He begins there (on 'Ha!') and comes back to it as frequently as decency and the laws of melody will permit. By my calculations Pizarro sings the note forty-nine times. Often the D is unusually prolonged: for two and a half bars on 'Wonne' and two and a quarter bars on 'Triumph'. Pizarro is also apt to hover on the tones half a note below and half a note above D. As a result the musical line is studded with emphatic, sustained C sharps and E flats, which, however, nearly always give way to the inescapable D. Through most of the aria these repeated Ds are sung over an orchestral accompaniment of swirling strings, blaring brass and rumbling timpani, all playing at full throttle. The orchestral turbulence serves to underline Pizarro's extraordinary energy, and the volume and thickness of the instrumental accompaniment demand that his high-lying trumpetings be consistently loud. It is an exhausting workout for the singer, and few performers can muster the vocal wherewithal to fulfil Beethoven's rigorous demands.

Pizarro's lines at the start of the prison quartet are an even more impressive example of the D principle. The text, once again, seems overblown:

> Er sterbe! Doch er soll erst wissen,
> wer ihm sein stolzes Herz zerfleischt.
> Der Rache Dunkel sei zerrissen!
> Sieh her! Du hast mich nicht getäuscht!
> Pizarro, den du stürzen wolltest,
> Pizarro, den du fürchten solltest,
> steht nun als Rächer hier.

> [Let him die! But first he shall know
> who hacks his proud heart from him.
> Revenge's dark veil be ripped away!
> Look here! You did not confound me!
> Pizarro, whom you sought to ruin,
> Pizarro, whom you should have feared,
> now stands here as avenger.]

The work of transforming these implausible utterances into an assertion of power is left to Beethoven's music. All but two of the notes to which Pizarro sings the self-congratulatory fifth and sixth lines of the passage are set on upper D, and the remaining two are on D an octave below. They come, furthermore, at the end of an ascending vocal line that finds him sustaining first C, then C sharp, and finally E, each through two full bars, before settling in to the unparalleled sequence of Ds. As in the aria, this monomaniacal assertion of a single tone (prefaced by its closest neighbours) is set above an accompaniment of singular energy and volume. Pizarro's shouted Ds assume the character of a code. They are the uniquely concentrated expression of his power.

The dungeon quartet that Pizarro initiates with this outburst stands at the heart of the opera's dramatic action. Indeed, it might legitimately be described as 'action packed', so compressed is its sequence of happenings. Its eventfulness is all the more striking because it comes in the middle of an opera that is otherwise relatively static – given to rumination rather than drama. Here Beethoven presents his audience with a breathless series of confrontations, physical as well as emotional, culminating in Leonore's 'Töt' erst sein Weib!' (First kill his wife!). It is a sustained essay in struggle, a distillation of the violent conflict marking the passage from oppression to liberty.

Beethoven succeeds remarkably in embracing the scene's actions within a single musical framework. The music itself is an exercise in sustained frenzy. Its violent fabric and headlong pace are interrupted only once – for Leonore's bloodcurdling cry. Throughout, the orchestra remains at an unremitting *forte* (Beethoven is, along with Verdi, one of the few composers who can get away with this kind of sustained loudness without embarrassment). Rushing strings and fanfares in the brass compete with the ever more excited and strenuous exertions of the singers. Leonore in particular repeatedly assaults the upper register, pounding away in the vicinity of high G (at one point she repeats this note for five straight bars). As the quartet reaches its climax, the individual voices increasingly overlap, singing against one another and creating the effect of a musical shouting match. For the final twenty-one bars, as Leonore and Pizarro utter their threats of mutual destruction, Beethoven jacks up the tempo and alternates vehemently descending runs in the strings with fanfares in the winds and brass. As a piece of sustained musical violence, the quartet might be compared to the first movement of Fifth Symphony. It is a remarkable instance of Beethoven's skill in the musical realization of heroic struggle.

Throughout the quartet Leonore is unambiguously the central force, the prime mover of the action. Her suitability for this decisive role has been carefully prepared in the earlier scenes of the opera. Indeed, virtually from the start Beethoven has conducted a systematic musical and dramatic campaign to empower her – to represent her as an adequate vessel for the extraordinary undertaking that falls to her. This empowering of Leonore, moreover, significantly shapes our understanding of the process of struggle that leads from oppression to freedom. It locates the seat of that transformative action not in the *deus ex machina* of the absent minister (absent, that is, until the final scene) but in an ordinary human being, a person distinguishable from other persons neither by rank nor by office but only by qualities of character. I am suggesting, in other words, that Leonore represents for Beethoven an essentially democratic principle. The liberating action celebrated in the opera is generated not from above but from below. *Fidelio* is a democratic opera in precisely the same sense that the French Revolution – to invoke R. R. Palmer's authority once again – was democratic: not because it installed or memorialized a particular form of government, but because it located significant historical agency in the popular domain. Leonore is the essential agent of the opera's liberating action, just as the Third Estate was the essential agent of the French Revolution. For both Beethoven and the Revolutionaries history is viewed from the bottom up.

Leonore is of course a woman. What is more, throughout most of the opera she is a woman disguised as a man. We might wonder about the significance of her sex and her male disguise, especially as it affects our view of her as a historically decisive actor. In the current intellectual climate her femaleness and transvestism are apt to prompt excited reflections about the ambiguity or 'constructedness' of sexual roles and to invite comparisons with cross-dressed figures in Shakespeare, Mozart or Richard Strauss. But these temptations should be resisted. The most important thing about Leonore's transvestism is that it interests Beethoven not in the slightest. It is for him nothing more than a necessity of the plot. He systematically rejects every opportunity to exploit it for dramatic or comic effects. Not for a moment, for example, will he titillate us with the sexual ambiguities of Marzelline's infatuation (unless it be in the mercifully deleted duet, 'Um in der Ehe', in which Marzelline looks forward to bearing Fidelio's child), even though audiences sometimes ignore his interdiction and give way to fits of nervous laughter. The truth is, Beethoven was a profoundly unsexual artist, with a sensibility of unparalleled austerity. We recall that he disliked *The Marriage of Figaro* and *Don Giovanni* because of their salaciousness. His art was desexualised on principle, the purest instance of sublimation, uncompromisingly spiritual and disembodied. Thus *Fidelio*, although an opera about marital devotion, is utterly untouched by eroticism. Significantly, Leonore and Florestan are well past the ardours of the first love. Theirs is essentially a companionship of the spirit, a union based on shared principles rather than physical passion. Leonore, accordingly, is unsexed in the opera. Not a bar of Beethoven's music is devoted to depicting her femininity. It would be unthinkable, for example, for her to reveal the emotional vulnerability of Pamina's 'Ach, ich fühl's'. In every meaningful musical and dramatic sense Beethoven treats her exactly as if she were a man. More precisely, he treats her as a generic human being. It is her humanity, not her gender or her sexuality, that interests him, and it is as a human being, rather than as a woman, that he makes her the fulcrum of the opera's democratic action.

Let us briefly trace the steps by which Beethoven empowers her in the opera. When, in the opening scene, Marzelline urges Rocco not to take Fidelio into the dungeon because he would be unable to bear the sight of the condemned prisoner, Leonore responds, 'Warum denn nicht? Ich habe Mut und Kraft!' (Why not? I have courage and strength!). This is no idle boast, and Beethoven takes the occasion to launch a trio (no. 5) in which he provides Leonore with the musical ammunition to back up her claim. Her opening gambit – the trio's second verse – represents the first time she sings alone in the opera, and Beethoven sees to it that she makes a memorable impression:

> Ich habe Mut!
> Mit kaltem Blut
> will ich hinab mich wagen;
> für hohen Lohn
> kann Liebe schon
> auch hohe Leiden tragen.

> [I have courage!
> In cold blood
> I will dare to go down there;
> for great reward
> love can
> bear even great suffering.]

He takes particular care with the significant opening assertion ('Ich habe Mut'). Save for the violas, playing *piano* quavers, he momentarily silences the orchestra so that the soprano's notes can sound out with uncompromised force. Nor is he afraid of the egoistic display. On the contrary, he sets the opening 'ich' on a confident D. From this moment of unembarrassed self-assertion, Leonore's heroism is never in doubt. The rest of her declaration is composed with athletic brio. The vigour of her musical self-presentation assures us that Leonore does indeed possess the emotional resources for the task before her.

Beethoven confirms this impression, emphatically, in the concluding Allegro of her act I aria. The aria provides us with our fullest portrait of Leonore, and its bracing conclusion establishes her activist credentials beyond doubt. Again, the text is an unembarrassed piece of self-advertising:

> Ich folg' dem innern Triebe,
> ich wanke nicht,
> mich stärkt die Pflicht
> der treuen Gattenliebe!

> [I follow an inner compulsion,
> I do not falter,
> I am strengthened by the duty
> of faithful married love!]

The repeated 'I's' are fully justified by the energetic music to which the declaration is set. Beethoven begins with an athletic upward E major arpeggio for the soprano, marching her from low E to a stunning G sharp above the stave, from which, on the same syllable ('*Ga*tten'), he drops her over an octave and a half to low B sharp – a baritonal note that any decent Leonore will boom out in chest register – only to carry her (still on '*Ga*tten') up a coloratura scale to C sharp in the middle of the voice. This technical description cannot begin to do justice to what is, in effect, a blatant flexing of the vocal muscles, an unapologetic display of her powers of voice – which the listener readily translates into powers of mind and character. Particularly striking here, as throughout the aria, is Beethoven's juxtaposition of the highest and lowest registers of the voice – the former piercing, the latter growling – in order to suggest Leonore's potent sense of resolve. Before the Allegro is complete he will send her down once again from high G sharp to low B sharp, and in the final phrase he takes her up a fifteen-note run from low E to a thrillingly sustained B natural *in alt*, the highest note she sings in the opera. It is a show of vocal power such as one rarely encounters in Mozart (Fiordiligi's 'Come scoglio' comes closest, and it of course is a *mock*-heroic aria). The raucous horn fanfares that accompany Leonore's vehement declaration have a decidedly military flavour and serve to convince us – if any further convincing were necessary – that she is a force to be reckoned with.

I have already mentioned Leonore's disquisition on freedom in the grave-digging duet with Rocco ('Wer du auch seist, ich will dich retten' [Whoever you may be, I will save you]). Both musically and textually it is of a piece with the impression we have gained of her from the first act. At its climax, as in that of the aria, Beethoven resorts to coloratura to express Leonore's readiness for action. Furthermore, in the immediately preceding moments we see her engaged in a most unladylike piece of manual labour, namely, shovelling earth, and Beethoven's music nicely conveys the sense of physical exertion this work requires of her. It is a small matter, but it contributes subtly to our sense of her humanity. Her heroism is not limited to rhetorical displays but encompasses bodily labour as well, whether carrying chains or digging a grave.

We are, then, fully prepared for Leonore's courageous and decisive acts in the climatic dungeon quartet where she confronts and ultimately defeats Pizarro. Much of the quartet is in fact composed as a violent musical battle between these two figures, with Pizarro's aggressive high Ds set against Leonore's even more altitudinous and penetrating F sharps, Gs and G sharps. For her most decisive act – when she reveals her identity and challenges Pizarro with 'Töt' erst sein Weib!' (First kill his wife!) – Beethoven interrupts the turbulent musical flow in order to let her stunning imperative ring out unaccompanied into the hall, and he sets it on an unexpected upward interval, E flat followed by a sustained B flat above the stave. That vertiginous B flat is both awkward and punishing for the soprano, and it sums up Leonore's extraordinary initiative with unrivalled conciseness. In the end Pizarro is no match for her, either vocally or temperamentally.

Following the quartet, with the issue now resolved, Beethoven writes the only possible duet for the triumphant Leonore and her liberated husband. 'O namenlose Freude' (O nameless joy) is a duet of surpassing athleticism, in which no distinction is drawn between the muscular upward arpeggios of the soprano and those of the tenor. The two sing as absolute equals – a parity already anticipated by their major arias, which are identical in format and dimension. In effect, the duet recapitulates and summarizes the musical evidence that has been accumulating over the course of the entire opera. Leonore is Beethoven's portrait of humanity in action, struggling in the face of deadly opposition, and ultimately prevailing.

5

Is Beethoven's prison opera, then, a metaphor for the French Revolution? I cannot claim to have demonstrated so conclusively, but I am nevertheless impressed by the structural parallels between the two. By drawing attention to the opera's dichotomous historical vision, its preoccupation with struggle and its democratically empowered protagonist, I hope to have suggested a plausible interpretation linking it to the epochal events of 1789. Perhaps I will be accused of grasping at straws if I remind readers that the Revolution itself began with the liberation of a prison: on 14 July the fortress of the Bastille was attacked by a Parisian crowd, and, after a battle in which more than a hundred civilians were killed, the prison was taken and (as in the opera) all its inmates were released. Ironically, their number contained not a single political martyr, only five convicted felons and two madmen. Yet the Revolutionaries insisted on regarding this strategically insignificant victory as the birthplace of their Revolution. They did so, of course, because the Bastille quickly became symbolically freighted: it was for them a metaphor for the old regime, just as its liberation, while practically meaningless, was a metaphor for the new order created by the Revolution itself. In this essay I have argued that we can plausibly read Beethoven's prison opera much as the Revolutionaries read the storming of the Bastille: as a symbolical representation of the great political drama with which the modern world began.

6 *Music as drama: structure, style, and process in* Fidelio

MICHAEL C. TUSA

1 Issues in genre and large-scale structure

In approaching the music of *Fidelio* it is helpful to remember that Beethoven was essentially an operatic novice, a fact repeatedly attested by the history of the work. Eager to conquer the prestigious genre, the composer applied himself to the study of the most intriguing models known to him, appropriating from them important principles and effects while striving to assert his own individuality.[1] Preparatory efforts in the related (but less risky) genres of concert aria, ballet, and oratorio provided useful practice in vocal and theatrical composition. His inexperience led him initially to accept an unpromising libretto; only after beginning to compose this text did he realize his error and seek out a libretto that truly responded to his artistic vision.[2] Disappointed by his opera's shaky premiere, he subjected the work to substantial revisions in an ongoing effort to master the peculiarities of the unfamiliar genre. Beethoven's lack of theatrical experience and the relatively weak condition of German opera in his day arguably prevented him from ever finding a wholly satisfactory form for his only opera. Nevertheless, many facets of his style lent themselves quite brilliantly to dramatic ends, and what he did achieve bears eloquent witness to his keen understanding of the possibilities of *musical* articulation of drama.

In many ways the 1805 version of the opera (insofar as it can be reconstructed from the extant sources[3]) allows us best to situate the opera in the context of Beethoven's development and the history of opera; after all, it was the work of a composer whose manifest ambition at the time was to establish credentials in opera as forcefully as he had in instrumental music. A comparison of the large-scale structure of the 1805 version with that of the Bouilly-Gaveaux *Léonore* of 1798 is highly instructive in this regard (table 6.1),

101

revealing the musical pretensions of Beethoven's setting to be significantly greater than those of the modest *opéra comique*.[4] Simple strophic pieces derived from the traditions of *Singspiel* and the simpler types of *opéra comique* stand beside large-scale arias in the most up-to-date forms of Italian serious opera. Pizarro, only a speaking role in the French libretto, gains a musical voice at a number of decisive points in the story. The most significant plot developments now unfold in action ensembles, the legacy of *opera buffa*, rather than in spoken dialogue. Sonnleithner and Beethoven subsume the dramatically static prisoners' chorus that concludes Bouilly's first act into a finale, another inheritance of *opera buffa*, that advances the plot through a series of linked movements in contrasting tempi, keys, and styles; likewise Beethoven's act III finale, comprising the last two pieces and intervening spoken dialogue of Bouilly's libretto, supplies a musical realization of the denouement.[5] The participation of the chorus is modestly expanded as well. On the whole, such adaptations are entirely consistent with cosmopolitan Viennese traditions demanding relatively great musical elaboration and a broad diversity of operatic types.[6]

Beethoven's dependence on models is also more evident in the original version of the opera than in its later incarnations. Many issues remain unsettled in this area, as historians are just beginning to sift through the operatic repertory and conventions in Beethoven's day; even the relatively straightforward question as to whether Beethoven consulted the printed score of Gaveaux's *Léonore* evades a definitive answer, since resemblances in certain pieces may well be coincidental, reflecting conventional responses to stimuli in the shared libretto rather than influence or modelling.[7] There can be no doubt, however, that the 1805 *Leonore* betrays a strong desire on Beethoven's part to emulate and compete with the two opera composers whom he is known to have most admired, Mozart and Cherubini. His fascination with the latter – whose works along with those of other French composers stormed the Viennese theatres in the 1802–3 season – is attested by anecdotes, letters, and excerpts from *Les deux journées* copied among his sketches for *Leonore*,[8] and the proximity of Beethoven's opera to Cherubini was noted by commentators almost from the outset.[9] Beethoven seems to have been attracted to the seriousness, forcefulness, and technical mastery of the older composer, and particularly keen to include in his own opera many of the effects found in Cherubini's operas. Like Antonio's *romance* at the start of *Les deux journées*

Table 6.1

Bouilly/Gaveaux. *Léonore* (1798)		Sonnleithner/Beethoven. *Leonore* (1805)	
Piece	Key	Piece	Key
Ouverture.	f–F	Ouverture ['*Leonore* No. 2']	C
Act I		*Act I*	
1 Couplets (Marcelline)	g/G	1 Arie (Marzelline)	c/C
2 Duo (Marcelline, Jacquino)	C	2 Duetto (Marzelline, Jaquino)	A
		3 Terzett (Marzelline, Jaquino, Rocco)	Eb
3 Chanson (Roc)	Bb	4 Canon [Quartet] (Marzelline, Leonore, Rocco, Jaquino)	G
		5 [Arie] (Rocco)	Bb
		6 Terzett (Rocco, Marzelline, Leonore)	F
		Act II	
		7 'Introduzione del Atto IIdo'	D
		8 [Arie] (Pizarro)	d–D
4 Duo (Marcelline, Léonore)	A	9 Duetto (Pizarro, Rocco)	A
5 Romance (Léonore)	f/F	10 Duetto (Marzelline, Leonore)	C
6 Air (Léonore)		11 Arie (Leonore)	E
7 Choeur (Prisonniers)	D	12 Finale	Bb/G/Eb/–/Bb
Act II		*Act III*	
8 Recitatif./Romance (Florestan)	c	13 Recitatio./Arie (Florestan)	f/Ab/F?/f
9 Duo (Roc, Léonore)	Eb	14 [Melodram?]/Duett (Rocco, Leonore)	a
10 Trio (Florestan, Roc, Léonore)	G	15 Terzett (Florestan, Rocco, Leonore)	A
		16 Quartett (Pizarro, Florestan, Leonore, Rocco)	D
11 Duo (Florestan, Léonore)	f–F	17 [Recit. &] Duetto (Florestan, Leonore)	G
12 Choeur (+ Florestan, Léonore)	Bb	18 Finale	c/A/F/–/C
13 Finale (Choeur general)	C		

(on another libretto by Bouilly) Marzelline's aria establishes a principal moral for the opera (the joy of marital love) and progresses from minor to major in each of its stanzas; in addition, both pieces entail imitative gestures between voice and winds in the dominant-prolongation phrase of each stanza.[10] As originally conceived, Florestan's aria starts with a slow movement in major and ends with a faster movement in minor, an unusual trajectory perhaps suggested by the title character's act II aria in *Lodoïska*, like Florestan's, an aria sung by an innocent victim of tyranny. Commentators have frequently pointed out Pizarro's stylistic dependence on *opéra-comique* villains:[11] what is more, the 1805 version of the act II finale concludes with Pizarro's raging entrance and subsequent *aria con coro* ('Auf euch will ich nur bauen'), an addition to the Bouilly libretto probably suggested by the conclusion of the act II finale in *Lodoïska*, where the villain Dourlinski brusquely enters and commands his followers to obey him. The use of Melodrama in the last act for a situation of hushed suspense looks to such pieces in *Les deux journées* and other *opéras comiques* for inspiration. Likewise, the original ending of the act III quartet on an unresolved dissonance points to *opéra-comique* models, like the act II *Morceau d'ensemble et choeur* no. 7 in *Les deux journées*. Interestingly, Beethoven seems to have turned his back on certain prominent elements in French opera of the 1790s. Wholly absent are any musical traces of the *couleur locale* that is a hallmark of the *opéra-comique* style: whereas Gaveaux sets Marzelline's aria as a 'Seguidilla' to establish the Spanish setting of his *Léonore* straight away, Beethoven avoids such particularization of time and place, perhaps so as not to limit the universality of the opera's humanitarian message. Practically ignored as well is the use of recurring motives and melodies, a prominent feature in Méhul's operas and Cherubini's *Les deux journées*, although we shall see Beethoven's use of related integrative devices.[12]

Mozart looms even larger in the 1805 *Leonore*, hardly surprising in view of Beethoven's lifelong admiration of his famous predecessor. The heterogeneity of the work is quintessentially Mozartian: just as *Die Zauberflöte* allegedly earned Beethoven's esteem in part for its universality of styles and genres, so too the 1805 *Leonore* employs a broad palette of available types.[13] The emphasis on action ensembles suggests a desire to compete with the master of such pieces, as does also the fact that Beethoven copied a number of Mozart ensembles as part of his study for the opera, with surviving excerpts in his handwriting from ensembles in *Don Giovanni* and *Die Zauberflöte* surely only a fragment of what he must have actually studied.[14] Some of the pieces that Sonnleithner added to Bouilly's libretto may have been suggested by specific Mozartian models. Like the Pamina-Papageno duet in *Die Zauberflöte*, the act I trio 'Ein Mann ist bald genommen' (no. 3 in 1805) is a sententious strophic ensemble about love. The canonic quartet in act I invokes the canon in the act II finale of *Così fan tutte*; common to both is the topic of marriage and the dissent of one of the participants.[15] And some of the texts taken over from Bouilly were modified in ways that make them more 'Mozartian'. For instance, the solo pieces for Leonore in the first act of the French libretto are consolidated into a multi-tempo aria of an Italianate mould; similarly, subtle changes in the text of Florestan's aria, treated as a strophic *romance* by Gaveaux, facilitate a through-composed multisectional setting.[16] The text of the act III trio is reshaped from one that prefigures an aBcB form in the French libretto to one that ultimately facilitates a sonata-like recapitulation of the *opening* music at a point of dramatic reprise, a typical gambit in Mozart's ensembles. Lastly, the overture of 1805 ('*Leonore* No. 2') follows and extends Mozartian models like the *Don Giovanni* and *Magic Flute* overtures in its use of quotation and suggestive musical processes to foreshadow the central emotional thrust of the drama.[17]

Large-scale tonal organization in the 1805 version is also consistent with practices that Beethoven must have observed in the mature operas of Mozart. The overture and the act III finale establish C major as a tonal frame for the opera; what is more, both the first vocal piece, Marzelline's aria, and the act III finale progress from C minor to C major.[18] Within this frame keys are chosen and deployed with evident care for their effective succession, despite the fact that spoken dialogue intervenes in the vast majority of cases. Adjacent pieces are normally related by either third or fifth, and the third act moves from the grave-digging duet to the finale by means of descent through the cycle of fifths (a–A–D–G–c/C).[19] The finales similarly link third-related movements within tonally closed frames. Perhaps more importantly, keys seem to be chosen according to Beethoven's understanding of their affective connotations, and many of the selections again suggest Mozartian precedents.[20] Pizarro's revenge aria shares the key of D minor with the revenge arias of Mozart's Elettra ('Tutto nel cor vi sento') and Queen of the Night ('Der Hölle Rache').

Topical and formal ties to 'Bei Männern welche Liebe fühlen' may have prompted the choice of E flat major (as well as the conspicuous use of horns) for 'Ein Mann ist bald genommen'. Like peasant choruses in *Figaro* and *Don Giovanni* the act I canon couples G major with compound metre, in this case to evoke the idyllic dreams of the working-class Marzelline. Leonore's great aria has been convincingly related to Fiordiligi's 'Per pietà, ben mio' in *Così fan tutte* by virtue of similarities of key (E major), instrumentation (virtuosic use of horns), and subject (fidelity).[21] The choice of A major in two duets (Marzelline–Jaquino; Pizarro–Rocco) recalls Mozart's preference for A major duets; what is more, both of these pieces can be seen as attempted 'seductions', like the Count–Susanna and Don Giovanni–Zerlina duets.

An especially important role attaches to C major, which emerges as a tonal symbol for the concepts of hope and marital love that lie at the heart of the drama. Just as the idea of marital love grows over the course of the opera from a daydream of petit-bourgeois domesticity to a driving force behind heroic self-sacrifice and all-embracing love of humanity, so too C major is gradually shifted from Marzelline's sphere to Leonore's. Early in the opera the key is associated with Marzelline's hopes for blissful union with Fidelio in her aria and the act II duet with Leonore. In the course of the opera, however, C major comes to be associated with Leonore and more noble manifestations of love: her self-sacrifice for the sake of Florestan (the transitional passage 'O du für den ich alles trug' in the 1805 version of her aria); her willingness to rescue the prisoner regardless of his identity (the passage 'Wer du auch seist' in the grave-digging duet); Florestan's amazement at her constancy and heroism (the start of the recitative 'Ich kann mich noch nicht fassen' preceding the duet no. 17); and her glorification as the epitome of spousal virtue in the act III finale ('Wer ein holdes Weib errungen'). By the end of the opera C major has attained the heroic stature frequently accorded to it by contemporary writers and reflected by triumphant uses of the key elsewhere in Beethoven's output (most notably in the finale of the Fifth Symphony).

A discussion of the revisions of 1806 and 1814 lies beyond the scope of the present essay, the remainder of which will focus on the 1814 version. For our purposes it must suffice to underscore some basic musical differences between the 1805 version and the 1814 revision, which Beethoven did view as a significant improvement.[22]

The quest for quicker dramatic pace and more concentrated focus on the principal characters led the composer to abandon certain premises of the opera's original large-scale organization. The 1814 version, like that of 1806, reverts to Bouilly's two-act plan, resulting in an imbalance between the acts (despite the removal of two pieces from act I) that has given rise to the unfortunate practice of performing the *Leonore* overture No. 3 immediately before the act II finale. The structural and symbolic roles of C major are mitigated by the new overture in E major and the reversal of the first two pieces,[23] and with the revised denouement, the act II finale no longer retraces the C minor/C major antithesis of Marzelline's aria but instead presents an unmitigated, cantata-like celebration of virtue triumphant. Some of the most extravagant gestures of the 1805 version were also tamed in 1814; for instance, the vocal demands in the role of Leonore were relaxed somewhat, and the original ending of the act II quartet on an unresolved diminished-seventh chord was converted into a full cadence on D major, an orthodox gesture of closure commensurate with the changed dramatic circumstances at the end of the 1814 version of the quartet. Lastly, Beethoven took advantage of the 1814 revision to eliminate or replace pieces that he may have come to feel were too obviously derivative of his operatic antecedents, such as the E flat major trio in act I and Pizarro's aria with chorus at the end of the act I finale, arguably the least inspired piece in the original version of the opera.

2 Characterization

Typical of German opera around 1800, *Fidelio* draws upon a wide range of available genres and forms in order to articulate the different social and spiritual planes in the drama: the strophic pieces that predominate in the first scenes reflect Rocco's modest working-class household, whereas the more Italianate forms in the second half of the opera signify the aristocratic characters and the life-or-death matters of the principal 'rescue' story. A comparable diversity of style and musical language serves the same end. For instance, the idioms of comic opera – tempered so as not to disrupt the basically serious tenor of the drama[24] – prevail at the start of the opera in the musical realizations of Rocco, Marzelline and Jaquino, and continue to be felt in subsequent passages in which Rocco interacts with the principal characters. Down-to-earth, sentimental descendants of comic archetypes, the members of Rocco's family express themselves through a consonant, diatonic tonal-harmonic language, a relatively rapid, syllabic delivery of the text, frequent reliance on staccato or detached articulations in the orchestra and voice, and relatively short-breathed vocal phrases; repeated tones, reminiscent of eighteenth-century patter, are quite conspicuous in Rocco's music. On the whole the members of Rocco's household avoid the kind of sustained, *bel canto* singing reserved for the heroic characters. That coloratura occasionally creeps into Marzelline's part as a sign of joy (no. 3, no. 5) or relief (no. 1) points to her descent from vivacious soubrettes like Despina and Blondchen.

The 'comic' pieces in *Fidelio* have frequently been faulted by critics as extraneous to the central thrust of the opera, and Beethoven himself seems to have reached a similar conclusion as he strove in 1814 to reduce the sentimental presence.[25] Nevertheless, one can only appreciate the care and ingenuity that Beethoven lavished on the lighter pieces. The strophic arias for Marzelline and Rocco incorporate imitative gestures between voice and orchestra and vary the accompaniments of their respective second stanzas. Rocco's gold aria contrasts the misery of poverty with the benefits of financial well-being, evoking the former through chromatic bass descent and a turn toward D minor (bars 8–14) and the latter through the ensuing shift to E flat major and 'rolling' compound-metre figure in the violins. A particularly witty detail is the allusion to the Papagena–Papageno duet in the trio no. 5 at the point where Marzelline imagines marriage to Fidelio to be imminent: 'in Kurzem sind wir dann ein Paar', she dreams (bars 87–91). The quotation of Papagena is doubtless Beethoven's commentary on the kind of relationship that Marzelline has in mind.[26]

The canon also belongs in Rocco's household, and though it ultimately transcends its surroundings with a solemnity inspired by the presence of Leonore, it too draws on styles appropriate to the class and character types of the participants, appropriately, since its principal *Affekt* is given by Marzelline's joyful incredulity. As noted earlier the choice of key and metre reflects longstanding traditions for pastoral/peasant music,[27] and the short phrases and triadic outlines of the first phrase can be heard in relationship to the start of Marzelline's aria. The use of canon to embody the *differing* perspectives of the participants at first glance seems odd, but the rigid form allows for some character differentiation and does in fact make a dramatic point.[28] In her role as Fidelio,

Leonore is trapped inside the canon and can do little but go along with Marzelline's plans (and melody); in effect, Leonore's music presents her 'public' expression of feigned joy, while her words, sung as an aside, betray her true feelings. With Rocco's entrance the *staccato* articulation characteristic of him and his family reappears; the introduction of bassoons and string basses in the orchestra reinforces his low register, thereby pointing up his paternal pride. Jaquino's seeming resistance to the canon is a natural consequence of his displeasure with the unfolding situation. He is the last to enter (and thus the first to break off), and the orchestral triplets that mark his entrance, an intensification of the duplets introduced by Rocco, are at odds with the rhythms of Marzelline's rhapsodic coloratura (ex. 6.1). In the coda (bars 43–51) Jaquino is further set apart from the others through his patter-like declamation.

Pizarro occupies a stylistic realm unto himself. On the whole the pieces in which he participates and those that refer to him contain irregularities that mirror the tyrant's disruptive effects on society. His vocal style is decidedly non-cantabile, its jagged contours easily related to precedents in the *opéra-comique* tradition. Brass instruments, long a symbol of political power, figure conspicuously in the pieces that emanate from his sphere. Persistent weak-beat accents in the orchestra characterize the rhythm of his aria, and the preceding *Marcia*, which brings him on stage, hints at his villainy through metrical ambiguities that are uncharacteristic of military music.[29] Throughout the opera, his villainy is suggested by diminished harmonies and by stepwise bass progressions that destroy or postpone key stability. The beginning of the duetto between Pizarro and Rocco, for instance, obscures the tonic by a rapid bass ascent from a to f, just as Pizarro seeks first to enlist Rocco's help through bribery and flattery before disclosing his true intentions. Consistent chromatic ascent undergirds the harmonic and melodic progressions of Pizarro's murderous boasts at the start of the act II quartet. Those who live in fear of him invoke him through chromaticism as well. Rocco's mention of 'the governor' in the act I trio effects an abrupt turn from a C major cadence at bars 71–3 to a hushed, unison chromatic ascent (c–c♯–d–d♯–e). A similar gesture is heard in the prisoners' chorus of the act I finale, where emphatic cries for freedom are suddenly suppressed through quiet, unison ascent from f to f♯ as the inmates are reminded of the constant surveillance in Pizarro's prison (bars 99–102). That even the guards fear Pizarro is suggested in the coda of his aria

Example 6.1 Quartet, no. 3, bars 32–8.

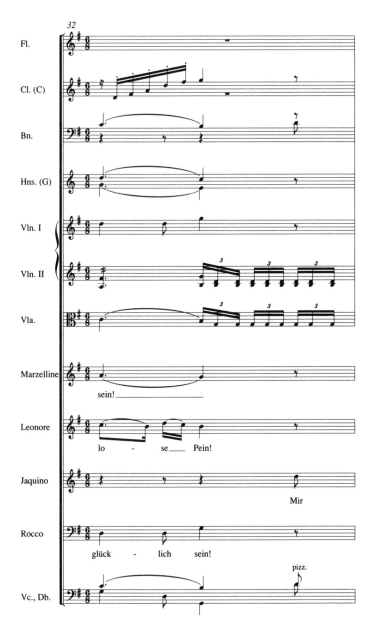

(bars 89–100, a section newly composed for the 1814 version), where chromatic motion in the bass from a to d supports their hushed expressions of concern for the governor's apparent rage. Though such gestures cannot be considered 'leitmotives' in the Wagnerian sense, they nevertheless contribute to a consistent musical portrait of the sadistic governor.[30]

Manipulations of form also characterize Pizarro as the villain. Not surprisingly, the ensembles in which he participates, nos. 8 and 14, are highly irregular with respect to tonal and melodic organization (see below). In contrast, his aria manifests a conventional two-part form analogous to a sonata form without development (table 6.2). It first presents the text with an exposition-like section of three main paragraphs that lead from D minor (bars 1–21, Pizarro's decision to seize the moment for revenge) via C major (bars 21–31, his reflections on nearly being exposed by Florestan) to the relative major, F major (bars 31–41, his delight in turning the tables on his old nemesis). In the manner of a recapitulation, the second presentation of the text restores D minor in the first paragraph (bars 45–57) and transposes to D major the third paragraph (bars 71–89), which is extended by additional text that graphically depicts Pizarro's deadly revenge and capped by an impressive coda that brings in the chorus. Such an approach to form was quite old-fashioned by Beethoven's time, harkening back to serious arias of the 1770s and 1780s;[31] in this instance the form, along with the trumpets and timpani in the orchestra, traditional perquisites of operatic rulers, identifies Don Pizarro as a member of the *ancien régime*. Further, the apparent paradox of the piece – the combination of large-scale formal rigidity with numerous local disruptions in rhythm and harmony – reflects the character of Pizarro himself, whose public, 'exterior', persona as a mainstay of social order conceals a malignant renegade.

In principle, the characterizations of the two heroes lead us into yet a third music-dramatic plane. Aristocrats endowed with spiritual nobility as well, Florestan and Leonore are the heirs to eighteenth-century figures like Tamino and Constanze. As befits their social status, their natural mode of expression is sustained diatonic lyricism that, in Leonore's case, occasionally blossoms into the coloratura traditionally reserved for operatic nobility. Indicative of their status as well is the fact that their soliloquies are cast in the three-part form of the Italian *rondò* aria (accompanied

Table 6.2. Formal Outline of Pizarro's Aria No.7

Bar number	1	7	21	31	41	45	57	71	89	101	119
Vocal forces		Solo							+Chorus		
Section	Ritornello	Exposition			Ritornello	Recapitulation			Coda, part 1	Coda, part 2	Ritornello
Text lines		1–5, 4–5	6–8	9–10		1–5	6–8	9–14	15–17, 1–2	9–10, 1–3, 14	
Material	x	A	B	C	(on C)	A' + x'	B'	C		C" + B"	
Accompaniment	♫	♪³	♪³	♫		♫	♪³	♫ ♫			
Key	d(V)	d–C	C–V/f	F	F–V/d	d–E♭	E♭–V/d D	D	♭VI–	D	D

recitative–slow section–fast section), in which each of the sections is motivated by a change in dramatic perspective.[32] The accompanied recitative at the start of Leonore's aria, for instance, leads her from consideration of the exiting Pizarro ('Abscheulicher, wo eilst du hin?') to contemplation of the goal that she pursues; the orchestra correspondingly changes from *agitato*, syncopated patterns in minor keys to calmer, more sustained music that pauses on the symbolically important key of C major ('So leuchtet mir ein Farbenbogen').[33] The Adagio movement is a prayer to a personified Hope to sustain her during her quest. Her resolve renewed, Leonore expresses her unwavering commitment to follow her 'inner impulses' in the concluding Allegro con brio; a character of heroic stature emerges through the brisk tempo, march-like rhythms, triadic contours in the vocal and instrumental parts, and closing coloratura.[34]

Yet, both Leonore and Florestan are caught in situations that impede their 'inner impulses'. Leonore's disguise as 'Fidelio' results in a musical disguise as well. As noted earlier, she adopts the manner of Rocco's family in the canonic act I quartet, unhappily caught in a deception of her own making; to conceal her femininity and aristocracy she breaks into coloratura only in the solitude of her aria or in asides that remain unheard by the other characters (e.g., act I trio, bars 112–17; the 'Wer du auch seist' episode in the grave-digging duet); in ensembles, 'Fidelio' is generally given a slightly lower tessitura than Marzelline, excepting again the asides, as at bars 164–82 of the act I trio; what is more, the instrumentation of the Marzelline–Leonore duet eliminated from the 1814 version supports the supposed gender difference between the two characters by associating obbligato solo violin with Marzelline and solo violoncello with 'Fidelio'.

Florestan's lyric-diatonic impulses are tempered, understandably enough, by his harsh surroundings. The orchestral *Introduzione* that precedes his aria paints an extraordinary portrait of horror by piling up the topoi from Pizarro's corrupt world: tonal instability through stepwise motion of the bass, diminished harmonies (underscored by the aberrant tuning of the timpani to a and e♭), syncopation, and additional brass instruments. Florestan's recitative gradually moves away from these symbols of fear towards a more sustained style, as his trust in the justice of God's will allows him to distance himself from the terror of his immediate surroundings. The slow A flat major movement of the aria follows his train of thought with great sensitivity as he contemplates the meaning of his suffering. The diatonic, major-mode music of his first phrase, clouded only at bar 58 by chromaticism in the orchestra, underscores his nostalgia for lost youth and happiness. Florestan's ironic reflection in the second phrase that his current imprisonment is the 'reward' for his political courage elicits musical features that bring us back into the present and suggest his anger: the hint of F minor at bar 62, the chromaticism and syncopation of bar 63, and the flare-up of agitated string figures in bar 64. To express his suffering, the third phrase (bars 66–9) moves in the chromatic orbit of C flat major/A flat minor and invokes 'sigh' figures of the eighteenth century. The consolation of his clear conscience, however, allows Florestan to rise above his suffering once again and to return to a diatonic A flat major in the fourth and fifth phrases of the movement.

Progressive upward extension of the singer's high notes, an important technique in Mozart's arias, serves to link the Adagio to the Poco allegro and shed light on Florestan's psyche.[35] The Adagio unfolds an ascent from his initial c^1 to the $g\flat^1$ at bar 64, which is reiterated at bars 66 and 78–9 as the upper boundary of this section of the aria. The transcendant Poco allegro, newly composed in 1814, continues this ascent through g^1 (bar 96) to a stratospheric $b\flat^1$ (first touched upon at bar 101), as the delirious Florestan imagines himself led into heavenly realms by a liberating angel in the image of Leonore. The obbligato oboe in this section is clearly a musical symbol for Florestan's vision.[36] It begins as a more or less undifferentiated line, suggesting an initially indistinct vision, but assumes greater motivic definition at bars 95–6 as Florestan recognizes the angel's features. At this point the oboe begins to 'lead' Florestan in quasi-imitative exchanges that persist until bar 114, when he and the oboe unite at the octave (ex. 6.2). This union seemingly gives him the strength to ascend twice to emphasized $b\flat^1$s in an imagined escape into heaven, before physical exhaustion finally overtakes him.

In contrast to the soloists, the choruses in *Fidelio* are not strongly characterized as to social plane, nor do they provide local colour. Rather, Beethoven treats the chorus – the brief chorus of guards in Pizarro's aria excepted – as the voice of humanity confronted by tyranny and subjugation, with the prisoners' chorus at the start of the act I finale a hymn for all who yearn for freedom and the choruses in the act II finale a celebration of the triumph of love and justice. While the celebratory chorus at the

Example 6.2 Florestan's aria, no. 11, bars 111–15.

start of the act II finale, an 1814 replacement for the revenge chorus of 1805, is somewhat perfunctory in its evocation of the heroic style, Beethoven's evident sympathy with the prisoners produced one of the most memorable choruses in all of opera. Its broad ternary form encompasses three basic feelings, each articulated by a different style. The lyrical opening section (bars 1–73) is given over to their joy and sense of rebirth, expressed tentatively at first and then more passionately; the ascending imitative entries at the start suggest their gradual emergence from the dungeon into the open air, which is itself evoked by the rising semiquaver patterns in the wind instruments. Only the recollection of the dungeon ('Der Kerker eine Gruft') disturbs the otherwise diatonic language of this section with unison chromatic motion and a menacing trill. At the start of the middle section the music invokes ecclesiastical style through 'walking bass', suspensions, and woodwind sonorities to express the prisoners' hopes for Divine justice and freedom (bars 74–99). Caught up in their own yearning they incautiously inquire at full voice about the return of freedom. The appearance of a guard on the ramparts, marked by sudden chromatic ascent, brings them back to the fearful reality of prison life, and the middle section continues at a hushed dynamic level with diminished-seventh harmonies and minor-mode inflections (bars 99–136); the descent of the bass at bars 125–8 can be heard as an inversion of the walking bass at the start of the section and thus an emblem of their suppressed hopes. The concluding section sums up the two poles of the prisoners' existence, their hopes for freedom and their awareness of present realities, with a compressed reprise of the opening music (bars 137–59) and a minor-tinged coda (bars 159–78) based on the second half of the middle section.

3 Musical process and dramatic action

Particularly indicative of Beethoven's ambitions and achievement in *Fidelio* are the ensembles that advance the dramatic action. Beethoven was doubtless attracted to pieces of this type in part because of their centrality to the dramaturgy of Mozart's master operas; we have already noted his extracts of examples from *Don Giovanni* and *Die Zauberflöte*. He doubtless appreciated the ways that his predecessor employs traditional musical symbols (choices of tempo, metre, key, instrumentation, and *figurae*) and basic musical processes (e.g., similarity versus contrast, motion versus stasis, tension versus resolution) to solve multiple dramatic tasks: to establish basic *Affekt* for the entire piece; to define and differentiate the characterization, power relationships, and emotions of the participants in the ensemble; and to enact physical and psychological change.[37] Mozart's virtuosic ability to weld the most diverse actions and jumbled emotions into coherent musical wholes must also have strongly appealed to a composer obsessed with musical integration as Beethoven unquestionably was. It must be acknowledged, however, that Beethoven's background in instrumental music and the emphatically developmental nature of his own approach lent themselves well to this kind of piece, with its complex interactions between characters and between voices and the orchestra.

As is often the case in Mozart's ensembles, a number of the action ensembles in *Fidelio* (nos. 1, 5, 8 and 13) exhibit affinities with so-called 'sonata form' of Classical instrumental style, coordinating dramatic content, poetic structure, and tonal, textural and melodic organization into three sections roughly analogous to exposition, development, and recapitulation, respectively. For example, the act II trio no. 13, similar in certain respects to the trio 'Ah, taci, ingiusto core' in *Don Giovanni*, has many points of contact with the sonata paradigm. Typical of such action ensembles, it begins with a solo, in this case a lyrical, A major melody for Florestan's expression of gratitude for the wine given to him in the prior dialogue. Rocco's and Leonore's reactions to Florestan's plight prompt new melodic elements and the initiation of modulation at bar 21. The establishment of E major as a secondary tonal area at measure 35 coincides with a new dramatic element, Florestan's observation of Rocco's and Leonore's expressions of sympathy. As is usually the case, this new key here is confirmed by a cadential period of simultaneous, reflective singing for all three characters. The middle section resumes the dramatic give-and-take, presenting the principal new action of the ensemble: Leonore persuades Rocco to allow her to give a piece of bread to the starving prisoner. Initially a new melody is introduced for this turn in the plot (bar 54), but music from the first section is recalled at bar 69 and led, development-like, through a number of keys as Leonore paraphrases Rocco's earlier compassionate words to strengthen her case ('Ach! Ihr labtet gern den armen Mann'); the rising tessitura, agitated semi-quavers in the strings, and accelerating rate of harmonic change between bars 79 and 82 provide indices for her increasingly urgent request (ex. 6.3). The climax of this middle section is marked by the arrival at the key of C major – doubtless chosen for its

Example 6.3 Trio, no. 13, bars 69–82.

symbolism – for Rocco's capitulation and Leonore's gift of bread to the prisoner. A strong gesture of musical reprise at bar 99 restores the tonic and the opening melody to point out a dramatic parallelism with the start of the piece: just as he had earlier thanked Rocco for the wine, he now thanks Leonore for the bread.

Naturally, analogies between vocal forms and instrumental sonata form should not be pushed too far.[38] The success of dramatic music, after all, depends less on the 'logical' internal development of music out of its own content than on its ability to follow and enhance the predetermined moods of the drama, and compositional techniques that serve primarily structural roles in instrumental music, such as 'thematische Arbeit' and recapitulatory gestures, are used in opera not as ends in themselves but as signposts for elements in the drama, though coherence of musical thought doubtless remains an important goal for composers like Mozart and Beethoven.[39] Nevertheless, a background awareness of sonata-like behaviour, or at least of the norms of large-scale Classical tonal syntax, can add interesting dimensions to one's appreciation of features that seem to underscore dramatic points precisely by evading or subverting sonata-form norms. Thus new events and variants in the reprise section of an ensemble point up changes in character, situation, and emotion. In the preceding example, the 'recapitulation' quickly begins to diverge from the 'exposition', and no transposition of the E major materials into the tonic ever occurs. Instead, a contrapuntal A minor development of motives from the first and second sections (bars 113–21; cf. bars 21 and 73–4) leads to a new coda-melody, presented in A major for Florestan's last expression of gratitude ('O daß ich euch nicht lohnen kann') and in A minor for Leonore's expression of unbearable anguish ('O mehr als ich ertragen kann'). The emphasis on the minor mode in the reprise section focusses our attention on the fear and sorrow felt by Rocco and Leonore as they contemplate the impending fate of the condemned prisoner. In the Marzelline–Jaquino duet the return of the 'first theme' at bar 118 underscores a parallelism with the start of the duet, as Jaquino resumes his awkward attempt to propose, but its setting in the very remote key of B flat major (flatted supertonic) suggests that he is far off course; only after Marzelline's emphatic refusal (bars 124–31) does the tonic return at bar 141 with a reprise of the 'second theme' as Jacquino finally acknowledges that Marzelline is not likely to reciprocate his interest ('So wirst du dich nimmer bekehren?').

From the perspective of traditional formal strategies, the Pizarro–Rocco duet presents an especially aberrant structure, emblematic of Pizarro's disruptive influence. At the start of the duet, key definition is delayed by a feint towards F major as Pizarro withholds his true intentions in soliciting Rocco's aid; the tonic, A major, is definitively established only with the honest Rocco's inquisitive reply (bar 21). As the 'exposition' unfolds, Pizarro leads Rocco through a number of shocking revelations, underscored by harmonic disjunctions (e.g., bar 42, bar 48), and the first section culminates with a dissonant passage of *a due* singing over a pedal G sharp (bars 64–81) that establishes the mediant, C sharp minor, as the secondary tonal area, a 'wrong' goal of modulation by any standard in the Classical style but an appropriate one in Pizarro's corrupt world.[40] The unorthodox treatment of the reprise section offers further commentary on the situation. After the modulating middle section, in which Rocco's refusal to murder the unnamed prisoner (bars 81–92) compels Pizarro to formulate an alternative plan (bars 92–127), A major returns in a second *a due* passage (bars 127–35), a tonal reprise that on first hearing could reasonably serve as the concluding section of the piece. The piece continues, however, with what seems like a second recapitulation, with a varied thematic and textual reprise of the opening gesture (bar 135), an amplified repetition of Pizarro's instructions (bars 137–47),[41] and an extended repetition of the second *a due* passage (bars 147–63). The unusual double recapitulation, perhaps inspired by the Donna Anna–Don Ottavio duet in *Don Giovanni*,[42] sheds light on Pizarro's psyche: unsettled by news of the impending arrival of the Minister and desperate to conceal his crime, he repeats himself in order to be sure that Rocco understands his assignment and the urgency of the situation.

Throughout the ensembles, Beethoven employs compositional techniques honed in instrumental music to expose the interior life of the drama. The opening duet characterizes Jacquino's single-minded pursuit of Marzelline by saturating the orchestral texture with derivatives of the semiquaver motive stated at the outset (e–c♯–e–f♯; see ex. 6.4). In the same piece, emphatic tonal disjunction, another essential element of Beethoven's musical vocabulary, supplies an analogy at bar 65 to the interruption caused by the knocking at the door. The duet also makes use of a common technique in middle-period Beethoven, the presentation of a harmonic puzzle or instability at the outset of a piece, to suggest the gulf

Example 6.4 Duetto, no. 1. Manipulations of basic motive

between Marzelline and her would-be suitor.[43] The brief introductory ritornello begins with the unharmonized pitches of the basic motive, and the first harmonies push towards B minor instead of the nominal tonic, A major. The opening exchange between Jacquino and Marzelline 'explains' this unstable beginning: Jacquino seeks to initiate a conversation with a phrase in A major, but the irritated Marzelline avoids him with a shift towards B minor. Doggedly, Jacquino follows her into B minor in his second phrase, and seeing that conversation is inevitable, Marzelline returns to the tonic as she agrees to hear him out.

Two action ensembles with little resemblance to sonata form, nos. 12 and 14, also exemplify the close coordination of musical and dramatic processes. The grave-digging duet, whose muted dynamics and dark scoring create an appropriately sepulchral atmosphere, takes as its starting point a rondo form implied by the poetic and dramatic structure, a characteristically French approach retained from the original Bouilly libretto. A refrain, consisting of Rocco's lines urging Leonore to hurry up and dig and her reply ('Nur hurtig fort, nur frisch gegraben . . .'/ 'Ihr sollt ja nicht zu klagen haben . . .'), is stated at the outset and reiterated at two later points in the piece to mark the resumption of excavation after interruptions that threaten to delay the completion of the task: (1) the episode with the heavy stone, and (2) Leonore's apostrophe to the as yet unknown prisoner. Beethoven turns the poetic repetitions to good use, varying the musical setting of the refrain to suggest the changing dynamic of the situation. At its initial appearance, the refrain comprises four phrases that differentiate Rocco's characteristic repeated-tone, quaver declamation in the first and third phrases (bars 9–14, 18–22) from Leonore's more arpeggiated, *cantabile* lines in the second and fourth phrases (bars 14–18, 22–6; ex. 6.5a); that Leonore's answering phrases basically follow the same harmonic progressions as Rocco's furnishes an underlying basis for musical coherence and symbolically lends credence to her assurances of dependability (ex. 6.5b). The second appearance of the refrain (bars 51–64) is truncated and elided with the second episode, as Leonore starts her address to the prisoner *before* Rocco has finished the third phrase (bar 62), figuratively tuning him out of consciousness as she focusses her attention on the prisoner (ex. 6.5c); unheard by Rocco, her selfless decision to save the prisoner regardless of his identity triggers appropriately heroic responses in the music, extended coloratura and modulation toward C major. Rocco's remonstrance (bar 78, 'Was zauderst du in deiner Pflicht') recalls Leonore to the task at hand and prompts

Example 6.5 Duetto, no. 12.

Example 6.5a The initial presentation of the refrain, bars 9–18.

the third statement of the poetic refrain (bars 86–98), which is significantly recomposed to reflect the altered situation at the end of the duet: in place of the original phrase structure in which the two characters alternate, Rocco's and Leonore's lines now overlap, a sign for increased urgency as Pizarro's arrival may be imminent; and Leonore assumes Rocco's quaver, repeated-tone style, perhaps to conceal from him her own, opposed agenda (ex. 6.5d).

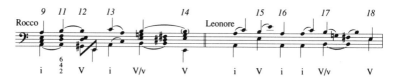

Example 6.5b Harmonic reduction, bars 9–18.

Example 6.5c The second presentation of the refrain, bars 60–4.

Leonore betrachtet den Gefangenen, während Rocco, von ihr abgewendet, mit gekrümmtem Rücken arbeitet.

Example 6.5d The third presentation of the refrain, bars 86–90.

The brief coda to the piece (bars 98–105) suggests, however, that Leonore has become the dominant personality, for the two characters sing their respective texts in unison to the rhythm previously associated with Leonore.

In no piece does musical process enact dramatic action and emotional change more emphatically than in the great act II quartet, the culminating point in the plot line and the ensemble that most clearly exemplifies Beethoven's merger of Mozartian technique with revolutionary *élan terrible* and his own sensibilities. Forged from spoken dialogue in the French original, the form of the piece is *sui generis*,[44] comprising a fast first section for Pizarro's assault on Florestan and Leonore's defence (bars 1–126), a slow second section for the two offstage trumpet calls and the initial, stunned reaction of the participants (bars 127–46), and a boisterous third section as the characters contemplate the revenge that will be visited on Pizarro and the triumphant union of love and courage (bars 147–213).

While the second and third sections are essentially contemplative, the first is furiously active, structured as a sequence of increasingly powerful surprises that in one way or another retard Pizarro's attack on Florestan: (1) before killing him, Pizarro reveals his identity to Florestan, who up to now has been ignorant of his captor ('Doch, er soll erst wissen'); (2) to stop Pizarro's lunge, Leonore interposes her body between Pizarro and Florestan ('Zurück'); (3) hoping that her gender will prevent an assault, Leonore reveals *her* identity as Florestan's wife ('Töt' erst sein Weib'); (4) since Pizarro is resolute in his murderous intention, Leonore pulls a pistol from her bosom to fend him off ('Noch einen Laut, und du bist tot'); and (5) the trumpet announces the arrival of the Minister, stopping everyone in his tracks. Each of these 'surprises' is matched to a harmonic twist that disrupts a preceding progression. At (1), the foregoing diatonic progression in D major is interrupted by a change of dynamic and the first chromatic event in the piece, a first-inversion B major chord at bar 9. At (2) a progression in A major (bars 53–9) is interrupted at bar 60 by the chromatic step in the bass to e$\sharp$, harmonized as V$^6_5$ of F sharp minor. Surprise (3) brings about a dramatic plunge from G major to a first-inversion E flat major chord (subsequently continued as a first-inversion seventh chord), a temporary cessation of orchestral activity, and a stunning leap up to b$\flat^2$ in Leonore's part (bars 79–80).[45] Points (4) and (5) are compressed into a single disruptive harmonic event, a deceptive cadence from V/D to B flat at measures 126–7 that effects an abrupt cessation of motion.[46]

The centrifugal, even chaotic tendencies of the first section – representative again of Pizarro's disruptive influence – are countered by integrative devices, summarized in a reduction in example 6.6a, that hold the piece together and at the same time highlight its dramatic-emotional core. For instance, two motives provide much of the orchestral substance of the first section (ex. 6.6b). The opening paragraph of the quartet, Pizarro's tirade, introduces a motive (x) that throughout the quartet is clearly associated with him and his murderous intentions. It returns at bar 53 as Pizarro reminds Florestan ('once again') of his past deeds before lunging at him with the dagger, and again at bar 69, as he shoves 'Fidelio' out of the way. A tonal reprise at bar 106 effects a motivic reprise as well as Pizarro now steels himself to kill both Florestan and

Example 6.6 Quartet, no. 14.

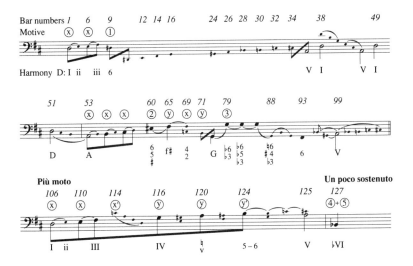

Example 6.6a Harmonic reduction, bars 1–127.

Example 6.6b Basic motives.

Leonore. The final appearance of the motive at the conclusion of the piece (bar 197) underlines a stage action, Pizarro's hasty exit and imperious gesture that Rocco follow him. Less prominent is a second figure (y) that furnishes the orchestral fabric for bars 65–8, 71–8 and 116–24; context in each case suggests that it is associated with Leonore's defiance of Pizarro, a point subtly reinforced by the insistence on *contrary* motion in the voice leading.

Equally important for the coherence and *Charakteristik* of the piece is a consistency of tonal-harmonic language that accrues through stepwise ascent of the bass. At the outset, motive (x) establishes this pattern by sequencing from I to ii to iii (bars 1–8); from Pizarro's digressive 'Doch' at bar 9 the bass slithers up a primarily chromatic scale from d♯ to a strong arrival on d at bar 49 that punctuates his tirade. In the subsequent course of the first section, ascent of the bass controls much of the harmonic progression. Bars 53 to 90 trace an octave rise from a to a that subsumes the chromatic progressions for surprises (2) and (3) discussed earlier and a sequential presentation of motive (y) in F sharp minor and G major. The reprise section (bars 106–26) spirals upward from d to b before settling on the dominant. As dramatic symbols, these long-range ascents, characteristic of many of Beethoven's middle-period development sections, create musical instability that is entirely apposite to the turbulence of the situation; that the bass consistently rises may also be heard as a reflex of the ever-mounting tension in the first section of the piece, an impression reinforced by the acceleration of tempo at bar 106. With rescue signalled by the trumpet calls, however, the denouement of the quartet resolves the instability of the rising bass, embedding it in a stable, key-defining progression (bars 158–69): instead of continuing on to iii, the sequential ascent from I to ii is now answered by the cadential continuation V^6-I-ii^6-V-I to effect closure. Like other examples we have discussed, the quartet thus adapts a technique that is vital to Beethoven's instrumental style – in this case the 'strategic reinterpretation' or 'thematic completion' of an initially unstable or open-ended gesture – to make a dramatic point.[47]

In writings about *Fidelio* one frequently encounters the opinion that Beethoven was not a 'natural' opera composer and that his musical imagination, boldly experimental in instrumental music, was essentially cramped by the demands and limitations of dramatic vocal music.[48] While it is true that Beethoven was temperamentally ill equipped to handle the many compromises and vexations that attend theatrical life and frustrated by his experiences with *Fidelio* to such an extent that he never again seriously ventured into opera, one must nevertheless admire the simple fact that he succeeded in his first and only opera – admittedly, after some tinkering – to create a work that still holds the stage, not just as a curiosity by a celebrated composer but as a powerful theatrical experience still capable of moving its audiences to share in the fates of its characters; in contrast, Gluck, Mozart, Rossini, Wagner, and Verdi required more or less extended apprenticeships in opera before hitting their stride. In point of fact, it was precisely Beethoven's vast experience with instrumental composition that allowed him to succeed in opera, despite his relative inexperience with the theatre. Through it he acquired an unrivalled understanding of the expressive potential of intrinsically musical elements and the technical means to forge such elements into satisfying wholes, the unity and cogency of which serve to focus and deepen their emotional impact. As a consequence of his background he alone among his German contemporaries fully comprehended and was able to build on Mozart's great compositional legacy in opera, the employment of sophisticated musical processes and intricate textures to elucidate character, emotion, and various kinds of dramatic action. Above all, his mastery of 'abstract' instrumental music gave him the means with which to endow the opera's Utopian message with a concrete, sonic presence that even today can still inspire audiences to believe in the possibility of a world based on love, hope, and freedom.

7 Augenblicke *in* Fidelio

JOSEPH KERMAN

'In a moment, in the twinkling of an eye . . .': *Augenblick* – a twinkling, a trice, an instant, a moment – is a word that must have especially appealed to Joseph Sonnleithner, the theatre functionary and amateur poet who provided Beethoven with the original libretto for *Fidelio*. The word appears with almost embarrassing frequency in Sonnleithner's text, often at the opera's most exposed moments. Momentous may, indeed, not be too grand a term for some of these *Augenblicke*, as far as their role in the opera is concerned. The instant becomes a turning-point, an epiphany, or an aporia.

Thus after the sensational climax of the opera's action, the confrontation in the dungeon in the act II quartet 'Er sterbe!', the stage directions indicate an *Augenblick* that is evidently crucial to the drama. The libretto of the original, 1805 version of the opera reads as follows:

(*Pizarro rushes out, Rocco following him.*)

Leonore (*running after Rocco, clutching at his clothes*) Can you desert me?

(*She falls at Rocco's feet; he seizes the moment to twist the pistol out of her hand; she emits a piercing cry.*)

(*Pizarro stürzt ab, Rocco folgt ihm nach.*)

Leonore (*Rocco nahlaufend, und sich an sein Gewand klammernd*) Du kannst mich verlassen?

(*Sie fällt zu Roccos Füßen, der den Augenblick benutzt, ihr die Pistole aus der Hand zu winden; sie stößt einen durchdringenden Schrei aus.*)

In the revised opera of 1814, the action differs significantly and Leonore does not speak:

(*Pizarro rushes out, giving Rocco a sign to follow him; Rocco seizes the moment, after Pizarro has already left, to take the hands of both spouses, press them to his breast, gesture towards heaven and hurry out. Soldiers* [who in 1814 have entered after the trumpet call] *light the way for Pizarro.*)

(*Pizarro stürtz fort, indem er Rocco einen Wink gibt, ihm zu folgen; dieser benutzt den Augenblick, da Pizarro schon geht, faßt die Hände beider Gatten, drückt sie an seine Brust, deutet gen Himmel und eilt nach. Die Soldaten leuchten Pizarro voraus.*)[1]

The *Augenblick benutzt* – the moment seized – has undergone a dramatic reversal. In 1805 Rocco's action is hostile and shocking; in 1814 his actions are supportive and sentimental.

The place marks one of the most important, in fact probably the most important, of the 1814 revisions of the libretto, a point emphasized by Winton Dean in his classic essay (see pages 22–50). In 1805, when Rocco has left wife and husband alone in the dungeon, their doom seems sealed, as they acknowledge when, after singing the duet 'O namenlose Freude', they respond to ominous cries of 'Rache' (revenge) in a C minor section of the original finale: 'O Gott! Nun ist um uns geschehn!', 'O god, now all is over for us!' They are still in doubt about their fate at the entrance of the Minister.

In 1814 they accept Rocco's mimed assurances with almost suspicious alacrity. The duet 'O namenlose Freude' that follows is a celebration of life together, not a prelude to impending doom, there is no C minor in the finale, and no tension as they face the Minister. The entire last scene in the prison courtyard is ceremonial rather than dramatic. *Fidelio* is a very different drama from *Leonore*.

The *Augenblick* in the 1805 stage direction was a realistic moment; Leonore falls and Rocco snatches the pistol. The 1814 business, still described as an *Augenblick*, consists of a dumb-show in three stages. This generous moment of action is obviously a makeshift, invented when the junta in charge of the revision ran out of ideas. One cannot imagine it in an original libretto.

Still, the stretched moment is a quintessential feature of operatic dramaturgy, as we know. Moments of shock, realization, or decision are stretched into minutes of song. Librettists routinely provide words for these prolongations and composers provide the music. In the typical solo aria we accept this as a meditation, as the character mulls over the experience of a moment at some length. In ensembles, the concept of group meditation is more problematic, and sometimes frankly implausible. It is no accident that when we think of the 'ensemble of perplexity' we think first of Rossini and farce.

Fidelio has an egregious example of such group meditation, the scene of liberation in the act II finale, the climax of the operatic drama. 'O Gott! welch' ein Augenblick!' Leonore exclaims, as she unlocks the fetters on Florestan's limbs. Don Fernando has invited her to do this in a highly formal, resonant passage leading to a grand cadence in A major; this cadence is undercut by a *pizzicato* F in the strings, expanding into off-beat wood-wind chords marked *sfp* – are these the chains falling away? – from which the famous slow melody emerges in the oboe. This moment lasts for two minutes – *five* minutes in the 1805 opera, which is more leisurely than the revision throughout, but never more leisurely than this.

The oboe melody, salvaged from an unpublished and unperformed cantata that Beethoven had written on the death of Emperor Joseph II in 1791, was there associated with the words 'Now mankind reaches to the light'. This sentiment is therefore enshrined in the opera, fixed by the simple, grave serenity of what Germans have called Beethoven's *Humanitätsmelodie*. It is shared by everyone on stage: after Leonore, the words 'O Gott! O welch' ein Augenblick' are sung by Florestan, Fernando, Marzelline, Rocco, and the chorus of townspeople and prisoners (including all the thieves, murderers, and laudanum pushers who are probably well represented among them, as Dean reminds us). Perhaps this is no more implausible than the traditional communal rejoicing that ends every comedy, and that is here stimulated by a great choral shout in C major, 'Wer ein holdes Weib errungen, stimm' in unsern jubeln ein': join in our jubilation.

One thinks of Leonore as a woman of action, strong feelings, and ideals. If there is a contemplative side to her character she has revealed nothing of it up to this point in the opera. Nonetheless the liberation scene is tinged with reflection, even irony. For Leonore here is quoting the words of Pizarro, 'Ha! welch' ein Augenblick', in his opening aria, an aria so fierce that it cows the soldiers who overhear it. Pizarro is anticipating the moment when he will murder Florestan – and sure enough, when the moment actually arrives, or so he thinks, and he lunges for Florestan in the dungeon, he repeats himself:

Just one more moment	Nur noch ein Augenblick
And this dagger —	und dieser Dolch —
(*he is about to stab Florestan*)	(*Er will Florestan durchboren*)

With Leonore's speech the villain's moment of darkness has been transmuted into humanity's moment of light.

Pizarro's key words are etched by the aria's most distinctive musical motif, developed, and transferred to the orchestra (see ex. 7.1). Leonore has not been on stage eavesdropping during 'Ha!

Example 7.1

welch' ein Augenblick', only during the duet between Pizarro and Rocco which follows (which prompts her recitative and aria 'Abscheulicher!' – 'Komm, Hoffnung'). If she had been, she might have remembered more than just the general outline of the motif (ex. 7.2). In any case, neither a scruple for not having been there nor any operatic performance tradition should inhibit Leonore from adding Pizarro's appoggiatura on the word *Augenblick*.

Reflective Leonore may be, but she is not responsible for a further, more subtle reference to Pizarro's aria in the liberation scene (neither is Sonnleithner). The lacerating D minor tonality of that aria is neutralized, as it were, or resolved into F major, an

Example 7.2

hour and a half after the piece is actually sung. This is part of a global resolution process put into play by Beethoven. The act II finale starts in C major (C minor in 1805/1806) and proceeds through Don Fernando's A major and Leonore's F major to C major at the end, making a grand large-scale plagal cadence; and on an even grander scale, it seems the three major keys were calculated to resolve all the minor keys that accommodated musical numbers earlier in the opera. In addition to D minor, in Pizarro's aria, these keys are C minor (Marzelline's aria), F minor (Florestan's recitative), and A minor (the grave-digging duet).[2]

All this was more cogent in the early version of the opera, where the move from C minor to C major was a central issue and where Florestan's recitative was followed by an aria ending (very exceptionally) in the same 'unresolved' minor key, F minor. In 1814 the new aria resolves to F major on the spot.

Though such long-range resolutions cannot mean much in the theatre, it seems that Beethoven took them seriously, for there are a number of thematic and other relationships linking the passages in question, in addition to the 'resolving' key relationships. The sections in A minor and A major share a type of accompaniment (ex. 7.3). In the scene of liberation, Florestan's aria is evoked most clearly by the obbligato oboe – a feature added in 1814 – and his recitative seems to be echoed by the off-beat wood-wind chords (ex. 7.4).[3]

Example 7.3

Example 7.4

Rocco

. . . No one could be more willing or smarter; indeed, I like you better every day, and your reward won't be long in coming, you can be sure. (*During the last words he casts looks back and forth between Leonore and Marzelline.*)

Leonore

Oh do not think that I do my duty only because of a reward –

Rocco

No more! Do you think I cannot see into your heart?

No. 3 Quartet (Canon)

Marzelline

I'm feeling so strange,
My heart seems all pent up;
He loves me, that is clear;
How happy I shall be!

Leonore

How great is the danger!
How faint the ray of hope!
She loves me, that is clear;
O unspeakable grief!

Rocco

She loves him, that is clear;
Yes, my girl, he shall be yours!
A fine young couple;
They will be happy.

Jacquino

My hair stands on end!
Her father consents.
I'm feeling so strange,
There's nothing I can do!

Rocco

Listen, Fidelio, even if I don't know who you are, or how and when you came into the world, or if you ever had a father, still I know what I am doing; yes, I am going to make you my son-in-law.

. . . Man kann nicht eifriger, nicht verständlicher sein; ich habe dich auch mit jedem Tage lieber, und sei versichert, dein Lohn soll dir nicht ausbleiben. (*Er wirft während der letzten Worten wechselnde Blicke auf Leonore und Marzelline.*)

O glaubt nicht, daß ich meine Schuldigkeit nur des Lohnes wegen –

Still! Meinst du, ich könnte dir nicht ins Herz sehen?

Nr. 3 Quartett (Canon)

Mir ist so wunderbar,
es engt das Herz mir ein.
Er liebt mich, es ist klar,
ich werde glücklich sein.

Wie groß ist die Gefahr,
wie schwach der Hoffnung
    Schein.
Sie liebt mich, es ist klar,
O namenlose Pein!

Sie liebt ihn, es ist klar;
ja, Mädchen, er wird dein.
Ein gutes, junges Paar,
sie werden glücklich sein.

Mir sträubt sich schon das
    Haar,
der Vater willigt ein.
Mir wird so wunderbar,
mir fällt kein Mittel ein!

Höre, Fidelio, wenn ich auch nicht weiß, wer und wo du auf die Welt gekommen bist, and wenn du auch gar keinen Vater gehabt hättest, so weiß ich doch, was ich thue – ich – ich mache dich zu meinem Tochtermann.

Roc

On n'a plus d'zele, et surtout plus d'intelligence. . . . [*ellipsis in the original*] Aussi je sens que chaque jour je m'attache à toi davantage; et quoique tu ignores ta naissance, que tu sois sans aveu, sans parens, je suis décidé à fair de toi mon gendre.

Figure 7.1

The other famous stretched moment in *Fidelio* is the canonic quartet in act I, which is indeed one of the opera's most famous numbers. The word *Augenblick* does not occur here, but I would award the piece a special prize for instantaneity: Sonnleithner, translating the libretto of Gaveux's *Léonore*, Beethoven's immediate model, slipped the canonic moment in half-way through a single continuous speech by Roc (figure 7.1).

The background of this canon in Viennese operatic history has been elucidated only recently.[4] It belongs to a strictly Italian, not a German tradition, one due to the much-travelled Spanish *opera-buffa* composer Vicente Martín y Soler, who worked in Vienna from 1785 to 1787, and whose *Una cosa rara* of 1786 is cited and named and mocked in a certain Mozartian masterpiece of the next year. After Martín had scored with two canons in this very popular opera, he included three in his next great hit, *L'Arbore di Diana* (1787). Vienna next heard canons by Antonio Salieri in *La Cifra* (1798) and *Falstaff* (1799), by Mozart in the wonderful A Flat Larghetto in the act II finale of *Così fan tutte* (1790), and by Ferdinando Paër in *Camilla* (1799), all of whom were content with a single canon; and there were others. A comparison of 'Mir ist so wunderbar' with these earlier canons is instructive, for it soon appears that Beethoven resolved to make his different from any and all.

In the text, first of all, the characters all sing different words – very different words – to the single canonic line. This is unlike almost all operatic canons, though another rare example occurs in the work by Paër.[5] Secondly, and the Mozart comparison is telling here, Beethoven's canon is not a tune. The canon's opening words 'Mir ist so wunderbar' are certainly too colloquial and prosaic to support lyricism, and no doubt Beethoven wanted them that way: his music begins with a featureless stammer that depicts Marzelline's confusion.[6] (It is interesting to compare this triadic stammer with another one by Marzelline, in her aria 'O wär' ich schon mit dir vereint'.) Next the line develops leaps of a fourth and a fifth that define it as a bass; the original bass has dropped out for Marzelline's stanza, replaced by precarious *pizzicato* strings doubling the voice *all' ottava*. The canonic line clarifies itself as a melody only in bars 5–6, where the words say 'it is clear' (with an accent on 'klar'); then it grows amorphous again for the off-beat cadence. The one lyric fragment, 'er liebt mich, es ist klar', is elegantly underlined by imitative lines that emerge in the first two stanzas (see ex. 7.5). The 'aside' quality of the canon was very important

Example 7.5

to Beethoven, then, and also explains the *fortissimo* cadence at the very end of the piece. Momentarily self-absorbed, the characters return to normal dialogue with a jolt. It is as though they had moved into the shadows for their respective brown studies, and now step forward briskly into the footlights.

By the time Rocco enters the canon (the third entry), it has accumulated a respectable contrapuntal texture, amplified by *Pastorale*-type wood-wind arpeggios, and the lack of a *Hauptstimme* causes no problem. In the early, exposed phrases for the women something is needed, and Beethoven provides it. The piece opens with a remarkable eight-bar phrase played by the orchestra alone, which repeats itself rather freely, up an octave, as a background for Marzelline when she begins to sing (or stammer). But this background music is not fully melodic either. The polyphonic complex is subtle: the orchestral line is melodic at the beginning, when Marzelline is unmelodic, and becomes accompanimental during her one clear melodic fragment, 'er liebt mich, es ist klar'.

Much depends on the opening phrase, with its hushed aura of meditation and its peculiar but moving accent. Scored for mellow divided violas and cellos above a bass *pizzicato*, it swells from *p* to *mf* and back to *p*. The cancellation of the dominant harmony by F natural is characteristic of Beethoven's depictions of absorption.[7] Without this orchestral phrase we would surely not have heard so much about this number as the first intimation of Leonore's soul, or as a pivot between the comic and serious plots, and the like. For whom does this music speak?

This is a real question when everyone sings the same music to very different words, sinking their several private thoughts into musical or at least linear anonymity. Nor is this the sort of situation that is often remarked in, say, the quintet of *Die Meistersinger*, where the characters all have their own private thoughts, but all these thoughts steer them towards a single mood. This is also what happens in Paër's *Camilla*. Most operatic characters can claim the music that introduces them as a matter of course, but even this customary perquisite is not available to poor Marzelline, who obviously lacks the necessary gravitas. The same is true of Rocco, whose words about looking into the heart have sometimes been suggested as a stimulus for this music. Many have wanted to associate the music with Leonore, of course, but this is hard to do also, not only because she sings second, but because by that time the music has moved all the way up to two flutes twittering an octave above her anxious song.

The canon's opening orchestra phrase is pure interiority; it speaks for none of the singers who follow. It speaks or sings in a suddenly arcane voice, a voice heard from outside the opera, or at least from outside the opera's normal discourse. Carolyn Abbate, in her much-discussed book *Unsung Voices*, has taught us to listen for such moments of fruitful rupture, *Bruchaugenblicke*, where the 'ordinary' constructed world of operatic discourse – arias, ensembles, recitative, even plain speech – is displaced by something other, something uncanny.[8] The voice in the canon is not, of course, the narrative voice that is the focus of Abbate's work, and that Beethoven knew from Pedrillo's Serenade in *Die Entführung aus dem Serail*, the truly uncanny 'In Mohrenland gefangen war'. He also knew another other-voiced operatic intrusion that is not narrative, the terzetto 'Soave sia il vento' from *Così fan tutte*, act I, and I venture to say that 'Mir ist so wunderbar' has more in common with that piece than with the actual canon in act II of *Così*, which is nearly always adduced in connection with his own canon.

In the above analysis I have wanted to establish that while the opening phrase of the canon derives its aura to a large extent from dynamics and orchestration, melodic indeterminacy is also a factor. Perhaps another comparison may shed some light. There is another strange and striking hushed piece in G major by Beethoven, the Praeludium in the Sanctus of the Missa Solemnis. Also marked *sostenuto* and also scored for divided violas and cellos, it is understood as an evocation of a rambling organ improvisation during the Elevation of the Host, prior to the Benedictus (the two low flutes and bassoon that double the low strings providing a very quiet 'chiff' to simulate organ sound) (ex. 7.6). In the *Fidelio* canon Beethoven's 6/8 tempo is not very churchy, it is true. But the melodic uncertainty, halting gait, changing texture (from three to five real parts), diapason sound, and even a swell-pedal effect create an unmistakable aura of sanctity.

The Praeludium of the Mass marks the sacrament of the Eucharist, and the canon in *Fidelio* can be read as a reference to another sacrament, the sacrament of Holy Matrimony. Just before the canon Rocco, in another of his dumb shows, has all but announced the betrothal of Marzelline and Fidelio (fig. 7.1). If we read the canon as ceremonial rather than expressive, the anonymity of the singers makes perfect sense. Whatever they are saying, we respond to them for the moment – for the stretched moment – as communications rather than as individuals.

Example 7.6

Praeludium

We too are communicants, enthralled by a ritual 'unsung voice'. Listeners and commentators from outside the opera are of course right to apprehend a deepening of mood when the canon appears from out of nowhere – our mood and Beethoven's, more than those of the various characters. The canon speaks for nobody, but its function in the drama is important. We reflect on the solemnity and the strangeness (as Beethoven saw it) of marriage. 'Conjugal Love' is the opera's subtitle. Marriage links the domestic and the heroic plots.[9]

Let us end where we began, with an observation about another difference between the 1805 and 1814 versions of the opera – a minor difference this time, no more than a note to Winton Dean's essay.

Next to the new conception of the ending, the major change was a sharp reduction of the domestic plot, the plot about Marzelline's false betrothal. In the original libretto, Marzelline fantasizes about marriage in her aria, no. 1, discourages the wrong groom in the duet, no. 2, repeats the discouragement in a terzetto (which was cut later), no. 3, acknowledges her betrothal in the canon, no. 4, and then confirms her new situation at the end of the act I finale, which in 1805 was the trio 'Gut, Söhnchen, gut,' no. 6. In the stretto of this number, just before the curtain, Rocco joins Leonore's hands with Marzelline's as Leonore's burning desire to accompany Rocco into the dungeon is confused with another kind of *Sehnen* on the part of Marzelline (and Rocco). See Table 7.1.

Table 7.1

1805		1814	
Act I		*Act I*	
1. Aria: Marzelline	Marzelline is in love	1. Duet	Marzelline rejects Jacquino
2. Duet	Rejects Jacquino	2. Aria	Marzelline is in love
3. Trio	Repeats rejection	—	
4. Canon	Betrothal	3. Canon	Betrothal
5. Aria: Rocco		4. Aria	
6. Trio	Confirms betrothal	5. Trio	Confirms betrothal
Act II			
7. March		6. March	
8. Aria: Pizarro		7. Aria	
9. Duet		8. Duet	
10. Duet	Contemplates married life and motherhood	—	

No. 5 Trio

Rocco
Just be on guard and all goes well,
Your desires will be gratified;
Hold hands and plight your troth
With sweet tears of joy.

Leonore
You are so good, you give me courage,
My desire will soon be gratified!
(*Aside*) I am giving my hand to a sweet
    alliance –
It costs me bitter tears.

Marzelline
O take courage, o what ardour,
O what deep longing!
A firm alliance of hearts and hands,
O what sweet tears!

Rocco
But now it is time for me to present my
report to the Governor.
Ah! here he comes himself.

No. 6 March

No. 5 Terzett

Nur auf der Hut, dann geht es gut,
gestillt wird euer Sehnen.
Gebt euch die Hand und schließt das
    Band
in süßen Freudentränen.

Ihr seid so gut, Ihr macht mir Mut,
gestillt wird bald mein Sehnen!
(*Für sich*) Ich gab die Hand zum
    süßen Band,
es kostet bittre Tränen.

O habe Mut! O welche Glut!
O welch ein tiefes Sehnen!
Ein festes Band mit Herz und Hand,
O süße, süße Tränen!

Aber nun ist es Zeit, dass ich dem
Gouverneur die Briefschaften
überbringe. Ah! er kommt selbst
hierher! . . .

No. 6 Marsch

Figure 7.2

Marriage was the focus of the whole first act – and was harped upon in a duet for Marzelline and Leonore near the beginning of act II (no. 10), another number that was cut.

In the final *Fidelio*, the stretto at the end of 'Gut, Söhnchen, gut' (now no. 5) seems somewhat inconsequential. Instead of cementing the modest action of an entire act, it introduces a slight glitch in the plot, for this now moves directly to Pizarro's business (fig. 7.2). In 1814 the domestic plot, with its focus on marriage and betrothal, has been confused a little as well as abbreviated, and the famous canon has become a little more enigmatic.

8   *An interpretive history*

From the start *Fidelio* has been a political opera, never more so than in the circumstances of its introduction to the world. Two months before the scheduled premiere in 1805 the police censors forbade the opera's performance. They apparently objected to the portrayal of Pizarro as a tyrannical representative of authority. The Viennese censorship was thus the first to consider Beethoven's opera politically subversive. Joseph Sonnleithner successfully allayed those fears by asserting, inaccurately, that the opera's action was set in the sixteenth century (and thus could have no possible bearing on contemporary events) and that the subject was chosen because Bouilly's original had so pleased the Empress – yet further testimony to its ideological inoffensiveness. As for Pizarro, he was inspired by entirely private motives of revenge. Sonnleithner anticipated the dominant nineteenth-century understanding of the opera when he suggested, finally, that *Fidelio* was not about politics at all but about 'wifely virtue'.[1]

The first performance of Beethoven's opera of oppression and liberation took place, significantly, a week after Napoleon occupied Vienna. Much of the city's aristocracy and wealthy bourgeoisie – Beethoven's natural constituency – had fled the capital, leaving the theatre to be attended largely by members of the French army. The work was poorly rehearsed and the cast, with one exception, undistinguished. The result was a predictable failure. 'A new Beethoven opera "Fidelio oder Die eheliche Liebe" has not pleased,' reported the correspondent for August von Kotzebue's *Freimüthige*. 'It was performed only a few times and after the first performance remained completely empty.'[2] To be precise, after just three performances the 1805 version of *Fidelio* disappeared from the stage until it was revived by Richard Strauss exactly a century later.

145

Very little is known about the premiere, which occurred on 20 November in the Theater an der Wien. The conductor was Kappelmeister Ignaz von Seyfried, although Beethoven may have indicated tempi from the pit.[3] What we learn of the original cast offers intriguing hints as to Beethoven's conception of the vocal roles. Principal interest attaches to the first Leonore, Anna Milder (later Milder-Hauptmann), for whom Beethoven wrote the part and who also sang Leonore at the 1806 and 1814 premieres (see fig. 8.1). She established one important precedent for the role: her voice was large and penetrating. Haydn reportedly said to her, 'My dear child! You have a voice like a house!'[4] On the other hand, she was only twenty when she sang Leonore, suggesting a less matronly sound (as well as figure) than would come to be associated with the role in the post-Wagnerian era. Contemporary reviewers describe her voice as 'beautiful' and 'lovely', but they also complain of its immaturity and lack of affect.[5] Her other roles as well as the greater florid demands of the 1805 score imply a soprano of some facility, which would again distinguish her from the generally sluggish singers who later assumed the part. Yet she was among the first to complain of Beethoven's unsingable writing for the voice, and in 1836 she told Anton Schindler of having forced Beethoven to compose a simplified version of her aria by flatly refusing to go on stage with the original.[6] In sum, the first Leonore appears to have possessed a voice of substantial dimensions but with more suppleness and bloom than many subsequent interpreters. Among modern singers perhaps Maria Callas had the ideal combination of power and agility for the part, and, although she never recorded Leonore's music, Callas in fact sang the role at the beginning of her career and was invited by Edward Johnson to perform it at the Met.[7]

None of the other participants in the 1805 premiere was a singer of consequence. Marzelline was taken by a soubrette, Louise Müller, thus establishing a prejudice in favour of a light-weight voice in the part, a prejudice against which certain conductors, notably, Gustav Mahler and Wilhelm Furtwängler, have reacted by assigning it to a lyric. The modern tendency to treat Rocco as an important singing role, undertaken by major artists like Alexander Kipnis, Gottlob Frick, or Kurt Moll, finds little support in its original assumption by a man named Rothe, who can be located in none of the usual sources for Viennese theatrical history.[8] The Pizarro was Mozart's brother-in-law Sebastian Mayer,

Figure 8.1 Anna Milder-Hauptmann, the first Leonore.
Watercolour sketch by Perger.

who doubled as stage manager at the Theater an der Wien and was known more as an actor than a singer. Finally, the first Florestan, Fritz Demmer – who according to one reviewer sang consistently flat[9] – enjoyed a reputation primarily as a comic tenor, which suggests a lighter, more agile voice than we now think of in the role. In the 1806 version of *Fidelio* Demmer was replaced by Joseph Röckel (in a cast that otherwise remained unchanged); Röckel was only twenty-two at the time, thus confirming the impression that Florestan was not meant for a Heldentenor. Indeed, the combination of Milder as Leonore and Demmer or Röckel as Florestan implies a vocal format for the two principals closer to Mozart than Wagner and contradicts our tendency to think of the typical Leonore as an Isolde and the typical Florestan as a Tristan.

Just as the 1805 premiere was overshadowed by the Napoleonic occupation, so the 1814 premiere benefited from the celebratory atmosphere that overtook Vienna following Napoleon's defeat. One might even read in this sequence an apt reflection of the opera's own trajectory from imprisonment to liberation. Beethoven himself conducted, but because of his deafness and excitability he often left the singers in the lurch.[10] Anna Milder-Hauptmann, whose Leonore had now achieved the maturity and expressiveness found lacking in her 1805 performance, was the sole survivor from the original cast; she was also, once again, the only singer of distinction. Nonetheless, all reports concur that the 1814 premiere was as great a success as the 1805 premiere had been a failure.

Appropriately, four months later, on 26 September 1814, *Fidelio* – still with its opening-night cast – became the first opera given for the assembled dignitaries of the Congress of Vienna.[11] As the Congress continued its deliberations, there were repeat performances, forging an almost official link between Beethoven's operatic celebration of freedom and the great diplomatic enterprise that fashioned post-Napoleonic Europe. Here lies the original association of *Fidelio* with moments of fundamental political transformation – its baptism, so to speak, as the opera of hopeful new beginnings. After the Second World War it would be chosen over and over as the work with which to reopen Central Europe's devastated opera houses, most famously the Vienna State Opera on 6 October 1945.[12]

2

The two most important figures in the nineteenth-century history of *Fidelio* are Wilhelmine Schröder-Devrient and Richard Wagner, whose richly intermingled careers were united precisely by Beethoven's opera. Schröder-Devrient (fig. 8.2) first sang Leonore in the Viennese revival of 3 November 1822, with Beethoven conducting the dress rehearsal (though not the performance).[13] She was

Figure 8.2 Wilhelmine Schröder-Devrient. Lithograph of H. Grevedon, Paris 1830.

even younger than Anna Milder at the 1805 premiere: just short of eighteen, again suggesting a more girlish sound and appearance than would be imaginable in the part today. Leonore quickly became the signature role of her remarkable career. In 1823 she performed it under Carl Maria von Weber in Dresden, and she later brought her Leonore to Paris (1830) and London (1832), always to ecstatic response.[14] She singlehandedly transformed the part into a major dramatic vehicle, investing it with an ideological message of historic significance. Her important modern successors have been Lilli Lehmann, Kirsten Flagstad, and, above all, Lotte Lehmann, who sang Leonore at Salzburg every year but one from 1927 to 1937, under Richard Strauss, Erich Kleiber and Arturo Toscanini.[15]

Vocally Schröder-Devrient may well have been the least gifted of famous singers. 'She had no "voice" at all', wrote Wagner.[16] Henry Chorley concurred: 'A singer the lady never was. . . . Her tones were delivered without any care, save to give them due force. Her execution was bad and heavy.'[17] Yet Wagner also said of her Leonore, which he claimed to have witnessed in Leipzig in 1829, 'If I look back on my life as a whole, I can find no event that produced so profound an impression upon me.'[18] Chorley, for his part, judged her 'far deeper and more moving' in the role than the vocally superior Maria Malibran.[19]

Schröder-Devrient began her career as an actress, and her success with Leonore was clearly more theatrical than musical. The Beethoven who so admired her performance in 1822 was completely deaf; he responded strictly to her physical dramatization of the role. Her most famous innovation was to speak rather than sing the final word in her threat to Pizarro: 'Noch einen Laut und du bist todt!' (see fig. 8.3).[20] The 'terrific effect' of this gesture Wagner attributed to the sudden and shocking return from the ideal world of music 'to the naked surface of dreadful reality'.[21]

Beyond its melodramatic extravagance and generalized pathos, Schröder-Devrient's performance was geared to convey a single passion: Leonore's unstinting devotion to her husband. She anxiously examined the faces of the prisoners as they entered the courtyard; she embraced Florestan rapturously at the moment of rescue; and in the final tableau, according to Chorley, 'there was something subduing in the look of speechless affection with which she at last undid the chains of the beloved one, saved by her love – the mere remembrance of which makes the heart throb, and the eyes fill'.[22] It is no exaggeration to say that through Schröder-Devrient *Fidelio* was absorbed into the nineteenth-century cult of domesticity. It became an opera about the ideal wife whose love for her husband all but exhausted her identity. In Schröder-Devrient's assumption *Fidelio*'s political edge was effectively blunted.

Wagner fully subscribed to the nineteenth century's domestic understanding of the opera, which conformed to his own obsession

Figure 8.3 Act 2, scene 1 (dungeon scene). Wilhelmine Schröder-Devrient as Fidelio. Lithograph by W. Santer. Text: Madame Schröder-Devrient, Royal Saxon Court Opera Singer, as Fidelio.

with chaste females abjectly devoted to their mates. Yet for all his admiration of Schröder-Devrient's Leonore, he found much in *Fidelio* to criticize. The libretto, he complained, was 'weakened and delayed by paltry details'.[23] Most famously, he argued that the opera's great subject was fully realized only in the *Leonore* overture No. 3, which 'sets the drama more completely and movingly before us than ever happens in the broken action that ensues'.[24] In thus demoting the opera proper, Wagner expressed the dominant conception of Beethoven as a purely instrumental genius – and, of course, reserved for himself the task of raising vocal music to the philosophical level achieved by Beethoven in his symphonies. Wagner's poor opinion of *Fidelio* was hardly unique among his contemporaries. Some of them even treated it with outright contempt. Berlioz (himself a great admirer) recalls a performance at the Théâtre-Lyrique in which the prison story was scrapped in favour of a Renaissance costume drama about Ludovico Sforza.[25]

Wagner's analysis of the *Leonore* No. 3 overture conveys his sense of the opera's ideal dramatic action. He detects in it four essential moments, without specifying their exact musical embodiments. The beginning plunges us directly into a gloomy dungeon, its stillness broken only by the prisoner's moans for freedom. The darkness is then pierced by 'the glance of [an] angel' whose own freedom seems intolerable because it has been denied her beloved. There follows the mounting resolve of the angel (who is 'but a loving woman') to tear down the prison walls. Finally, 'the last bolt falls', and redeemed and redeemer shout 'Freedom! Godlike freedom!' as sunlight floods the dungeon.[26] Perhaps the most striking feature of this reading of the Leonore overture is its elimination of the entire first act of the opera with its petty-bourgeois intrigue. With characteristic radicalism Wagner thus 'solves' the problem of the opera's dramatic and stylistic schizophrenia. At the same time his interpretation has the effect of restoring something of the opera's political muscle – its charting of the progress from oppression to liberation – which had been dissipated in the prevailing domestic construction.

Wagner also complained of Beethoven's failure to set the dialogue of *Fidelio* to music.[27] It was a failure that others aimed to correct. Thus in 1851 Michael Balfe composed recitatives for a London production, which Wagner heard in 1855, and which continued to be performed for decades.[28] This effort to regularize the opera – to bring it into conformity with the through-composed prejudices of the age – did not end with the nineteenth century. Artur Bodanzky produced recitatives for the Met's *Fidelio* in 1927, and they were still in use when Kirsten Flagstad sang her first Leonore there in 1936.[29] A similar irreverence, unthinkable nowadays, is implied by performances in unlikely languages: Balfe's London *Fidelio* was sung in Italian, as was the Met's version of 1892, even though the Leonore was the great German soprano Lilli Lehmann.[30] The piety that has descended on the opera would seem to be a fairly recent phenomenon.

3

The modern history of *Fidelio* begins with Gustav Mahler's and Alfred Roller's Vienna production of 1904. In contrast to his nineteenth-century predecessors (Wagner in particular), Mahler considered *Fidelio* a masterpiece, indeed the 'opera among operas'.[31] To reveal its greatness he instituted a number of musical and dramatic changes and inspired Roller – a charter member of the Vienna Secession who sought to replace traditional realistic stage-craft with a stylized theatre of space, light and colour – to design a strikingly new mise-en-scène. Mahler's and Roller's innovations in effect liberated *Fidelio* from its domestic fetters and revealed its repressed political logic. Our lofty contemporary estimate of the opera as well as our tendency to interpret it as an allegory of human liberation date from this production.

Mahler's first step was to cordon off, diminish and sanitize the *Singspiel* elements. Reaching back to the three-act version of 1805, he reinstituted a change of scene at Pizarro's entrance. Thus isolated, the domestic comedy of the opening was played in the drastically reduced space of a Biedermeier interior. So as not to darken Rocco's character (and perhaps because he considered the piece musically inferior) Mahler eliminated the gold aria. At the same time Marzelline was lent more gravity by assigning her to a lyric soprano, while Jaquino's exaggerated teasing was reduced to a bare minimum.[32] The first scene's comic realism was thus tamed and miniaturized so as to contrast with the epic *opera seria* that followed.

One number was exempted from this treatment: the canon. Mahler instinctively recognized its music as belonging to the serious idiom of the 'real' opera. He therefore sought to isolate it from its plebeian surroundings. In order to suggest that the singers were in the grip of a single idea – the idea of hope – he froze them in a 'holy immobility' throughout the course of the piece. Hope was conveyed more precisely by a ray of sunlight shining through the window and falling, in a 'supernatural burst', on a vase of flowers.[33] So italicized, the canon prefigured the opera's denouement, scenically as well as musically. This was the first instance of Roller's use of light to specify the opera's ideological import.

The change to the second scene took place during the march (no. 6), and the curtain rose on the immense courtyard of the prison with Pizarro's guard already in place. The set was the first of three remarkable above all for their monumentality, which carried unmistakably political overtones: by locating the drama in large and weighty architectural spaces, Mahler and Roller suggested its world-historical significance. The massiveness of the sets also corresponded to the heavier musical manner of Beethoven's second period, which displaced the Mozartian lightness of the opening numbers.

The second tableau was designed to convey 'the terrible tyranny of the prisons of old Spain'.[34] A massive tower dominated the high, thick, blackish walls, and the lighting conjured up an atmosphere at once cold, dreary and suffocating. The whole of the stage picture, including the guards deporting themselves like automatons, implied the utmost dehumanization. The central episode of the scene for Mahler was not Leonore's aria but the prisoners' chorus, which he staged so as to convey the men's utter pitiableness. Instead of the traditional mass of choristers disposed in a semi-circle and singing robustly, a mere eight figures crept on stage 'feeling the walls like poor earthworms blinded by the daylight and intoxicated by the pure air'.[35] Their suffering was made the more abject so as to lend their ultimate liberation its full force.

The two tableaux of the second act were distinguished less by their shared monumentality than by their antithetical lighting. In the first – a claustrophobic vault carved out of an old cistern – Florestan sang his aria in near complete darkness; the set was lit only by a small oil lamp, which echoed the ray of sunshine in the act I canon.[36] By contrast, the final scene, before the prison's main gate, was brilliantly illuminated, marking the drama's progress, as Roller put it, 'from night to light'.[37] Arguably more than any other opera, *Fidelio* was transformed by the electrification of the theatre in the late nineteenth century. Beethoven's metaphorical contrast between darkness and light could now be realized with spectacular literalness, and Roller was among the first to exploit this possibility. The conceit has been repeated in virtually all modern productions, and it is in no small part responsible for their subliminal political message. Roller fell short of the extreme black-and-white aesthetic of the typical twentieth-century production only in retaining a good deal of colour in his costumes and in deploying a vivid pastoral backdrop for the final tableau.

The most famous (and influential) of Mahler's innovations was to insert the *Leonore* No. 3 overture between the two scenes of the second act. Recent scholarship has argued that he may have been anticipated in this practice by Otto Nicolai, and earlier conductors are known to have incorporated the Leonore overture at other points in the opera, notably, before the dungeon scene: in 1862 Berlioz reported its being played there in the principal theatres of Germany and England, and Mahler himself conducted it between the two acts in a London performance of 1892.[38] Nonetheless, the modern practice of playing *Leonore* No. 3 between the dungeon scene and the final tableau owes its authority to Mahler's Vienna production.

According to some witnesses, Mahler inserted the overture only because Roller's last set was so heavy and complicated that the overture's full fifteen-minute duration was needed to move the set into place.[39] But in fact the decision was both principled and of a piece with the cordoning off of the opening scene and the monumentalizing of the rest. Whether consciously or not, Mahler embraced Wagner's conception of the Leonore overture as a symphonic apotheosis of the opera's central action. Placed between the scenes of act II – at the story's turning point – it recapitulated the drama in condensed and purified form. The overture thus contributed to the 'Wagnerization' of *Fidelio*, appropriating the Bayreuth Master's imprimatur for the opera itself while adding to its musical gravitas. As the Viennese critic Max Graf observed, Mahler made Beethoven 'Wagner's ancestor' by transforming the *Singspiel* into a full-fledged *Musikdrama*.[40] Most importantly, the overture's binary structure underscored Mahler's political reading of the opera as an allegory of oppression and liberation.[41]

4

The most important twentieth-century interpretations of *Fidelio* have stood in Mahler's shadow, not least in their domination by strong conductors. Indeed, since Mahler *Fidelio* has generally been thought of as a conductor's opera. The first of Mahler's successors was Otto Klemperer, who inaugurated his tenure at the Wiesbaden Opera in 1924 and, more significantly, at Berlin's Kroll Opera in 1927 with new productions of *Fidelio*. Klemperer's collaborator in both instances was Ewald Dülberg, who, like Roller, was influenced by Adolph Appia's stylized notions about space, form and colour. Dülberg went beyond Roller in designing massive cubist sets whose severe abstraction conveyed an even more deracinated and universalized conception of the opera. Huge rectangular blocks were arranged in different configurations to suggest the opera's various locales (see fig. 8.4). In the courtyard scene the blocks towered above the prisoners, while in the final tableau they were rolled aside to leave a barren stage – the most universal and his- torically unspecific of spaces. Dülberg's Wiesbaden and Kroll settings differed from one another mainly in their colouration: the first was garish – a kind of Fauvist *Fidelio* – while the second used a range of greys, blues and whites recalling the austere tonality of Picasso's and Braque's early cubist paintings.[42]

Klemperer's directorship at the Kroll is generally associated with the progressive or even radical impulses of the Weimar Republic,[43] and his productions often came under right-wing attack. The Nazi *Völkischer Beobachter* called him a 'head musical Jew' (Obermusikjude), and Paul Zschorlich, later a member of the NS-Reichsmusikkammer, alluded menacingly to 'German shame everywhere one looks' – thereby linking Klemperer's *Fidelio* to the humiliation of Versailles.[44] Yet this supposedly left-wing version of the opera was curiously authoritarian. Not just the prisoners in the first act but the 'liberated' populace of the finale were deployed in static blocks, their movements stiffly choreographed to suggest puppets. As the various sections of the chorus cried 'Heil', their arms shot into the air, while Leonore, whose heroism had provided the opera's *raison d'être* in the nineteenth century, was swallowed up by the crowd.[45] Klemperer's and Dülberg's modernist aesthetic led them to repress the opera's bourgeois sentimentality. But, ironically, their abstract monumentalism seemed to anticipate the totalizing inhumanity of the Nazis. Klemperer also drilled his per- formers to obtain absolute conformity with his musical conception; the efforts of the individual artists were ruthlessly subordinated to the ensemble. Alfred Einstein complained of the conductor's 'fanatical exactitude' and 'tyranny': 'In this opera about freedom there is no sense of freedom.'[46] The impression is confirmed by Klemperer's commercial recording of *Fidelio*, made four decades later, which offers the most monumental and uncompromising of interpretations.

From a strictly musical viewpoint the greatest figure in the modern history of *Fidelio* is Wilhelm Furtwängler. Unlike Mahler and Klemperer before him or Karajan afterward, Furtwängler had little interest in how the opera was staged, so long as the pro- duction was sufficiently orthodox not to detract from Beethoven's music. Accordingly his *Fidelio* is linked to no scenic designer of the stature of Roller, Dülberg or, later, Schneider-Siemssen. His close identification with the opera extended from 1915, when he

Figure 8.4 Scenery sketch by Ewald Dülberg for the Kroll Opera *Fidelio*, 1927.

led a concert version in Lübeck, until 1953, a year before his death, when he performed it for the last time at the Vienna State Opera and recorded it for EMI. During his long tenure as Germany's premiere musician, he conducted it more often than any other opera.[47]

Furtwängler's indifference to the opera's staging reflected his symphonic conception of the work: he thought of *Fidelio* in almost purely musical terms, which also meant purely spiritual terms. One could say he advanced the same claims for the opera that Wagner had advanced for the *Leonore* overture a century before. As an exploration of human psychology, he felt, *Fidelio* could not be taken seriously. Its action was improbable and tended even to be 'unpleasant' (by which he meant the relationship between Leonore and Marzelline). Above all, the conception of the heroine was, to modern sensibilities, 'totally abstract and theoretical'. To be sure, the idea of the opera deeply engaged Beethoven, but ultimately *Fidelio*, like the *Missa Solemnis*, pursued a musical logic: the text merely supplied an excuse for the composer's imagination. Furtwängler found the clearest evidence for this view in the canon, 'a magnificent inspiration born from an insignificant cue'. Rocco's question, 'Meinst du, ich könnte dir nicht ins Herz sehen?' was not even well founded psychologically. Yet his inconsequential – even wrong-headed – remark inspired Beethoven to a stunning compositional achievement.[48] Furtwängler's radically musical conception of the opera meant that in performance he sought to underline the work's sonic architecture, even at the risk of tempos too slow or dynamics too extreme for the singers' comfort. He stripped the opera of its melodramatic accretions, permitting the score to emerge, in his concentrated and ethereal reading, as an expression of pure *Geist*.

This rigorously musical approach might seem to imply an apolitical conception of *Fidelio*. But that is only superficially the case. Furtwängler had remained in Germany and continued to perform under Hitler because he believed – naively, his critics said – that the great masterpieces of German music offered the sole emotional bulwark against the barbarism of the regime.[49] After the war *Fidelio* became the linchpin of his effort to redeem German culture in the eyes of the world. Thomas Mann, who in contrast to Furtwängler went into exile, charged that *Fidelio* under the Nazis was an obscenity: 'What obtuseness it took to listen to *Fidelio* in Himmler's Germany without covering one's face and fleeing the hall.'[50] To which Furtwängler responded, in a letter to Mann, '*Fidelio* never has been presented in the Germany of Himmler, only in a Germany raped by Himmler'.[51] The opera was the ultimate anti-Nazi gesture, not just because it celebrated human freedom but because its profound spirituality embodied all that was noblest in Germany's heritage. More than any other artifact, it refuted the equation of German culture with Nazism. Furtwängler's reasoning – which echoed Mann's own earlier defence of the unpolitical German – may have inspired the widespread practice of reopening Germany's opera houses with *Fidelio*, in order to mark a symbolic break with the Nazi past.

5

If Furtwängler pursued the musical impulse of Mahler's *Fidelio* to its logical conclusion, Wieland Wagner realized most completely the universalist assumptions of Roller's staging. Wieland's version of the opera was premiered at Stuttgart in 1954 and travelled thence to Paris and London, where Ernest Newman pronounced it 'the greatest musical experience in twenty years'.[52] It was the most abstract of *Fidelio*s, dispensing even with Dülberg's geometrical blocks. A barren stage centred on the disc made famous in the new-Bayreuth productions of the *Ring*. The sole prop was a huge, fence-like grid – a clear reminder of prison bars – which was variously disposed to suggest the opera's different spaces. The director's only other resource was lighting, whose scenic possibilities (and ideological import) Wieland explored more thoroughly than anyone since Roller.

Wieland sought to liberate *Fidelio* from its 'bourgeois fetters'.[53] He dealt ruthlessly with the opera's *Singspiel* elements: the dialogue was eliminated and a Speaker introduced to give a minimal précis of the action. Reaching back to Beethoven's 1805 version, he replaced the genial *Fidelio* overture with the dramatic *Leonore* No. 2, reversed the order of the first two numbers, and inserted the trio 'Ein Mann ist bald genommen' before the canon. Most importantly, he turned the characters into archetypes: Rocco became a symbol of greed, Pizarro of hate, Florestan of humanity, Leonore of love, and Don Fernando – dressed in gold and flooded with light – of 'goodness itself'.[54] The aim of these personifications was to transform *Fidelio* into a 'scenic oratorio' and thus reveal its philosophical essence.[55]

Yet for all its abstractness and its striving for universality, Wieland's production also carried a precise, historically specific allusion: namely, to the concentration camps, and hence to the criminality of Germany's recent past. The camps were brought to mind not only by the towering, ubiquitous fence and the often glaring lights but also by the mechanical, alienated movements of the figures, especially the prisoners, with their modern uniforms, their shorn heads, and their bodies chained together, marching in lock-step (see fig. 8.5).[56] Wieland's *Fidelio* – a *Fidelio* in the manner of Brecht – was thus as much a response to Germany's historical predicament as was Furtwängler's, but where Furtwängler aimed to exonerate by recalling the spiritual depths of Germany's musical heritage, Wieland forced a cathartic encounter with the ugly political reality.

Figure 8.5 Act 1, scene 2, prisoners' chorus, courtyard scene. Stuttgart Opera, 1954. Production by Wieland Wagner.

Herbert von Karajan dominated the post-war history of *Fidelio* much as he did the German musical scene in general. During the Third Reich Karajan had been Furtwängler's nemesis: a Party member and glamorous prodigy, he became the main vehicle of the Nazis' efforts to undermine the older conductor.[57] Like Furtwängler, he was closely associated with the music of Beethoven: in 1938 he conducted a new production of *Fidelio* in Aachen to celebrate Hitler's birthday, and *Fidelio* was also the work of his memorable debut at the Berlin Staatsoper that same year.[58]

In 1957 Karajan began his long reign as artistic director of the Salzburg Festival with his own version of the opera, assisted by the designer Helmut Jürgens. Karajan performed his *Fidelio* in the Felsenreitschule, Salzburg's vast open-air theatre, carved out of granite, whose three-story galleries of ninety arcades were festooned with bars so as to transform the stage into a gigantic prison.[59] The outdoor setting, open to the heavens, situated Beethoven's drama in the largest conceivable space and gave it a benign, cosmic ambience utterly alien from the claustrophobic barrenness of Wieland's Stuttgart production three years earlier. Karajan's preference for traditional costumes and gestures also kept the burdens of recent German history out of mind; instead, a timeless allegory of oppression of liberation was sung beneath the stars. The production's visual sumptuousness was aptly reflected in Karajan's mellifluous, homogenizing way with the score, from which he extracted the utmost surface beauty. The finale paid tribute to the influence of Roller, as the arcades, their grates now down and filled with Don Fernando's retinue, were spectacularly illuminated (see fig. 8.6). Karajan even adopted the idea – entertained but ultimately rejected by Mahler – of cutting the opening chorus, so that the Leonore overture led directly from the 'Namenlose Freude' duet to the address of Don Fernando.[60]

Karajan staged *Fidelio* again for the Salzburg Easter Festival in 1971. This time his collaborator was the favoured designer of his later career, Gunther Schneider-Siemssen, whose sets were distinguished (like Karajan's music) by their great physical beauty as well as their tasteful stylization. Performed indoors at the Neues Festspielhaus built expressly for Karajan, the new *Fidelio* separated the drama yet more completely from any particular time or place in order to stress its eternal significance. Even the allusion to prison – so central a feature of the Felsreitenschule production – was eliminated in the massive set constructed of hammered metal

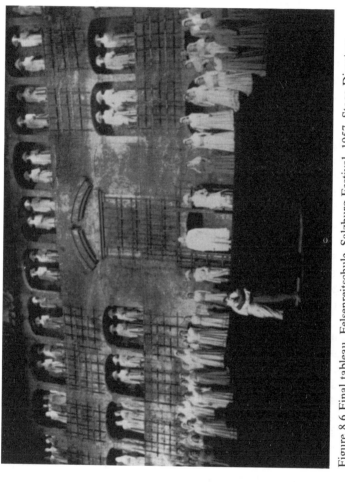

Figure 8.6 Final tableau, Felsenreitschule, Salzburg Festival, 1957. Stage Director: Herbert von Karajan; scenery: Helmut Jürgens; Lenore: Christl Goltz; Florestan: Giuseppe Zampieri.

plates and oversize rivets. The scenery projected into the auditorium on both sides of the pit to suggest that we are all prisoners – perhaps 'prisoners of the ozone layer'.[61] At the same time, the theme of liberation was sharply muted: the finale adhered to the sombre lighting of the whole, as the darkly clad chorus appeared before a cloudy sky on a stage empty save for an ominous black tower. Arguably the production reflected the diminished hopes and weary pessimism of the Cold War, as if Karajan shared Gary Schmidgall's persuasion that, under conditions of ongoing tyranny, *Fidelio* is 'the saddest opera'.[62]

6

The most recent past has brought an attempt to link *Fidelio* to the artistic and intellectual world of its conception. This possibility was anticipated by Roller, who originally suggested a design for the dungeon scene modelled on Piranesi's prison etchings.[63] A similar impulse lay behind Andrei Serban's 1986 Covent Garden *Fidelio*, which was inspired by the designs of Blake.[64] But perhaps the most interesting of the historical *Fidelio*s has been Jonathan Miller's, produced at Kent Opera in 1982 and revived at Glimmerglass in 1991. The particular connection Miller draws is between Beethoven and Goya. In Miller's view Goya's prints, especially of shackled prisoners, belong to the same ideological universe as Beethoven's opera, the universe of the Enlightenment: 'Goya and Beethoven are almost indistinguishable figures – great romantic figures extolling Enlightenment and liberty.'[65] His production conveyed their affinity above all in its colouration: Bernard Culshaw, the designer, fashioned sets out of gauzes dipped in tea-coloured dye and spattered with sepia to lend them the aquatint texture and chiaroscuro effect of the Goya prints. In the final scene tricolour banners explicitly associated both Goya and Beethoven with the French Revolution.[66]

Musically as well as scenically, Miller's *Fidelio* was informed by a historicizing ethos. His conductor at Kent was Roger Norrington, soon to gain world-wide fame for extending the historical performance movement from the Baroque to the music of the nineteenth century. In Norrington's view the proper point of reference for an authentic *Fidelio* was the past rather than the future: 'The score should sound light, more like Mozart, not slow and boring as it does when people try to turn it into Mahler and Wagner.'[67]

One might say Norrington resolved the dilemma of *Fidelio*'s schizophrenic musical character by approaching the whole of it from the perspective of the eighteenth century. Put another way, he took his musical cue from the opera's much abused opening scene rather than from the bombastic finale, as had previous conductors.

In Miller's and Norrington's hands *Fidelio* completed nearly two centuries of performance history with a resounding return to its origins. Yet one suspects their enterprise will remain quixotic. Future *Fidelio*s seem more likely to honour the monumentalizing interpretive tradition that extends from Wagner to Karajan.

Notes

1 Introduction

1 A case might be made for Schumann, whose ill-fated *Genoveva* was his sole completed opera. *Bluebeard's Castle* was also Bartok's only opera. Liszt's student effort *Don Sanche* is generally considered an operetta. Sibelius composed his single opera, *The Maiden in the Tower*, in 1896. Finally, *Dido and Aeneas* is 'the one work of Purcell which may properly be classed as an opera' (*The Concise Oxford Dictionary of Opera*, ed. Harold Rosenthal and John Warrack, 2nd edn [London, 1979], p. 401).

2 John Steane, 'Beethoven: *Missa Solemnis*', in Alan Blyth (ed.), *Choral Music on Record* (Cambridge, 1991), p. 140.

3 Edward Dent, *Mozart's Operas*, 2nd edn (London, 1947), pp. 88–9.

4 See David Galliver, '*Léonore, ou L'amour conjugal*: A Celebrated Offspring of the Revolution', in Malcolm Boyd (ed.), *Music and the French Revolution* (Cambridge, 1992), pp. 166–7.

5 Joseph Kerman, 'It Was His Only Opera but He Wrote It Twice', *San Francisco Opera Magazine 1978*, p. 20.

6 Ibid., p. 87.

7 Stephen Spender, *World within World* (New York, 1951), p. 65.

8 In his memoirs Bouilly wrote that he based his play on 'a sublime deed of heroism and devotion by one of the ladies of the Touraine, whose noble efforts I had the happiness of assisting' (*Mes récapitulations* [Paris, 1836–7], vol. II, p. 81.). But David Galliver has cast doubt on Bouilly's claim: 'No record of occurrences in the Touraine during the Revolution has been found to support his statement.' (David Galliver, '*Léonore, ou L'amour conjugal*', p. 162. Also pp. 164–5.)

9 Ernst Bloch, *The Principle of Hope* (Oxford, 1986 [German original *Das Prinzip Hoffnung* (Frankfurt, 1959)]), pp. 1102–3.

3 Beethoven and Opera

From 'Beethoven and Opera', in Winton Dean, *Essays on Opera* (Oxford, Oxford University Press, 1990), pp. 123–41, 145–54. (Originally published in Denis Arnold and Nigel Fortune (eds.), *The Beethoven Reader*, [New York, 1971], pp. 331–56, 361–73.)

1 There are curiously few references to Gluck in the Beethoven literature. Czerny says Beethoven played through *Iphigénie en Tauride* for some French officers in 1805. His letters never mention Gluck's name; the only two allusions are problematical. In February 1808 he lent Collin an *Armide* that did not belong to him; about the same time he borrowed an *Iphigénie* from Zmeskall and lost it (see Emily Anderson (ed.), *The Letters of Beethoven* [London, 1961], henceforward cited as *LA*, letters 163, 263, and 264). But he must have been familiar with Gluck's music.

2 According to Alfred Loewenberg, *Annals of Opera*, 2nd rev. edn (Geneva, 1955), col. 553, the last finale of Winter's *Marie von Montalban* (1800) is supposed to have influenced *Fidelio*. This claim will not bear inspection. Beyond the fact that Winter's finale contains a rescue and ends in C major there appears to be no resemblance.

3 *Allgemeine musikalische Zeitung*, quoted in E. Forbes (ed.), *Thayer's Life of Beethoven* (Princeton, 1967), henceforward cited as *TF*, p. 326.

4 They were not wholly reciprocated. Cherubini said of *Fidelio* that Beethoven paid too little heed to the art of singing, and he found the modulations in the overture (*Leonore* No. 2) so confusing that he could not recognize the principal key. See *TF*, p. 399.

5 'On the Road to Fidelio (1814)' *Opera*, 12 (1961), 82, and 'Beethoven's Operatic Plans', *Proceedings of the Royal Musical Association*, 88 (1961–2), 62.

6 He wrote to Alexander Macco on 2 November 'I am only now *beginning to work at my opera*.' See *LA*, letter 85.

7 *LA*, letter 87a.

8 Quoted in *TF*, p. 340.

9 For a summary see W. Hess, *Beethovens Bühnenwerke* (Göttingen, 1962), pp. 32–4. Hess published the complete libretto in *Beethoven-Jahrbuch*, 2nd ser., vol. III (1957–8), 63–106.

10 The score has been completed and edited by Hess (Wiesbaden, 1953; vocal score, Kassel, 1957). Gustav Nottebohm discussed the fragment in *Beethoveniana: Aufsätze und Mittheilungen* (Leipzig, 1872), pp. 82–99, and the sketches, which are associated with those for the 'Eroica' Symphony and the opening scenes of the 1805 *Fidelio*, in P. Mies (ed.), *Zwei Skizzenbücher von Beethoven aus den Jahren 1801 bis 1803* (Leipzig, 1924), pp. 56–7. See also Anderson, 'Beethoven's Operatic Plans', pp. 63–6.

11 Before the discovery of the complete libretto Nottebohm, followed by Ernest Newman in *More Opera Nights* (London, 1954), p. 254, and others, mistook the fragment for a final scene. They should have been alerted by the occurrence in the sketches, after the trio, of a vengeance aria for the slave, which Beethoven never completed.

12 For parallel quotations, see ex. 3.5, p. 39. The second strain ('Mein Mann an meiner Brust') had been set to the words 'Gute Götter, blickt herab' in *Vestas Feuer*.

13 *Vestas Feuer* was subsequently set by Weigl and produced at the Theater an der Wien on 10 August 1805.

14 *LA*, letter 88.

15 Treitschke's personal knowledge was confined to the 1814 revival, and he is not always accurate about that.

16 For quotations see *TF*, p. 387.

17 *LA*, letter 128.

18 The 1810 vocal score, arranged by Czerny, over which, of course, the theatre had no control, also bore the title *Leonore*. This was the 1806 version without the overture and the two finales. Three numbers had been published separately in 1807.

19 *LA*, letters 129 and 130.

20 The Pizarro, Rocco, and Don Fernando of the 1814 cast.

21 *LA*, letter 479.

22 See below, p. 49.

23 Bouilly tells the story in his memoirs, *Mes Récapitulations* (Paris, 1836–7), vol. II, pp. 81ff.

24 This was common practice during the revolutionary period, when realism in all the arts was a matter of pride. The score has 'fait historique espagnol'.

25 He is listed as second tenor, but has not a note to sing.

26 Gaveaux's *Le petit Matelot*, a great success in Germany, had been produced at the Theater auf der Wieden in 1801.

27 The opera belonged to the *semiseria* category, which sought to combine the old *seria* and *buffa* styles. It was an important stage in the development of Romantic opera.

28 'Paers "Leonora" und Beethovens "Fidelio"', *Neues Beethoven-Jahrbuch*, 4 (1930), 118.

29 Mosco Carner, 'Fidelio', in *Major and Minor* (London, 1980), pp. 186–252, also believed that Beethoven used Paer's opera as a model, but curiously does not mention this parallel.

30 Not until the last of the seven incipits quoted by Nottebohm does it begin to resemble either its eventual form or Paer's.

31 This was Nottebohm's opinion; Douglas Johnson, Alan Tyson, and Robert Winter, *The Beethoven Sketchbooks* (Berkeley and Los Angeles, 1985), p. 150, opt for 1805.

32 See L. Schiedermair, *Beiträge zur Geschichte der Oper* (Leipzig, 1907), vol. II, pp. 39–50.

33 In this summary I have retained the familiar names of the characters rather than confuse the reader with their Polish equivalents.

34 By a curious coincidence Mayr was invited to set a German libretto by Schikaneder in April 1803, just when Beethoven was about to take up *Vestas Feuer*. See the interesting letter from Hubert Rumpf to Mayr (Schiedermair, *Geschichte der Oper*, vol. II, p. 191) informing him, among other Viennese theatre gossip, that Schikaneder is working on an opera 'mit, und für Pethoven' (sic).

35 The 1805 version, reconstructed after great labour from scattered manuscripts, many of which had been used by Beethoven for his revisions, was edited by Erich Prieger under the title *Leonore* (full score, six copies only without critical apparatus, Leipzig, 1908–10; vocal score 1905, 2nd edn, 1907; neither score contains the spoken dialogue). This material was used for the Berlin revival under Richard Strauss on

20 November 1905, the centenary of the first performance. In 1967 Willy Hess brought out a new full score in two supplementary volumes (xi and xii) to the complete Beethoven edition, with a scholarly critical commentary that identifies all the sources. The basis of this score is a reproduction of Prieger's; although many corrections have been made to the text, others could not be incorporated and must be supplied from the notes. Hess's preface promises a later supplement containing the 1806 version, which has never been published in full, although as early as 1853 Otto Jahn attempted a vocal score (published by Breitkopf & Härtel), indicating the 1805 text where it differed. This was a fine achievement for its date, but later scholarship has modified some of Jahn's conclusions. Certain details remain in doubt; it is not always possible to distinguish Beethoven's changes before the first performance from those for the 1806 revival. Other disputable points are mentioned below. The best account of the various versions is Hess's *Beethovens Oper Fidelio und ihre drei Fassungen* (Zürich, 1953), which includes a line-by-line comparison of the 1805 and 1806 librettos. Adolf Sandberger, in *Ausgewählte Aufsätze zur Musikgeschichte*, vol. II (Munich, 1924), reprinted the Bouilly and Sonnleithner librettos and compared them in detail with Treitschke, but ignored 1806 and consequently attributed some of Breuning's work and even Sonnleithner's to Treitschke. The most reliable account in English is in Mosco Carner's 1980 study, cited above (n. 29). Ernest Newman's in *More Opera Nights*, pp. 253ff., is misleading in several important particulars.

36 With the single exception of the March, which (apart from a different treatment of repeats in 1814) remained unchanged throughout. Treitschke's statement that it was composed in 1814 is wrong.

37 Beethoven subsequently shortened it, but apparently not till 1814; see A. Tyson, 'Yet Another "Leonore" Overture?', *Music & Letters*, 58 (1977), 192–203. For a full account of the overtures see J. Braunstein, *Beethovens Leonore-Ouvertüren* (Leipzig, 1927).

38 Beethoven also drew on this for the first four bars of the ritornello before Florestan's monologue.

39 A report in *Opera*, 28 (1977), 1134, stated that a hitherto unknown score of this version, with notes, corrections, and deletions by the composer, had been discovered by Oldrich Pilkert in the archives of the National Theatre, Prague. According to another account it was used as a conducting score by Weber and Smetana and carried their annotations as well as Beethoven's.

40 Jahn prints both sets with the 1805 music.

41 The confusion is partly due to the fact that Jahn, when he prepared his score, had not seen the 1806 libretto and was unaware of the changed order of movements. Elliot Forbes falls into the same trap in *TF*: see his footnotes to p. 572. Georg Kinsky, *Das Werk Beethovens: Thematisch-bibliographisches Verzeichnis*, ed. Hans Halm, (Munich and Duisburg, 1955) is also wrong about the 1806 order.

42 A mysterious (and superior) second setting of this and the three following lines was copied in a score of the 1814 version prepared for Dresden in 1823 (see Hans Volkmann, *Beethoven in seinen Beziehungen*

zu Dresden [Dresden, 1942], p. 106). The lines belong only to 1806; but they were in the original 1814 libretto from which Beethoven worked, and he may have set them again in that year.

43 The exceptions appear to have been Marzelline's aria, both quartets, the March, and the Pizarro–Rocco duet. Some of these were changed in detail.

44 Jahn did not print the 1805 version. Hess restored the recitative and ritornello from fragmentary sources, but the 1805 Adagio, if it differed from that of 1806 (as is very likely), is lost. Hess's score diverges from Prieger's more sharply here than elsewhere because Prieger backdated to 1805 alterations made in 1814.

45 The double bassoon in Hess's 1805 score, like the direction for scaling down the dynamics of the whole duet (also added in 1806), is an uncancelled relic of Prieger's.

46 So did Pizarro's 'Ha! welch' ein Augenblick!' – but it appears to have gained a second pair of horns, which were removed in 1814.

47 This may explain Beethoven's reference to the libretto of *Fidelio* as 'a French and Italian book' in conversation with Benedict in 1823.

48 *LA*, letter 479. This was not always his opinion. On 19 April 1817 he wrote to Charles Neate that 'the book and the text left much to be desired': see *LA*, letter 778.

49 The words, too, take a step nearer, especially in the two lines repeated by Don Fernando: 'Es sucht der Bruder seine Brüder, Und kann er helfen hilft er gern' ('Brother seeks out his brothers and gladly helps whom he can').

50 Sketches survive for all the new music of the 1814 score except the fifty bars before the second prisoners' chorus. They are discussed in *Zweite Beethoveniana: Nachgelassene Aufsätze* (Leipzig, 1887), henceforward cited as *NZB*, pp. 293–306. At one time Beethoven thought of using the trumpet call in the new overture.

51 Thus reversing the tendency of the 1804 sketches, where Beethoven began with B flat and a mild dissonance. The 1810 vocal score has B flat. Possibly the singer found it difficult to keep the B natural in tune.

52 *LA*, letter 483.

53 Quoted in *TF*, 588.

54 Printed in *NZB*, p. 304.

55 Much of Treitschke's account is in *TF*, pp. 572–4.

56 Described in Sotheby's sale catalogue, 29 April 1969, lot 204A.

57 This fascinating libretto, which has escaped notice elsewhere, has many further points of interest. Beethoven himself altered the title from *Leonore* to *Fidelio* and made changes in the words. Many of the ideas rapidly (and not always legibly) noted were subsequently adopted, but not all. He seems to have considered a new recitative before 'O namenlose Freude'. Pizarro was still to be on stage during the removal of Florestan's fetters.

58 Moser's plan (*Neues Beethoven-Jahrbuch*, 2 (1925), 56) may be quoted as a morphological curiosity. It was to have three acts, act I in the 1805 version, act II (from the March) in that of 1814. Act III was to follow 1814 with the following exceptions: the F minor (1805) Andante

un poco agitato of Florestan's aria inserted between the A flat and F major section of 1814; the 1805 recitative introducing the 1814 duet; the opening of the 1805 finale, accompanied by a visible scene-change after the *Parsifal* manner, leading from the revenge chorus to the 1814 finale with its orchestral introduction cut; the F major Sostenuto assai ('O Gott, O welch' ein Augenblick!') restored to its 1805 form.

4 The French theatrical origins of *Fidelio*

1 Bruce Alan Brown, 'La Diffusion et l'influence de l'opéra-comique en Europe au XVIIIe siècle', in Philippe Vendrix (ed.), *L'Opéra-comique en France au XVIIIe siècle* (Liège, 1992), pp. 283–342.

2 These four sample topics are addressed in, for example, *Silvain* by Jean-François Marmontel; *Les Trois fermiers* by Jacques-Marie Boutet de Monvel; *Julie* by Monvel; and *Félix, ou L'enfant trouvé* by Michel-Jean Sedaine.

3 Jean-Nicolas Bouilly, *Mes Récapitulations* (Paris, 1836–7), vol. I, pp. 260–5, and vol. II, pp. 13–35. Sedaine's 'method' as retailed here does not convincingly correspond with the results as seen in his published librettos, however.

4 i.e. 'The Innocent *Philosophe*', or perhaps 'The Natural *Philosophe*'; the title implies both approval of Enlightenment ideas and the desire for their dissemination in society.

5 Robert Dodsley, *The King and the Miller of Mansfield*, translated into French by Charles-Pierre Patu in 1756; Memoirs of the Comte de Ségur, recounting an incident in 1767 which Sedaine reportedly took as source for *Le Déserteur*. See Michel Noiray, '*Le Déserteur, ou l'orée du romantisme*', *Théâtre Impérial de Compiègne. Le Déserteur* (unpaginated programme-book, 3 and 10 October 1993).

6 Further background to the Sedaine–Grétry works is in David Charlton, *Grétry and the Growth of Opéra-Comique* (Cambridge, 1986), pp. 226–51.

7 Louis Petit de Bachaumont, *Mémoires secrets* (London, 1777–89), vol. XXXIV, pp. 141–2 (13 February 1787); Maurice Tourneux (ed.), *Correspondance littéraire, philosophique, et critique par Grimm, Diderot, Raynal, Meister, etc.* (Paris, 1877–82), vol. XV, p. 9.

8 Information from Johann Friedrich Reichardt's *Theaterkalender*, as reported in W. H. Bruford, *Theatre, Drama and Audience in Goethe's Germany* (London, 1950), pp. 199–201. This remarkable accomplishment was not repeated, for various reasons. The bells of the palace in Bonn played music from *Le Déserteur*, until 1777: *Thayer's Life of Beethoven* rev. edn by Elliot Forbes (New Jersey, 1967), vol. I, p. 40; the reference to 'Kein Dienst bleibt unbelohnt' is in ibid., vol. I, p. 98.

9 Herbert Lindenberger, *Historical Drama: The Relation of Literature and Reality* (Chicago and London, 1975), p. 31.

10 From an unsigned review of *Marcel* by A. J. Grétry *le neveu* in *Journal des théâtres*, issue of 29 Germinal III (18 April 1795), p. 281. All translations in this chapter are my own.

11 Martyn Lyons, *France Under the Directory* (Cambridge, Mass., 1975), p. 236.

12 Michel Foucault, *Discipline and Punish: The Birth of the Prison*, tr. Alan Sheridan (Harmondsworth, 1991), p. 130; see also pp. 115–19.

13 Statistics taken from Raphaëlle Legrand, 'L'information politique par l'opéra: l'exemple de la prise de Toulon', in Jean-Rémy Julien and Jean Mongrédien (eds.), *Le Tambour et la harpe. Oeuvres, pratiques et manifestations musicales sous la Révolution, 1788–1800* (Paris, 1991), pp. 111–21.

14 'Ta gloire t'a survécu . . . Tu renais une seconde fois': César Ribié, *Le Cachot de Beauvais, Fait historique en un acte* (Rouen, An II), final speeches.

15 André-Pépin Bellement, *Cange, ou Le commissionnaire de Lazare, fait historique en un acte*, music by Hyacinthe Jadin (Paris, An III), scene 17.

16 The libretto was by Benoît-Joseph Marsollier des Vivetières; unsigned review in *Journal des théâtres*, issue of 26 Nivôse III (15 January 1795), pp. 261–7.

17 (John Rose), *The Prisoner. A Musical Romance in Three Acts* (London, 1792). The female leading roles were taken by Mrs Crouch and Mrs Bland.

18 Dianne Dugaw, *Warrior Women and Popular Balladry 1650–1850* (Cambridge, 1989).

19 'L.C.' (A.E.X. Poisson de La Chabeaussière) in *La Décade philosophique, littéraire et politique*, An VI, vol. II, pp. 549–53. Identification of authorial initials 'L.C.' provided in Joanna Kitchen, *Un journal philosophique: "La Décade" (1794–1807)*, (Paris, 1965), especially pp. 237–44. My thanks to Dr Anselm Gerhard for this reference.

20 We do not as yet know definitely for which company – if any – Bouilly initially imagined his text.

21 'Sweet Palma [in Charles-Henri Plantade's eponymous opera], jealous Calypso [in Jean-François Le Sueur's *Télémaque*], Proud Medea, mischievous sailor [in Gaveaux's *Le petit matelot*], Leonora, affecting wife, And always kindly Scio, After such long expectation, You appear at last on the stage before our eyes . . .' Extract from poem by Ange Vieillard, *Journal des théâtres, de littérature et des arts*, issue of 19 Pluviôse VII (7 February 1799), p. 278.

22 Laura Mason, *Singing the French Revolution: Popular Songs and Revolutionary Politics, 1787–1799* (Ph.D. dissertation, Princeton University, 1990), pp. 224ff.

23 Ibid., p. 227.

24 Ibid., p. 249.

25 Referring to 'la présence obscène / Du brigand le plus odieux / . . .sur les rives de la Seine'; quoted in Arthur Pougin, *L'Opéra-Comique pendant la Révolution de 1788 à 1801* (Paris, 1891), p. 165.

26 David Galliver, '*Léonore, ou L'amour conjugal*: A Celebrated Offspring of the Revolution', in Malcolm Boyd (ed.), *Music and the French Revolution* (Cambridge, 1992), p. 167.

27 David Galliver, '*Fidelio* – Fact or Fantasy?', *Studies in Music*, 15 (1981), 83.

28 David Galliver, 'Jean-Nicolas Bouilly (1763–1842), Successor of Sedaine', *Studies in Music*, 13 (1979), 22–3.

29 The literary career of the Marquis de Sade was furthered by the Revolution; *Philosophie dans le boudoir* (including scenes of appalling cruelty), for example, was issued in 1795.

30 His orchestral writing here seems to have been influenced by Cherubini's powerful entr'actes in *Médée*, still in the Théâtre Feydeau repertory.

31 Gaveaux's instruction is 'Le pavillon l'un contre l'autre'. According to Berlioz in *A travers chants* (Paris, 1862), p. 185, Gluck experimented with the same technique in the 1776 *Alceste*, act 3, for the fanfares signalling 'Caron t'appelle'. This is open to doubt only for lack of other evidence. See also Charles-Simon Catel, *Sémiramis* (1802) and Jean-François Le Sueur, *La Mort d'Adam* (1809).

32 Jean-Nicolas Bouilly, *Léonore, ou L'amour conjugal* (Paris, An VII) pp. 23–4.

33 See note 19 above.

34 'Théâtre lyrique rue Feydeau', in *La Décade philosophique, littéraire et politique*, An VI, part 2, pp. 493–5. The phrase 'to our eyes at least' signifies that in Bouilly's *drame* dramatic reasoning and logic have been replaced by merely visual, superficial dramatic criteria. La Chabeaussière did not address some elements mentioned by other critics (e.g., the fate of Marcelline), while they, in turn, did not explicitly connect *Léonore* with the Terror.

5 *Fidelio* and the French Revolution

1 Maynard Solomon, *Beethoven* (New York, 1977), p. 199; Editha and Richard Sterba, *Beethoven and his Nephew: A Psychoanalytical Study of their Relationship* (New York, 1971), p. 111.

2 Alan Tyson, 'Beethoven's Heroic Phase', *Musical Times*, 110 (1969), 141.

3 Solomon, *Beethoven*, p. 199.

4 Ibid., p. 200.

5 Irving Singer, *Mozart and Beethoven: The Concept of Love in their Operas* (Baltimore, 1977), pp. 120, 135.

6 See, for example, Bishop Fan S. Noli, *Beethoven and the French Revolution* (New York, 1947) and Frida Knight, *Beethoven and the Age of Revolution* (London, 1973).

7 Solomon, *Beethoven*, p. 34.

8 Ibid., p. 40.

9 Ibid., p. 38.

10 Ibid., p. 198.

11 Ibid., p. 198.

12 R. R. Palmer, *The Age of the Democratic Revolution*, vol. II (Princeton, 1964), pp. 425–56.

13 Hegel, *Lectures on the Philosophy of History*, tr. J. Sibree (New York, 1956), p. 447.

14 François Furet, *Interpreting the French Revolution*, tr. Elborg Forster (Cambridge, 1981), especially pp. 14–19, 22–8. See also Keith Michael Baker, *Inventing the French Revolution* (Cambridge, 1990), pp. 218–23.

15 M. H. Abrams, *Natural Supernaturalism* (New York, 1971), pp. 35–7, 64–5, 329–47.

16 Alfred Heuss, 'Die Humanitätsmelodien im "Fidelio"', *Neue Zeitschrift für Musik*, 91 (1924), 545–52.

6 Music as drama: structure, style, and process in *Fidelio*

1 On Beethoven's lessons with Salieri and his efforts to master recitative, for instance, see Richard Kramer, 'Beethoven and Carl Heinrich Graun', in Alan Tyson (ed.), *Beethoven Studies*, vol. I (New York, 1973), pp. 18–44.

2 Beethoven's criticisms of Schikaneder's *Vestas Feuer* and his decision to turn to an established French libretto are voiced in a letter to Friedrich Rochlitz of 4 January 1804, in Emily Anderson (tr. and ed.), *The Letters of Beethoven* (London, 1961), vol. I, pp. 105–6. Beethoven later reworked some of the material that he composed for *Vestas Feuer* as the duet 'O namenlose Freude' in *Fidelio*.

3 The valuable reconstruction edited by Willy Hess in *Beethoven. Leonore. Oper in drei Aufzügen. Partitur der Urfassung vom Jahre 1805*, vol. XI–XII of *Beethoven. Supplemente zur Gesamtausgabe* (Wiesbaden, 1967), proposes hypothetical solutions for several pieces for which no 1805 musical sources survive. Recent studies examining the text-critical problem of the 1805 version include: Helga Lühning, '"Fidelio" in Prag', in Sieghard Brandenburg and Martella Gutiérrez-Denhoff (eds.), *Beethoven und Böhmen. Beiträge zu Biographie und Wirkungsgeschichte Beethovens* (Bonn, 1988), pp. 349–91, especially 365, 368; Clemens Brenneis, 'Beethovens "Introduzione del IIdo Atto" und die "Leonore" von 1805', *Beiträge zur Musikwissenschaft*, 32 (1990), 181–203; and Michael C. Tusa, 'The Unknown Florestan: The 1805 Version of "In des Lebens Frühlingstagen"', *Journal of the American Musicological Society*, 46 (1993), 175–221.

4 The extant sketches for the 1805 *Leonore* suggest that Beethoven decided to divide Bouilly's first act into two acts at a relatively late stage of composition; see Brenneis, 'Beethovens "Introduzione del Atto IIdo"', pp. 193–4. The contents of table 1 require a few additional comments: (1) The printed score of Gaveaux's *Léonore* does not contain a setting of the 'Air' for Léonore in the first act of Bouilly's libretto. (2) For the 'Introduzione del Atto IIdo' in the 1805 *Leonore* and the original form of Florestan's aria, see below, notes 29 and 32, respectively. (3) Sketches for the melodrama are found in the *Leonore* sketchbook, but no performable source for the original version of the piece survives.

5 As is well known, Beethoven borrowed the melody for the slow F major section of the act III finale from his early cantata on the death of Emperor Joseph II, WoO 87.

6 In *Die Entführung aus dem Serail* Mozart faced a comparable task a generation earlier in adapting Bretzner's *Belmont und Constanze* to suit Viennese tastes and his own sensibilities. See Thomas Baumann, *W. A. Mozart. Die Entführung aus dem Serail* (Cambridge, 1987), pp. 20–6, 36–61.

7 The stylistic evidence for Beethoven's borrowing from Gaveaux is given by Winton Dean in 'Beethoven and Opera', in D. Arnold and N. Fortune (eds.), *The Beethoven Reader* (New York, 1971), pp. 343–4 (also chapter 3 of this book). For excellent overviews of the contemporary operatic scene see Dean, 'French Opera' and 'German Opera', in Gerald Abraham (ed.), *The Age of Beethoven*, New Oxford History of Music, no. 8 (London, 1982), pp. 26–119 and 452–522, as well as M. Elizabeth C. Bartlet, 'Etienne Nicolas Méhul and Opera during the French Revolution, Consulate, and Empire: A Source, Archival and Stylistic Study' (Ph.D. dissertation, University of Chicago, 1982).

8 On the Cherubini excerpts, taken from the act I trio and finale, see Alan Tyson, 'Das Leonoreskizzenbuch (Mendelssohn 15): Probleme der Rekonstruktion und der Chronologie', *Beethoven-Jahrbuch*, Zweite Reihe, 9 (1973/77), 490.

9 For instance, Amadeus Wendt noted in 1815 general affinities between Beethoven and Cherubini and a close relationship between *Fidelio* and *Lodoïska* in particular. See 'Gedanken über die neuere Tonkunst, und van Beethovens Musik, namentlich dessen Fidelio', *Allgemeine musikalische Zeitung*, 17 (1815): cols. 387 and 398; reprinted in Stefan Kunze (ed.), *Ludwig van Beethoven. Die Werke im Spiegel seiner Zeit* (Laaber, 1987), pp. 187, 190.

10 Gaveaux's setting of Marcelline's *couplets* entails a comparable minor/ major antithesis but lacks the contrapuntal interest of Beethoven's setting.

11 Dean, 'Beethoven and Opera', pp. 374–7.

12 The only use of true musical quotation in the 1814 version of the opera occurs in the Melodrama, which quotes from the act I finale and Florestan's aria. Although the 1805 version of the Melodrama has not survived, sketches for the piece in the *Leonore* Sketchbook of 1804–5 suggest that Beethoven planned to quote from the finale in the original version of the Melodrama. See Gustav Nottebohm, 'Ein Skizzenbuch aus dem Jahre 1804', in *Zweite Beethoveniana: Nachgelassene Aufsätze*, (Leipzig, 1887), pp. 423–4.

13 Anton Schindler, *Biographie von Ludwig van Beethoven*, 3rd edn (Münster, 1860), vol. II, pp. 164–5.

14 For a listing of surviving passages from Mozart's works copied in Beethoven's hand see Bathia Churgin, 'Beethoven and Mozart's Requiem: A New Connection', *Journal of Musicology*, 5 (1987), 475–6.

15 Other possible precedents include canons embedded in multi-tempo pieces in the Viennese operas of Martín y Soler and Salieri. See Dorothea Link, 'The Viennese Operatic Canon and Mozart's "Così fan tutte"', *Mitteilungen der Internationalen Stiftung Mozarteum*, 38 (1990), 111–21. Writers on the canon, beginning with an anonymous review in the *Allgemeine musikalische Zeitung*, 16 (1814, quoted in Kunze (ed.), *Ludwig van Beethoven. Die Werke im Spiegel seiner Zeit*, p. 152), have also singled out the canonic trio 'Sento che quelli sguardi' in Paer's *Camilla* (1799) as especially close to Beethoven's piece. The A major, compound-metre melody is quoted in Richard Engländer's 'Paers "Leonore" und Beethovens "Fidelio"', *Neues Beethoven-Jahrbuch*, 4 (1930), 129–30; see also Winfried Kirsch,

'Zur musikalischen Konzeption und dramaturgischen Stellung des Opernquartetts im 18. und 19. Jahrhundert', *Die Musikforschung*, 27 (1974), 193–4.

16 On the adaptation of Florestan's aria text, see Tusa, 'The Unknown Florestan', pp. 177–82.

17 On Mozart's mature practice, see Daniel Heartz, 'Mozart's Overture to *Titus* as Dramatic Argument', *Musical Quarterly*, 64 (1978), 29–49, and Constantin Floros, 'Das "Programm" in Mozarts Meister-ouvertüren', *Studien zur Musikwissenschaft*, 26 (1964), 140–86. On the programmatic conception of the 'second' and 'third' *Leonore* overtures see Wolfgang Osthoff, 'Zum dramatischen Charakter der zweiten und dritten Leonoren-Ouvertüre und Beethovenscher Theatermusik im allgemeinen', in Heinz Becker (ed.), *Beiträge zur Geschichte der Oper* (Regensburg, 1969), pp. 11–24. The so-called '*Leonore* overture No. 1' was written in 1807 for a projected performance of the opera in Prague; see Alan Tyson, 'The Problem of Beethoven's "First" *Leonore* Overture', *Journal of the American Musicological Society*, 28 (1795), 292–334.

18 Philip Gossett notes that Beethoven at one point sketched a version of the aria entirely in C major, perhaps to downplay the parallel with the act III finale and the attendant tonal-dramatic symbolism; see 'The Arias of Marzelline: Beethoven as a Composer of Opera', *Beethoven-Jahrbuch*, Zweite Reihe, 10 (1978/81), 170–4 and 182–3.

19 Douglas Johnson, '*Fidelio*', in *New Grove Dictionary of Opera* (London, 1992), vol. II, p. 186. Changes of mind about the keys of certain pieces evidenced in the *Leonore* sketchbook show, however, that Beethoven did not begin with an inflexible plan for the opera's tonal organization.

20 On theoretical descriptions of conventional associations of keys with *Affekt* see Rita Steblin, *A History of Key Characteristics in the Eighteenth and Early Nineteenth Centuries*, Studies in Musicology, no. 67 (Ann Arbor [Michigan], 1983); for Beethoven's purported views on the subject see Schindler, *Biographie*, vol. II, pp. 162–8, and Bruce Edward Clausen, 'Beethoven and the Psyches of the Keys' (Ph.D. dissertation, University of Southern California, 1988).

21 See Wolfgang Osthoff, 'Beethovens "Leonoren"-Arien', in *Bericht über den internationalen musikwissenschaftlichen Kongress: Bonn 1970* (Kassel, 1971), pp. 192–3.

22 Beethoven wrote in the diary that he kept from 1812 to 1818, 'Die Oper Fidelio 1814 statt März bis 15ten May neu geschrieben und verbessert.' ('The opera *Fidelio* 1814, instead of March, newly written and improved by 15 May.') See Maynard Solomon, 'Beethoven's Tagebuch of 1812–1818', in Alan Tyson (ed.), *Beethoven Studies*, vol. III (Cambridge, 1982), p. 224. For comparisons of the different versions see Willy Hess, *Beethovens Oper Fidelio und ihre drei Fassungen* (Zürich, 1953), expanded and revised as *Das Fidelio-Buch* (Winterthur, Switzerland, 1986); in general Hess invokes primarily musical criteria of form and large-scale rhythm to argue for the superiority of the 1805 version. For an opposed view, see Jens Brincker, '*Leonore* and *Fidelio*', in *Festskrift Jens Peter Larsen* (Copenhagen, 1972), pp. 351–68.

23 Other changes that lessen the role of C major include the removal of the Marzelline–Leonore duet and the accompanied recitative before the Leonore–Florestan duet, and the elimination of the striking C major passage at the beginning of the allegro in Leonore's aria ('O du für den ich alles trug'). Note, however, that C major is symbolically incorporated in Leonore's new accompanied recitative of 1814 (see below).

24 Wendt, in comparing Beethoven's Marzelline to the Marcellina of Paer's *Leonora*, noted that the German Marzelline 'approximated more closely the nobler fundamental tone of [the opera's] colouring'. *Allgemeine musikalische Zeitung*, 17 (1815), col. 414; reprinted in Kunze (ed.), *Ludwig van Beethoven. Die Werke im Spiegel seiner Zeit*, p. 195. With respect to the libretto one notes as well that all the members of Rocco's family speak High German, whereas the French counterparts in Bouilly's libretto speak a form of peasant dialect.

25 In addition to removing the Marzelline–Fidelio duet and the trio for Marzelline, Jaquino, and Rocco, Beethoven initially planned to eliminate Rocco's aria as well and reinstated it only at the seventh performance on 18 July 1814 at the wish of the singer; according to the librettist of 1814, G. F. Treitschke, the piece was subsequently omitted from Viennese performances. See Manfred Schuler, 'Unveröffentlichte Briefe von Ludwig van Beethoven und Georg Friedrich Treitschke: Zur dritten Fassung des "Fidelio"', *Die Musikforschung*, 35 (1982), 53–62, and 'Die "Fidelio"-Partitur des k. k. Hofoperntheaters Wien', *Archiv für Musikwissenschaft*, 49 (1992), 52–3.

26 See Mark Brunswick, 'Beethoven's Tribute to Mozart in *Fidelio*', *Musical Quarterly*, 31 (1945), 29–32.

27 See, for instance, the peasant choruses in *Le nozze di Figaro* ('Giovani liete') and *Don Giovanni* ('Giovinette che fate all'amore'). Of course, the relatively slow tempo of the *Fidelio* canon (Andante sostenuto) tends to mitigate the pastoral symbolism.

28 Kirsch, 'Zur musikalischen Konzeption', p. 189.

29 Brenneis, 'Beethovens "Introduzione del IIdo Atto"', argues persuasively on the basis of paper type that a D major orchestral piece formerly thought to have been composed in 1813 as an entr'acte for Christoph Kuffner's tragedy *Tarpeja*, WoO 2b, was performed at this point in the 1805 version of the opera. Accordingly, the familiar B flat major *Marcia* was probably composed for the 1806 revival.

30 Interpretations of the chromatic element as a kind of proto-leitmotive include those by Ernst Bücken, *Ludwig van Beethoven* (Potsdam, 1934), pp. 95–6, and Erich Schenk, 'Über Tonsymbolik in Beethovens "Fidelio"', in *Beethoven-Studien, Festgabe der österreichischen Akademie der Wissenschaften zum 200. Geburtstag von Ludwig van Beethoven* (Vienna, 1970), pp. 223–52; but see the cautionary comments against reading Beethoven's procedures as precursors of Wagner in Carl Dahlhaus, *Ludwig van Beethoven: Approaches to His Music* (Oxford, 1991), pp. 188–93.

31 Arias in this form include numerous examples in *Idomeneo*, Constanze's 'Traurigkeit' in *Die Entführung aus dem Serail*, and Don Ottavio's 'Il

mio tesoro' in *Don Giovanni*. The revenge arias of Elettra and the Queen of the Night both allude to the form as well, but with deviations that connote their villainy.

32 Florestan's aria was originally drafted in 1805 as a four-section piece: (1) Introduzione and recitative; (2) A flat major Adagio; (3) F major Moderato; (4.) F minor Andante. For an argument that this version was performed at the premiere, see Tusa, 'The Unknown Florestan'.

33 The possible influence of Paer's *Leonora* on the new recitative of 1814 is discussed in Engländer, 'Paers "Leonore" und Beethovens "Fidelio"', p. 126.

34 For a comparative dramaturgical analysis of different versions of the aria see Osthoff, 'Beethovens "Leonoren"-Arien'.

35 For this aspect of Mozart's approach see James Webster, 'The Analysis of Mozart's Arias', in Cliff Eisen (ed.), *Mozart Studies* (Cambridge, 1991), pp. 101–99, especially 166–8. That Beethoven struggled with precisely this issue in the different versions of Marzelline's aria is shown in Gossett, 'The Arias of Marzelline', pp. 166–9, 179–82.

36 This symbolism is repeated in the ensuing melodrama, during which the oboe quotes the aria to reveal the contents of the motionless Florestan's thoughts.

37 From the enormous literature on Mozart's operas, the following studies have provided particularly illuminating analyses and interpretations of active ensembles; Joseph Kerman, *Opera as Drama* (New York, 1956), pp. 73–98; Charles Rosen, *The Classical Style* (New York, 1971), pp. 288–325; Julian Rushton, *W. A. Mozart. 'Don Giovanni'* (Cambridge, 1981), pp. 92–9; Tim Carter, *W. A. Mozart. 'Le nozze di Figaro'* (Cambridge, 1987), pp. 95–104; Daniel Heartz, 'Constructing *Le nozze di Figaro*', *Journal of the Royal Musical Association*, 112 (1987), 77–98; and James Webster, 'To Understand Verdi and Wagner We Must Understand Mozart', *19th-Century Music*, 11 (1987–8), 175–93.

38 Recent writings cautioning against overreliance on instrumental paradigms in the analysis of Mozart's operatic music include John Platoff, 'The Buffa Aria in Mozart's Vienna', *Cambridge Opera Journal*, 2 (1990), 99–120, especially 117–20, and Webster, 'To Understand Verdi and Wagner We Must Understand Mozart'.

39 I take this to be implied in Mozart's well-known dictum, apropos the unusual dramatic effects in Osmin's aria 'Solche hergelauf'ne Laffen', that music 'even in the most terrible situations, must never offend the ear, but must please the listener, or in other words must never cease to be *music . . .*', Letter of 26 September 1781 to Leopold Mozart in Emily Anderson (ed.), *The Letters of Mozart and His Family*, 3rd edn (London, 1985), p. 769.

40 Schindler, *Biographie von Ludwig van Beethoven*, p. 167, relates an alleged conversation between Beethoven and the composer-critic Friedrich August Kanne in which Beethoven himself singled out the unusual key choice for this passage in the piece:

'Wenn ich den Pizarro dort, wo er seine verruchten Anschläge auf Florestan dem Kerkermeister offenbart, in grellen Tonarten (auch in Gis-dur [by which is presumably meant the prolongation of V/c♯]) singen lasse, so liegt der psychische Grund in seiner individuellen Charakteristik, die sich in dem Duett mit Rocco in voller Blöße entfaltet, für welchen Ausdruck jene Tonarten mir die entsprechendesten Farben gegeben.'

41 The possibility that Pizarro's words 'Hast du mich verstanden?' at bars 137–8 were Beethoven's own contribution to the libretto is raised by the fact that they are not given in the libretto of 1805 and that they interrupt the otherwise regular versification of the ensemble.

42 A suggestion made by Douglas Johnson in the *New Grove Dictionary of Opera*, vol. II, p. 186.

43 For analyses of the piece see Peter Benary, 'Beethovens Personalstil in dramaturgischer Funktion: Zur ersten "Fidelio"-Szene', *Musica*, 42 (1988), 265–7; and Peter Gülke, 'Kompositorisch genau kalkulierte Unmöglichkeit: Marzelline und Jaquino singen ein Anti-Duett', *Österreichische Musik-Zeitung*, 44 (1989): 346–9. On the role of such 'problems' as an opening gambit in middle-period Beethoven, see Carl Dahlhaus, 'Beethoven's neuer Weg', *Jahrbuch des Staatlichen Instituts für Musikforschung Preußischer Kulturbesitz 1974* (Berlin, 1975), pp. 46–62.

44 However, in a paper presented at the fiftieth annual meeting of the American Musicological Society at Philadelphia in 1984 Philip Gossett argued that Beethoven may have taken hints about certain aspects of organization from the trio no. 7 in *Le nozze di Figaro*. I wish to thank Professor Gossett for sharing his paper with me.

45 According to Hess's edition of the 1805 *Leonore*, there was originally an even more shocking harmony at this point, the highly dissonant simultaneity G–B–D♭–E♭, and Leonore leaped up to a high b♮.

46 In the 1805 version the quartet subsequently concluded with yet another surprise, Rocco's confiscation of Leonore's pistol, which justified the unorthodox original ending on an unresolved diminished seventh chord.

47 On Beethoven's propensity to use the coda as a place to resolve inherent instabilities and tensions in the principal thematic materials of a movement see Joseph Kerman, 'Notes on Beethoven's Codas', *Beethoven Studies*, vol. III, especially pp. 148–50; and Lewis Lockwood, '"Eroica" Perspectives: Strategy and Design in the First Movement', *Beethoven Studies*, vol. III p. 99.

48 Paradigmatic is the view of the anonymous Vienna correspondent in the *Berlinische musikalische Zeitung*, 2 (1806), 42–3 (reprinted in *Ludwig van Beethoven: Die Werke im Spiegel seiner Zeit*, pp. 171–2), who sought to explain the relative lack of success of the 1805 version of *Fidelio* as a necessary consequence of the difficulties that specialists in instrumental composition face when confronted by the specified expressive demands of vocal music. A related strain of criticism is found in Richard Wagner's well-known novella of 1841, 'A Pilgrimage to Beethoven', wherein Beethoven himself is made to express his severe dissatisfaction with the traditional expectations of the genre.

7 *Augenblicke* in *Fidelio*

1 The English translations in this chapter are my own. In 1806 the stage directions are the same as in 1805, with Leonore's words changed slightly to 'Verlass uns nicht! O hilf –' See Kurt E. Schürmann (ed.), *Ludwig van Beethoven: Alle betonten und musikalisch bearbeiteten Texte* (Münster, 1980), pp. 69–70, 120, 171.

2 'Abscheulicher!', Leonore's recitative, begins in G minor, of course, but the sense of key centre is lost almost immediately.

3 For a discussion of these resolutions in a larger context, see Joseph Kerman, *Write All These Down* (Berkeley, 1994), chapter 13, 'Beethoven's Minority,' pp. 217–37.

4 See Dorothea Linke, 'The Viennese Operatic Canon and Mozart's "Così fan tutte"', *Mitteilungen der Internationalen Stiftung Mozarteum*, 38 (1990), 111–21, summarized in Stanley Sadie (ed.), *The New Grove Dictionary of Opera*, under 'canon'.

5 Different words are sung by Max and Agathe in the little canon in *Der Freischütz*, no. 9. This was doubtless influenced by *Fidelio*.

6 We hope featureless; some opera-goers might have thought (and still might think) 'cuckoo'. Contemporaneous opera-goers might also have thought they were hearing a false start of Paisiello's 'Nel cor non più mi sento', an enormously popular piece of the time that is also in G and in 6/8 time. Beethoven had written variations on it (WoO 70).
   Elsewhere *Fidelio* sings 'Three blind mice'.

7 See Joseph Kerman, 'Remarks from the Chair', in *Atti del XIV Congresso della Società Internationale di Musicologia [1987]* (Turin, 1990), pp. 677–84.

8 Carolyn Abbate, *Unsung Voices: Opera and Musical Narrative in the Nineteenth Century* (Princeton, 1989).

9 The importance of keys, to Beethoven, is shown by the fact that the theme of conjugal love in its various aspects is associated with a single key, G major: 'Mir ist so wunderbar' (the mystery of conjugal love), 'O namenlose Freude' (its rapture), and if I am not mistaken the flute and bassoon duet in the overture *Leonore* No. 3, after the trumpet calls (its pleasure, two at play).

8 An interpretive history

1 Joseph Sonnleithner, 2 October 1805, cited in Willy Hess, *Das Fidelio-Buch* (Winterthur, Switzerland, 1986), p. 54.

2 *Der Freimüthige*, 14 January 1806, cited in Elliot Forbes (rev. and ed.), *Thayer's Life of Beethoven* (Princeton, 1964) p. 387; Hess, *Das Fidelio-Buch*, p. 60.

3 Hess, *Das Fidelio-Buch*, p. 60n.

4 *Thayer's Life of Beethoven*, p. 383.

5 *Leipziger allgemeine musikalische Zeitung*, 8 January 1806; *Zeitung für die elegante Welt*, 20 May 1806, cited in Hess, *Das Fidelio-Buch*, pp. 60, 73.

6 Anton Schindler, *Beethoven as I Knew Him* (*Biographie von Ludwig van Beethoven*, 1860), ed. Donald W. MacArdle (London, 1966), p. 133.

7 Michael Scott, *Maria Meneghini Callas* (Boston, 1991), p. 22; Irving Kolodin, *The Metropolitan Opera, 1883–1966* (New York, 1966), p. 535.
8 Hess, *Das Beethoven-Buch*, p. 58.
9 *Leipziger allgemeine musikalische Zeitung*, 8 January 1806, cited in Hess, *Das Beethoven-Buch*, p. 60.
10 Forbes (ed.), *Thayer's Life of Beethoven*, p. 583.
11 Ibid., pp. 594, 597.
12 Alexander Witeschnik, *Wiener Opernkunst* (Vienna, 1959), p. 230. The performance took place at the old Theater an der Wien because the opera house had been destroyed by bombs on 12 March 1945. Ten years later the rebuilt opera house was opened, again with a performance of *Fidelio*.
13 Claire von Glümer, *Erinnerungen an Wilhelmine Schröder-Devrient* (Leipzig, 1904), p. 22.
14 Ibid., pp. 24, 30, 44.
15 Josef Kaut, *Festspiele in Salzburg* (Salzburg, 1969), pp. 411–41.
16 Richard Wagner, 'On Actors and Singers' (1872), *Richard Wagner's Prose Works*, tr. William Ashton Ellis (London, 1896; reprinted New York, 1966), vol. V, p. 219.
17 Henry F. Chorley, *Modern German Music* (London, 1854; reprinted New York, 1973), vol. I, p. 342; *Thirty Years' Musical Recollections* (London, 1862; reprinted New York, 1926), p. 39.
18 Richard Wagner, *My Life* (1865–80) (New York, 1911), p. 44. Recently scholars have questioned Wagner's recollection, arguing that no such performance occurred and insinuating that he may have concocted the story to project his image as Beethoven's natural successor (Barry Millington, 'Myths and Legends', in Millington (ed.), *The Wagner Compendium* [London, 1992], p. 133). But the specificity of Wagner's description makes clear that he must have seen Schröder-Devrient's Leonore, although perhaps at a later date.
19 Chorley, *Thirty Years' Musical Recollections*, p. 9.
20 The accounts vary from source to source (reflecting, perhaps, the artist's changing practice), though all focus on the confrontation with Pizarro. In one of his essays Wagner states that the shift from singing to speaking occurred precisely on the word 'todt'; yet in his autobiography he claims that Schröder-Devrient 'almost whispered' the entire line ('The Destiny of Opera' [1871], *Richard Wagner's Prose Works*, vol. V, p. 152; *My Life*, p. 345). According to Claire von Glümer, the shift to speech came rather on 'Töt' erst sein Weib!' – which would have spared the singer a painfully exposed high B flat – but Glümer also mentions her 'famous unmusical cry' at the sounding of the trumpet (Glümer, *Erinnerungen an Wilhelmine Schröder-Devrient*, p. 23). Berlioz, by contrast, speaks of Schröder-Devrient's electrifying the house in this scene 'with her convulsive laugh' (*The Memoirs of Hector Berlioz* [1870], tr. and ed. David Cairns [London, 1969], p. 269). On Leonard Bernstein's recording of *Fidelio* (Deutsche Grammophon Gesellschaft, 1978), Gundula Janowitz shouts the word 'todt' in what may be a conscious imitation of Schröder-Devrient.
21 Wagner, *My Life*, p. 345.

22 Chorley, *Modern German Music*, vol. I, p. 344; *Thirty Years' Musical Recollections*, p. 39.
23 Wagner, 'On the Overture' (1841), *Richard Wagner's Prose Works*, vol. VII, p. 159.
24 Ibid., p. 157.
25 Hector Berlioz, *A travers chants – études musicales, adorations, boutades, et critiques* (Paris 1862), republished as *Beethoven* (Paris, 1970), p. 114.
26 Wagner, 'On the Overture'. p. 160. Nowhere in his essay does Wagner mention the trumpet call, which is the most obvious narrative borrowing from the opera; nor does he undertake the sort of tonal analysis by which Joseph Kerman and Alan Tyson link the overture to the opera (see *The New Grove Beethoven* [New York, 1983], p. 115).
27 Wagner, 'On Actors and Singers', p. 206.
28 Hess, *Das Beethoven-Buch*, p. 103; Wagner, *My Life*, p. 631.
29 *The Annals of the Metropolitan Opera* (Boston, 1989), pp. 388, 410, 476, 501, 522.
30 Ibid., p. 44. See also Irving Kolodin, *The Metropolitan Opera 1883–1935* (New York, 1936), p. 49.
31 Gustav Mahler, cited in Henry-Louis de La Grange, *Gustav Mahler: Chronique d'une vie* (Paris, 1983), vol. II ('L'Age d'or de Vienne [1900–1907]'), p. 465.
32 Ibid., p. 466.
33 Ibid., pp. 466–7.
34 Alfred Roller, cited in ibid., p. 467. Roller's costuming played off the antithesis between seventeenth-century authoritarianism and eighteenth-century Enlightenment. Pizarro was dressed in a black military uniform 'à l'ancienne mode' (p. 467) while Don Fernando wore a blue and gold courtly outfit and an eighteenth-century blond wig (p. 472).
35 Alfred Roller, cited in Ludwig Karpath, *Begegnung mit dem Genius* (Vienna, 1934), p. 126.
36 La Grange, *Gustav Mahler*, vol. II, pp. 469–70.
37 Alfred Roller, 'Die Fidelio Bühne' (1923), in Franz Willnauer, *Gustav Mahler und die Wiener Oper* (Vienna and Munich, 1979), p. 308.
38 Berlioz, *A travers chants*, pp. 112–13; Hess, *Das Fidelio-Buch*, p. 106. According to Hess (p. 106), Hans von Bülow played the overture at the end of the opera.
39 La Grange, *Gustav Mahler*, vol. II, p. 471; Hess, *Das Fidelio-Buch*, p. 105.
40 Max Graf, cited in La Grange, *Gustav Mahler*, vol. II, p. 477.
41 Following the example of Felix Weingartner, Mahler's successor in Vienna, certain critics have attacked the insertion of the *Leonore* overture as motivated by nothing more than the conductor's appetite for applause. Mahler actually inhibited applause by keeping his arms raised at the overture's conclusion and plunging directly into the finale. (See Hess, *Das Fidelio-Buch*, p. 107; La Grange, *Gustav Mahler*, vol. II, p. 471.) The inclusion of *Leonore* No. 3 has been warmly defended by, among others, Richard Strauss and Wilhelm Furtwängler. Mahler's practice became so standard that when Otto Klemperer's recording of *Fidelio* appeared in 1961, the producers felt obliged to apologize for the overture's omission. Only recently has the practice begun to wane,

in all likelihood because advanced stage machinery now permits a virtually instantaneous transformation of the dungeon scene into the closing parade ground.

42 Peter Heyworth, *Otto Klemperer: His Life and Times* (Cambridge, 1983), vol. I, pp. 200–3, 259–61.

43 Hans J. Reichhardt, *Bei Kroll 1844 bis 1957* (Berlin, 1988), p. 85.

44 *Völkischer Beobachter*, 24 March 1928; Paul Zschorlich, *Deutsche Zeitung*, 21 November 1927, cited in Heyworth, *Otto Klemperer*, p. 261.

45 Heyworth, *Otto Klemperer*, pp. 260–1.

46 Alfred Einstein, *Berliner Tageblatt*, 20 November 1927, cited in Heyworth, *Otto Klemperer*, p. 260.

47 Sam H. Shirakawa, *The Devil's Music Master: The Controversial Life and Career of Wilhelm Furtwängler* (New York and Oxford, 1992), p. 348. At least four complete Furtwängler *Fidelios* are (or have been) available: a 1948 Salzburg performance with Erna Schlüter, a 1950 Salzburg performance with Kirsten Flagstad, the EMI studio recording (without dialogue) with Martha Mödl, and a live version of the 1953 Vienna performance on which the studio recording was based. Taken together they represent the most significant musical documentation of the opera.

48 Wilhelm Furtwängler, *Gespräche über Musik* (Wiesbaden, 1948); Programme essay for *Fidelio* (Salzburg, 1948), in the Fonit Cetra recording (1950), p. 6.

49 See Fred K. Prieberg, *Kraftprobe: Wilhelm Furtwängler im Dritten Reich* (Wiesbaden, 1986), *passim*; Shirakawa, *The Devil's Music Master*, pp. 145–369.

50 Thomas Mann, *Briefe 1937–1947*, ed. Erika Mann (Frankfurt, 1979), p. 444.

51 Wilhelm Furtwängler to Thomas Mann, 4 July 1947, cited in Shirakawa, *The Devil's Music Master*, p. 343.

52 Ernest Newman, *Sunday Times*, cited in Walter Erich Schäfer, *Wieland Wagner: Persönlichkeit und Leistung* (Tübingen, 1970), p. 38.

53 Schäfer, *Wieland Wagner*, p. 36.

54 Walter Panofsky, *Wieland Wagner* (Bremen, 1964), p. 88.

55 Ibid., p. 87.

56 Ibid.; Schäfer, *Wieland Wagner*, p. 37.

57 Shirakawa, *The Devil's Music Master*, pp. 236–8, 241–6, 414.

58 Prieberg, *Kraftprobe*, pp. 301, 308–9.

59 Kaut, *Festspiele in Salzburg*, pp. 152–3, 172; Gisela Prossnitz, Imre Vincze, Renate Wagner, *Herbert von Karajan Inszenierungen* (n.p., 1983), p. 47.

60 To be precise, Mahler contemplated cutting not the chorus ('Heil sei dem Tag') but its orchestral introduction (La Grange, *Gustav Mahler*, vol. II, p. 471). A pirate recording of Karajan's opening-night performance on 27 July 1957 (Hunt Productions 222) confirms his suppression of both.

61 Prossnitz, Vincze, Wagner, *Herbert von Karajan Inszenierungen*, p. 143.

62 Gary Schmidgall, 'Is *Fidelio* the Saddest Opera?', *Opera News*, 7 January 1984, pp. 13–16.

63 La Grange, *Gustav Mahler*, vol. II, p. 469.
64 Mike Ashman, 'Serban, Andrei', in Stanley Sadie (ed.), *The New Grove Dictionary of Opera* (London and New York, 1992), vol. IV, p. 316.
65 Jonathan Miller, cited in Michael Romain, *A Profile of Jonathan Miller* (Cambridge, 1992), p. 54.
66 Ibid., also pp. 55, 82, 109–110, 203–5.
67 Roger Norrington, cited in Romain, *A Profile of Jonathan Miller*, p. 205.

Select bibliography

The most comprehensive *Fidelio* bibliography, through 1986, is contained in Willy Hess, *Das Fidelio-Buch* (Winterthur, Switzerland, 1986), pp. 393–414.

Anderson, Emily, 'Beethoven's Operatic Plans', *Proceedings of the Royal Musical Association*, 88 (1961–2), 61–71.

Anderson, Emily (tr. and ed.), *The Letters of Beethoven*, 3 vols. (London, 1961).

Berlioz, Hector, *A travers chants – études musicales, adorations, boutades, et critiques* (Paris, 1862).

Bockholdt, Rudolf, 'Freiheit und Brüderlichkeit in der Musik Ludwig van Beethovens', in Helga Lühning and Sieghard Brandenburg (eds.), *Beethoven zwischen Revolution und Restauration* (Bonn, 1989), pp. 77–107.

Braunstein, Josef, *Beethovens Leonore-Overtüren* (Leipzig, 1927).

Brunswick, Mark, 'Beethoven's Tribute to Mozart in *Fidelio*', *Musical Quarterly*, 31 (1945), 29–31.

Carner, Mosco, 'Fidelio', in *Major and Minor* (London, 1980), pp. 186–252.

Cerf, Steven R. '*Fidelio*, Ideology and the Cold War', *Opera News* (11 December 1993), 20–4.

Charlton, David, 'On Redefinitions of "Rescue Opera"', in Malcolm Boyd (ed.), *Music and the French Revolution* (Cambridge, 1992), pp. 169–88.

Conrad, Peter, *Romantic Opera and Literary Form* (Berkeley, 1977).

Dahlhaus, Carl, '*Fidelio*', in *Ludwig van Beethoven: Approaches to His Music*, tr. Mary Whittall (Oxford, 1991), pp. 181–93.

Dean, Winton, 'Beethoven and Opera', in Denis Arnold and Nigel Fortune (eds.), *The Beethoven Reader* (New York, 1971), pp. 331–86.

Dent, Edward, *Mozart's Operas*, 2nd edn (London, 1947).

The Rise of Romantic Opera, ed. Winton Dean (Cambridge, 1976).

Engländer, Richard, 'Paers "Leonora" und Beethovens "Fidelio"', *Neues Beethoven-Jahrbuch*, 4 (1930), 118–32.

Forbes, Elliot (ed.), *Thayer's Life of Beethoven* (Princeton, 1967).

Galliver, David, '*Fidelio* – Fact or Fantasy?', *Studies in Music*, 15 (1981), 82–92.

'*Léonore, ou L'amour conjugal*: A Celebrated Offspring of the Revolution', in Malcolm Boyd (ed.), *Music and the French Revolution* (Cambridge, 1992), pp. 157–68.

Gossett, Philip, 'The Arias of Marzelline: Beethoven as a Composer of Opera', *Beethoven-Jahrbuch*, Zweite Reihe, 10 (1978/81), 141–83.

Grout, Donald Jay, *A Short History of Opera*, 2nd edn (New York, 1965)

Harewood, George Henry Hubert Lascelles, 7th Earl of, '*Fidelio*', in Alan Blyth (ed.), *Opera on Record* (Salem, New Hampshire, 1979), pp. 119–30.

Hess, Willy, *Das Fidelio-Buch* (Winterthur, Switzerland, 1986). (A revised and enlarged edition of *Beethovens Oper Fidelio und ihre drei Fassungen* [Zurich, 1953].)

Heuss, Alfred, 'Die Humanitätsmelodien im "Fidelio"', *Neue Zeitschrift für Musik*, 91 (1924), 545–52.

Johnson, Douglas, '*Fidelio*', in Stanley Sadie (ed.), *The New Grove Dictionary of Opera* (London, 1992), vol. II, pp. 182–7.

Kerman, Joseph, 'It Was His Only Opera but He Wrote It Twice', *San Francisco Opera Magazine 1978*, 14–20, 84–7.

Opera as Drama (New York, 1956).

Kerman, Joseph and Alan Tyson, *The New Grove Beethoven* (New York, 1983).

Knight, Frida, *Beethoven and the Age of Revolution* (London, 1973).

Kropfinger, Klaus, *Wagner and Beethoven*, tr. Peter Palmer (Cambridge, 1991).

Kufferath, Maurice, *Fidelio de L. van Beethoven* (Paris, 1913).

Lindenberger, Herbert, *Opera: The Extravagant Art* (Ithaca, 1984).

Lühning, Helga, 'Florestans Kerker im Rampenlicht: Zur Tradition der Sotterraneo', in Helga Lühning and Sieghard Brandenburg (eds.), *Beethoven zwischen Revolution und Restauration* (Bonn, 1989), pp. 137–204.

Marx, Hans Joachim, 'Beethoven as Political Person', in *Ludwig van Beethoven 1770–1970* (Bonn, 1970), pp. 24–33.

Mayer, Hans, 'Beethoven und das Prinzip Hoffnung', in *Versuche über die Oper* (Frankfurt, 1981), pp. 71–89.

Newman, Ernest, '*Fidelio*', in *Seventeen Famous Operas* (New York, 1955), pp. 245–88.

Noli, Bishop Fan S., *Beethoven and the French Revolution* (New York, 1947).

Pahlen, Kurt, *Ludwig van Beethoven Fidelio* (Munich, 1979).

Robinson, Paul, *Opera and Ideas: From Mozart to Strauss* (New York, 1985).

Rolland, Romain, 'Leonora', in *Beethoven the Creator*, tr. Ernest Newman (New York, 1929), pp. 207–60.

Rosen, Charles, *The Classical Style: Haydn, Mozart, Beethoven* (New York, 1971).

Ruhnke, M., 'Die Librettisten des "Fidelio"', in *Opernstudien: Anna Amalie Abert zum 65. Geburtstag* (Tutzing, 1975), pp. 121–40.

Sandberger, Adolf, 'Beethovens Stellung zu den führenden Geistern seiner Zeit in Philosophie und Dichtung', in *Ausgewälte Aufsätze zur Musikgeschichte* (Munich, 1924), vol. II, pp. 263–91.

'Léonore von Bouilly und ihre Bearbeitung für Beethoven durch Joseph Sonnleithner', in *Ausgewälte Aufsätze zur Musikgeschichte* (Munich, 1924), vol. II, pp. 141–53.

Schenk, Erich, 'Über Tonsymbolik in Beethovens "Fidelio"', in Erich Schenk (ed.), *Beethoven-Studien* (Vienna, 1970), pp. 223–52.

Schiedermair, Ludwig, *Die Gestaltung weltanschaulicher Ideen in der Vokalmusik Beethovens* (Leipzig, 1934).

Schmidgall, Gary, 'Is *Fidelio* the Saddest Opera?', *Opera News* (7 January 1984), 13–16.

Schmitz, Arnold, *Das romantische Beethovenbild* (Berlin, 1927).

'Zur Frage nach Beethovens Weltanschauung und ihrem musikalischen Ausdruck', in Arnold Schmitz (ed.), *Beethoven und die Gegenwart* (Berlin, 1937), pp. 266–93.

Singer, Irving, *Mozart and Beethoven: The Concept of Love in their Operas* (Baltimore, 1977).

Solomon, Maynard, *Beethoven* (New York, 1977).

'Beethoven and the Enlightenment', *Telos*, 19 (1974), 146–54.

'Beethoven, Sonata, and Utopia', *Telos*, 9 (1971), 32–47.

Stoverock, Dieter and Dietrich, *Fidelio von L. van Beethoven* (Berlin, 1960).

Sullivan, J. W. N., *Beethoven: His Spiritual Development* (London, 1927).

Tovey, Donald Francis, 'Dungeon Scene from *Fidelio*', in *Essays in Musical Analysis*, vol. 5 (London, 1937), pp. 185–93.

Tusa, Michael C., 'The Unknown Florestan: The 1805 Version of "In des Lebens Frühlingstagen"', *Journal of the American Musicological Society*, 46 (1993), 175–221.

Tyson, Alan, 'Beethoven's Heroic Phase', *Musical Times*, 110 (1969), 139–41.

'The Problem of Beethoven's "First" Leonore Overture', *Journal of the American Musicological Society*, 28 (1975), 292–334.

Wagner, Richard, 'On Actors and Singers' (1872), *Richard Wagner's Prose Works*, tr. William Ashton Ellis, 8 vols. (London, 1896; reprinted New York, 1966), vol. V, pp. 157–228.

'The Destiny of Opera' (1871), *Richard Wagner's Prose Works*, tr. William Ashton Ellis, 8 vols. (London, 1896; reprinted New York, 1966), vol. V, pp. 127–55.

'On the Overture' (1841), *Richard Wagner's Prose Works*, tr. William Ashton Ellis, 8 vols. (London, 1896; reprinted New York, 1966), vol. VII, pp. 151–66.

Index